Essays on dignity, shame and trauma in modernity

Terry Dawson

Contents

Sexuality and the superego

in Freudian theory

Fantasy and Reality in Freud's Seduction Theory

On 1 January 1896 Freud sent to his close friend Wilhelm Fliess a draft entitled 'The Neuroses of Defence', ironically subtitled 'A Christmas Fairy Tale', outlining the argument of his emerging childhood seduction theory. In this attempt to develop a unified theory of the neuroses Freud claims that hysteria, obsessional neurosis and one of the forms of paranoia have in common two necessary conditions: '(t)he precipitating cause must be of a sexual nature and it must occur at a time before sexual maturity has been reached.'[1] What is particularly damaging about such 'presexual' sexual experiences is that they evade our normal processes of defence which direct psychical energy away from sources of unpleasure. Freud explains, 'Here, indeed, we have the one possibility of a memory subsequently producing a more powerful release than that produced in the first instance by the corresponding experience itself. Only one further condition must be fulfilled, namely, that puberty should have occurred between the experience and its repetition – an event which very greatly intensifies the effect of the revival. The psychical mechanism seems unprepared for dealing with this exception, and it is consequently a *sine qua non* of being free from defensive neuroses that one should have undergone no considerable sexual irritation before puberty…'. Typically, the memory of the original experience is restimulated by an

[1] J. W. Masson (ed.), *The Complete Letters of Sigmund Freud to Wilhelm Fliess 1888-1908*, Belknapp Press, (Cambridge Mass: Harvard University Press, 1980), pp. 162-9.

event occurring after puberty, the subsequent formation of a primary symptom which is then for a time successfully repressed and lies latent, followed by the return of the repressed ideas, the onset of fresh symptoms and the illness proper. The different neuroses are primarily distinguished by the manner in which the repressed ideas return.

On 30 March 1896 Freud went on to make public his seduction theory for the first time in an article entitled *L'Hérédité et l'étiologie des névroses* in the *Revue neurologique*, and then on 15 May 1896 in 'Further Remarks on the Neuro-Psychoses of Defence'. In both articles he claimed that in the 13 cases of diagnosed hysteria he had treated (2 men and 11 women), all had suffered severe illness originating in childhood sexual abuse:

> The childhood traumas which analysis uncovered in these severe cases had all to be classed as grave sexual injuries; some of them were positively revolting. Foremost among those guilty of abuses like these, with their momentous consequences, are nursemaids, governesses and domestic servants, to whose care children are only too thoughtlessly entrusted; teachers, moreover, figure with regrettable frequency. In seven out of these thirteen cases, however, it turned out that blameless children were the assailants; these were mostly brothers who for years on end had carried on sexual relations with sisters a little younger than themselves.[2]

The fullest account of the seduction theory is then set out in a paper delivered to the Vienna Society for Psychiatry and Neurology on 21

---

[2] *The Standard Edition of the Complete Psychological Works of Sigmund Freud*, trans. By James Strachey, Vol. III, (London: The Hogarth Press and the Institute of Psychoanalysis, 1958), p. 164.

April 1896. Freud seeks to persuade his audience that every case of hysteria is caused by premature sexual experience, declaring somewhat immodestly that he has discovered the *caput Nili* (the source of the Nile) in neuropathology.[3] In attempting to assuage the doubts of his fellow clinicians, he assures them that it is not possible that he has forced these scenes upon his patients or that they have invented or imagined them:

> In the first place, the behaviour of patients while they are reproducing these infantile experiences is in every respect incompatible with the assumption that the scenes are anything else than a reality which is being felt with distress and reproduced with the greatest reluctance. Before they come for analysis the patients know nothing about these scenes. They are indignant as a rule if we warn them that such scenes are going to emerge. Only the strongest compulsion of the treatment can induce them to embark on a reproduction of them. While they are recalling these infantile experiences to consciousness, they suffer under the most violent sensations, of which they are ashamed and which they try to conceal; and, even after they have gone through them once more in such a convincing manner, they still attempt to withhold belief from them, by emphasizing the fact that, unlike what happens in the case of other forgotten material, they have no feeling of remembering the scenes. This latter piece of behaviour seems to provide conclusive proof. Why should patients assure me so emphatically of their unbelief, if what they want to discredit is something which – from whatever motive – they have themselves invented?

[3] *SE*, III, p. 203.

> It is less easy to refute the idea that the doctor forces reminiscences of this sort on the patient, that he influences him by suggestion to imagine and reproduce them. Nevertheless it appears to me equally untenable. I have never yet succeeded in forcing on a patient a scene I was expecting to find, in such a way that he seemed to be living through it with all the appropriate feelings. Perhaps others may be more successful in this.[4]

He goes on to claim that the uniformity of detail in his patients' descriptions seems to indicate the reality of infantile sexual scenes, along with telling details which they mention in passing and 'which only someone of experience in life can understand and appreciate as subtle traits of reality.' Patients also describe horrific events as harmless, failing to understand their significance. Most revealing, perhaps, of Freud's 'proofs' is the account he gives of his psychoanalytic method. The infantile scenes convince, he asserts, because of the way they fit the case history:

> It is exactly like putting together a child's picture puzzle; after many attempts, we become absolutely certain in the end which piece belongs in the empty gap; for only that one piece fills out the picture and at the same time allows its irregular edges to be fitted into the edges of the other pieces in such a manner as to leave no free space and to entail no overlapping. In the same way, the contents of the infantile scenes turn out to be indispensable supplements to the associative and logical framework of the neurosis, whose insertion makes its course of

[4] *SE*, III, p. 204-5.

> development for the first time evident, or even, as we might often say, self-evident.[5]

Whereas the article published in March referred to 13 patients, the April lecture has 18 patients (6 men and 12 women), all of whom suffered sexual abuse in childhood, and an additional category of abuser is included, namely, strangers who practised isolated instances of abuse, mainly upon female children, and who 'knew how to avoid inflicting gross, mechanical injury.'[6] Freud also adds an assertion that children who abuse other children have in all cases themselves been previously abused by adults. The very brief interval between the two papers, during which Freud appears to have completed the diagnosis of a further five patients, and the inconsistencies in the identities of the alleged seducers have, as is well known, occasioned a great deal of scepticism as to the veracity of his account, which was never supported by the publication of clinical details for these patients.[7]

Freud's own subsequent recollections, published after his renunciation of the seduction theory, have served only to deepen the confusion. In 1925, in *An Autobiographical Study*, blatantly contradicting his early accounts which made no reference to the role of father as abuser, Freud wrote in connection with his previous adherence to the seduction theory:

> Under the influence of the technical procedure which I used at that time, the majority of my patients reproduced from their childhood scenes in which they were sexually seduced by some

[5] *SE*, III, p. 205.

[6] *SE*, III, p. 208.

[7] See for example Frederick C. Crews, *The Memory Wars: Freud' Legacy in Dispute*, (London: Granta, 1995) and *Unauthorized Freud: doubters confront a legend*, (London: Viking,1998).

> grown-up person. With female patients the part of the seducer was almost always assigned to their father. I believed these stories, and consequently supposed that I had discovered the roots of the subsequent neurosis in these experiences of sexual seduction in childhood. If the reader feels inclined to shake his head at my credulity, I cannot altogether blame him; though I may plead that this was at a time when I was intentionally keeping my critical faculty in abeyance so as to preserve an unprejudiced and receptive attitude towards the many novelties which were coming to my notice every day.[8]

In the *New Introductory Lectures on Psychoanalysis* (1933), Freud again stated:

> In the period in which the main interest was directed to discovering infantile sexual traumas, almost all my women patients told me that they had been seduced by their father. I was driven to recognize in the end that these reports were untrue and so came to understand that hysterical symptoms are derived from phantasies and not from real occurrences. It was only later that I was able to recognize in this phantasy of being seduced by the father the expression of the typical Oedipus complex in women. And now we find the phantasy of seduction once more in the pre-Oedipus prehistory of girls; but the seducer is regularly the mother. Here, however, the phantasy touches the ground of reality, for it was really the mother who by her activities over the child's bodily hygiene inevitably stimulated,

[8] *SE*, XX, p. 34.

> and perhaps even roused for the first time, pleasurable sensations in her genitals.[9]

In 1924, in additional footnotes written for the reprint of *Studies on Hysteria* in the *Gesammelte Schriften*, Freud admitted having on two occasions deliberately suppressed the involvement of the father as abuser.[10] In the case of Katharina, not a patient but a barmaid in an Alpine tavern whom Freud chanced upon while on holiday, he reveals that she claimed to have been sexually abused not by her uncle, as stated in the case history, but by her father. As Freud comments in his added footnote, 'Distortions like the one which I introduced in the present instance should be altogether avoided in reporting a case history. From the point of view of understanding the case, a distortion of this kind is not, of course, a matter of such indifference as would be shifting the scene from one mountain to another.'[11] Indeed not, but neither is Freud's presumed discretion in these two cases sufficient to resolve the theoretical confusion regarding the role of the father as seducer revealed by this inconsistency, leaving aside questions of his personal integrity and professional competence.

The letters to Fliess, however, do indicate an increasing conviction in the role of the father as abuser. On December 6, 1896, Freud tells Fliess, 'It seems to me more and more that the essential point of hysteria is that it results from *perversion* on the part of the seducer, and *more and more* that heredity is seduction by the father.' In other words, what has been ascribed to heredity should be ascribed to paternal seduction. He goes on to cite the example of a patient whose younger brother exhibited hysterical symptoms as a result of abuse by

[9] *SE*, XXII, p. 120.
[10] *SE*, XXII, pp. 120-1, n.1.
[11] *SE*, II, p. 134.

his perverse father.[12] In a letter of 8 Feb, 1897 Freud writes, '(u)nfortunately my own father was one of those perverts and is responsible for the hysteria of my brother (all of whose symptoms are identifications) and those of several younger sisters. The frequency of this circumstance often makes me wonder.'[13]

Freud's renunciation of the seduction theory

In the famous letter of 21 Sept, 1897, Freud reveals to Fliess, 'the great secret that has been slowly dawning on me in the last few months. I no longer believe in my *neurotica* [theory of the neuroses].' He goes on to list his reasons for abandoning the seduction theory. First, that he has failed to bring a single analysis to a successful conclusion. 'Then the surprise that in all cases the *father*, not excluding my own, had to be accused of being perverse… [*Dann die Überraschung, dass in sämtlichen Fällen der* Vater *als pervers beschuldigt warden nusste, mein eigener nicht ausgeschlossen…*]'.[14] As Esterson points out, Freud does not write 'had been accused' but, 'had to be accused', transforming what had been previously put forward as a statement of fact into what is now presented as an unacceptable consequence of his speculative theory.[15] The 'surprise' to which Freud refers is 'the realization of the unexpected frequency of hysteria' from which it would follow, on Freud's theory, that the sexual abuse of children by their fathers would be improbably widespread, particularly since, he argues, sexual abuse only results in hysteria where there are other

---

[12] Masson (ed.), pp. 212-3.

[13] Masson (ed.), p. 231. Letter omitted from earlier editions.

[14] Masson (ed.), p.264.

[15] Allen Esterson, 'Jeffrey Masson and Freud's seduction theory: a new fable based on old myths', *History of the Human Sciences*, Vol. 11, No. 1, (pp. 1 – 21), p. 9.

contributory factors. Thirdly, and most importantly for the development of Freudian theory, 'the certain insight that there are no indications of reality in the unconscious, so that one cannot distinguish between truth and fiction that has been cathected with affect. [Accordingly, there would remain the solution that the sexual fantasy invariably seizes upon the theme of the parents.]'[16] The fourth reason put forward for the failure of the seduction theory is that 'in the most deep-reaching psychosis the unconscious memory does not break through, so that the secret of childhood experiences is not disclosed even in the most confused delirium.'[17]

Freud declares his readiness to give up the possibility of completely resolving neurosis and 'the certain knowledge of its origin in childhood.' He continues, 'Now I have no idea of where I stand because I have not succeeded in gaining a theoretical understanding of repression and its interplay of forces. It seems once again arguable that only later experiences give the impetus to fantasies, which [then] hark back to childhood, and with this the factor of a hereditary disposition regains a sphere of influence from which I had made it my task to dislodge it – in the interest of illuminating neurosis.'[18] The letter to Fliess must be considered the most reliable explanation we have for his rejection of the seduction theory, since he did not disclose this in any publication until 1905[19], and his later explanations are clearly misleading and inconsistent. As this was a private letter to his close friend and confidant there seem to be no grounds for believing that Freud is misrepresenting his own motives, yet it is difficult to see anything in these explanations of which Freud would not have been

---

[16] Masson (ed.), pp. 264-5.
[17] Masson (ed.), p. 265.
[18] Masson (ed.), p. 265.
[19] Jeffrey Masson, *The Assault on Truth: Freud's Suppression of the Seduction Theory*, (New York: Farrar, Straus and Giroux, 1984), p. 129.

aware for some time and which would have had sufficient force to lead him to overturn a firmly held theory that, as his letter makes clear, he had hoped to bring him eternal fame and wealth.

Masson's attribution of the abandonment of the seduction theory to 'a personal failure of courage,' without theoretical or clinical grounds, is not however, convincing. His interpretation of Freud's 'turn' appears to rest upon two separate arguments. The first is that following the scandalous (mis)treatment of Emma Eckstein by Freud and Fliess in which Freud persuaded his patient to submit to an unnecessary and botched operation on her nose by Fliess which left her permanently disfigured, Freud and Fliess convinced themselves that the repeated bouts of bleeding that followed her operation were a symptom of hysteria in which she was 'bleeding out of longing.' Since Emma Eckstein was the 'Emma' whose subjection to a sexual assault at the age of eight had been analyzed in Freud's *Project for a Scientific Psychology* (1895), Masson claims that the cover-up of the botched operation led Freud to re-interpret her sexual assault as a fantasy arising from a '*wish* to be seduced.'[20] Yet, however disreputable Freud's behaviour in this episode it is difficult to believe that it could have played a significant role in Freud's abandonment of the entire seduction theory.

The second thread of Masson's argument is that Freud 'suffered emotional and intellectual isolation as long as he held to the reality of seduction.'[21] Masson claims that '(i)n accepting the reality of seduction, in believing his patients, Freud was at odds with the entire climate of German medical thinking.'[22] Yet this fits badly with the fact that Freud did not publicly disclose his abandonment of the seduction

[20] Masson, *The Assault on Truth*, p. 134.
[21] p. 134,
[22] p. 137.

theory until 1905. Sulloway's biography of Freud examines in detail the reception of Freud's theories, revealing as a 'myth' created by the psychoanalytic movement, started by Freud himself, the claim that Freud's contemporaries were outraged and implacably hostile to his views. Rather than regarding Freud as a radical revolutionary, the modernizing group among Austrian psychiatrists regarded Freud's theory as reactionary and 'old wives' psychiatry' in its insistence upon the sexual aetiology of neuroses and its resemblance to attempts to exorcise sexual demons from the body of the hysteric. Sulloway also observes, 'The fact that Freud's medical colleagues remained in the dark until 1905 concerning his important decision, reached eight years earlier, to abandon his seduction theory of psychoneurosis, only added to the reactionary image Freud had already acquired around the turn of the century.'[23] Contrary to the myth, Sulloway notes, some of Freud's opponents were arguing prior to 1905 for the existence of normal sexuality in childhood against what they considered to be Freud's reactionary theory of the sexual aetiology of the neuroses.

Macmillan's account of the failure of the seduction theory focuses upon the deficiencies in Freud's method which are plainly evident in the paper 'The Aetiology of Hysteria' quoted earlier in which, as we saw, Freud warned his patients before analysis about the distressing scenes he expected to emerge, the 'strongest compulsion' needed to elicit them and the patients' subsequent disavowal of them. As Macmillan shows, Freud was able to believe that this was sound practice because he based it upon Meynert's psychological associationism, a form of psychological determinism which he believed ruled out the possibility of suggestion. The logical and associative structure of a neurosis linking infantile scenes with

[23] F. J. Sulloway, *Freud: Biologist of the Mind*, (Cambrdge Mass: Harvard University Press, 1992), p. 455.

hysterical symptoms, Freud believed, revealed its aetiology. As Macmillan puts it, 'the causal role of the memory was inferred from its logical and associative ties with the symptom.'[24] A 'complex of associational pathways running from the symptom to the memory of the core trauma to related memories' was linked by determined connections which could not be influenced by the therapist, except by the removal of obstacles. 'If a memory of a childhood seduction was at the core of the memory structure, a real seduction must have occurred.'[25]

Freud's essay on infantile sexuality in the *Three Essays on Sexuality* of 1905 shows his reluctance to acknowledge publicly the major shift that had occurred in his thinking. He argues there that 'great and lasting importance attaches at this period to the accidental *external* contingencies.'

> In the foreground we find the effects of seduction, which treats a child as a sexual object prematurely and teaches him, in highly emotional circumstances, how to obtain satisfaction from his genital zones, a satisfaction which he is then usually obliged to repeat again and again by masturbation. An influence of this kind may originate either from adults or from other children. I cannot admit that in my paper on 'The Aetiology of Hysteria' (1896) I exaggerated the frequency or importance of that influence, though I did not then know that persons who remain normal must have had the same experiences in their childhood, and though I consequently overrated the importance of seduction in comparison with the factors of sexual constitution

[24] Malcolm Macmillan, *Freud Evaluated: the Completed Arc*, (Cambridge Mass: M. I .T. Press, 1997), p. 209.
[25] Macmillan, p. 210.

> and development. Obviously seduction is not required to arouse a child's sexual life; that can also come about spontaneously from internal causes.[26]

First, Freud's denial that he exaggerated the frequency of seduction as a causative factor in hysteria contradicts his admission in the 1897 letter to Fliess. Second, in 'The Aetiology of Hysteria', Freud acknowledges that there are many people who have a clear recollection of infantile seduction who do not suffer from hysteria, but responds that this objection has no weight since *ex hypothesi* only individuals with *unconscious* memories of childhood seduction can suffer from hysteria.[27] The only evidence cited by Freud here is the autobiographical narratives published by Havelock Ellis in 1903, which clearly consist of the conscious recollections of adults who, as Freud notes, have not suffered mental illness. In any case, Freud's argument was never that all children who suffered sexual abuse became hysterics, but rather that all hysterics had suffered sexual abuse as children.

Besides the publication of the *Three Essays on Sexuality* in 1905, Freud also wrote 'My Views on the Part Played by Sexuality in the Aetiology of the Neuroses', dated June, 1905. Here, for the first time Freud publicly acknowledges his 'error' and abandons the childhood seduction theory. Contradicting his remarks in the former essay of the same year, he writes of his earlier belief in the seduction theory:

> At that time my material was still scanty, and it happened by chance to include a disproportionately large number of cases in which sexual seduction by an adult or by older children played

[26] *SE VII*, pp. 190-191.
[27] *SE III*, p. 211.

> the chief part in the history of the patient's childhood. I thus over-estimated the frequency of such events (though in other respects they were not open to doubt). Moreover, I was at that time unable to distinguish with certainty between falsifications made by hysterics in their memories of childhood and traces of real events. Since then I have learned to explain a number of phantasies of seduction as attempts at fending off memories of the subject's *own* sexual activity (infantile masturbation).[28]

The decisive shift has now occurred in that instead of explaining the aetiology of hysteria in terms of external, contingent, *traumatic* events, it is now infantile sexual experience itself which is the driving force. In this important essay Freud argued that hysterical symptoms were no longer to be regarded as directly derived from repressed memories of childhood seduction, but 'between the symptoms and the childish impressions there were inserted the patient's *phantasies* (or imaginary memories), built up and worked over from childhood memories and only then transformed into symptoms. Only once this mediating role was recognized did 'the texture of the neurosis and its relation to the patient's life become intelligible.'[29]

The factors of heredity and constitution which the early Freud had sought to downplay were now reinstated as originating causes, but with Freud still insisting upon the determining role of the *sexual* constitution. A further modification of the theory is also elaborated. Freud had always insisted that no experience could have a pathogenic effect unless 'it appeared intolerable to the subject's ego and gave rise to efforts at defence,' thereby bringing about the 'splitting' of the psyche. Illness ensued when defence failed and the unconscious

[28] *SE VII*, p. 274.
[29] *SE VII*, p. 274.

memory pushed its way back into consciousness in the form of a symptom. With the abandonment of the seduction theory Freud argues that what he previously explained through the concept of 'defence' [*Abwehr*] against an external, accidental threat, is now to be explained as 'repression' [*Verdrängung*]. The question now became not what sexual experiences an individual had undergone but of how the individual had responded to them – whether the individual had repressed those experiences. A masturbatory phantasy might then be 'repressed' in the same way as the experience of rape. The threat to the psyche originated from the 'inside' rather than the 'outside'.

Masson, rather tendentiously, describes Freud's position as 'saying that whether seduction actually took place or was only a fantasy does not matter.'[30] He points out, quite rightly, that to the patient who has been the victim of childhood sexual violence it matters a great deal whether his or her experience receives recognition. While Freud could properly insist that for him the issue of seduction was a question of psychoanalytic theory rather than a forensic matter, the introduction of systematic doubt concerning the testimony of those claiming to be the victims of sexual assault, especially when coupled with prejudiced views on female psychology could easily produce invidious results.

Forrester, in particular, has drawn attention to the fact that, from the first, Freud uses the term 'seduction' [*Verführung*] to describe the form of sexual assault he believed his patients to have suffered. Why did he consider it appropriate to describe cases which included assaults including those inflicting 'grave sexual injuries' upon children as 'seduction'? This was because, in Forrester's view, Freud was concerned with the traumatic effects of the event as *remembered*, rather than the events themselves, memories which might suggest to the subject a degree of complicity in the event, manifested as guilt or

[30] *The Assault on Truth*, p. 133.

shame. A child cannot, of course *consent* to sexual relations with an adult, but, as Forrester suggests, Freud recognized that the child may well be drawn into 'the *dialectic* of authority and servitude, of power and helplessness, of mutual dependence, of expectation and disappointment, of shame and embarrassment, which characterises the relationship *and which leaves its mark on the child*.'[31]

Freud's renunciation of the childhood seduction theory was, in the words of his biographer Ernest Jones, 'one of the great dividing lines' in Freud's development as a thinker.[32] Freud had, he observes, 'just recognized something of the significance of phantasies'. As Freud describes it in 1914, 'Analysis had led back to these infantile sexual traumas by the right path, and yet they were not true. The firm ground of reality was gone...If hysterical subjects trace back their symptoms to traumas that are fictitious, then the new fact which emerges is precisely that they create such scenes in *phantasy*, and that this psychical reality requires to be taken into account alongside practical reality. This reflection was soon followed by the discovery that these phantasies were intended to cover up the auto-erotic activity of the first years of childhood, to embellish it and raise it to a higher plane. And now, from behind the phantasies, the whole range of a child's sexual life came to light.' [33] The inherited disposition of the child, he adds, may lead it to exaggerate what would otherwise be commonplace impressions 'so that they become traumas giving rise to stimulations and fixations.'

---

[31] John Forrester, *The Seductions of Psychoanalysis*, (Cambridge: Cambridge University Press, 1992), p. 80.
[32] Ernest Jones, *Sigmund Freud: Life and Work*, (London: Penguin, 1974) p. 291.
[33] *SE*, XIV, pp. 17-18.

Freud singles out Karl Abraham's paper of 1907, 'The Experiencing of Sexual Traumas as a Form of Sexual Activity', as 'the last word on the subject of traumatic aetiology.' Freud's emerging position, centring upon the existence of a pre-pubescent infantile sexuality generating sexual phantasies which, in individuals of abnormal disposition, produce traumatic effects, is indeed stated in a very explicit form in Abraham's paper. Abraham writes:

> For a child disposed to hysteria or dementia praecox a sexual experience constitutes a sexual aim… It undergoes the trauma in consequence of a tendency in its unconscious. If there is an underlying wish for it, the experiencing of a sexual trauma in childhood is a masochistic expression of the sexual impulse. It represents therefore one form of infantile sexual activity.[34]

Such children, he claims, exhibit an abnormal desire for obtaining sexual pleasure and actively seek out situations productive of sexual trauma, not once but often repeatedly. It is their sense of guilt at having done so and having submitted to sexual abuse without resistance which gives rise to neurotic consequences. These tendencies persist into adulthood. 'Female hysterics in particular are constantly meeting with adventures. They are molested in the public street, outrageous sexual assaults are made on them, etc. It is part of their nature that they must expose themselves to external traumatic influences. There is in them a need to be constantly subjected to external violence. In this we

[34] Karl Abraham, *Selected Papers on Psychoanalysis*, trans. D. Bryan & A. Strachey, (London: Hogarth Press and the Institute of Psychoanalysis, 1927), p. 54.

recognize a general psychological characteristic of women in an exaggerated form.'[35]

In a letter written to Abraham dated 5th May 1907, Freud commends Abraham's 'acute' and 'conclusive' observations, pointing out that the latter had been 'spared the mistake I made of believing the real aetiology of neurosis to be sexual traumas.'[36] '(I)t is an excellent thing', he adds, 'that work on these sexual traumas should be undertaken by someone who, unlike me, has not been made uncertain by that first great error.' Yet, if Freud was content to cede to Abraham 'the last word' on the issue of child seduction it was because all his own earlier certainties had evaporated. Freud writes, 'a proportion of the sexual traumas reported by patients are or may be phantasies; distinguishing them from the so frequent genuine ones is not easy, and the complication of this situation and the relationship of sexual traumas to forgetting and remembering is one of the chief reasons why I cannot persuade myself to undertake a conclusive account of them.' Later traumas are 'mostly genuine' whereas earlier ones are '*prima facie* doubtful,' and sexual traumas are more likely to have occurred in lower than in higher social classes. While accepting Abraham's arguments concerning unconscious intention and abnormal constitution in victims of sexual traumas, Freud adds the reservation, 'only to me everything seems less clear-cut, *i.e.* more graded in intensity.'

John Toews argues that Freud's abandonment of the seduction theory occurred not because the accumulated evidence failed to support it but

[35] Abraham, p. 57.

[36] *A Psychoanalytic Dialogue: the Letters of Sigmund Freud and Karl Abraham 1907-1926*, ed. Hilda C. Abraham and Ernst L. Freud, tr. Bernard Marsh and Hilda C. Abraham, (London: Hogarth Press and the Institute of Psycho-analysis, 1965, pp.1-4.

because he began to interpret the available evidence in a new way.[37] Prior to 1897, Freud had sought to explain hysterical symptoms by reconstructing, 'a causally connected sequence of objective processes or events that were ultimately set in motion by a first cause – the originating sexual trauma.' Despite the fragmented and distorted character of such recollections, along with fantasies which were 'sublimations and embellishments of the facts'[38], Freud remained convinced that the 'associative and logical framework of the neurosis' could be reproduced intact. Toews correctly points out that the letter of September 21, 1897 marks Freud's loss of faith in his ability to distinguish fact from fantasy in his patients' disclosures, but goes on to quote Freud's remark in the letter, 'I have more the feeling of a victory than a defeat (which is surely not right),' as evidence that Freud had already evolved a new method in which psychoanalysis had for the first time found its proper theoretical object, namely 'psychic reality'. That this was evidently not the case is, however, indicated in the passage just prior to this remark where Freud writes, 'Now I have no idea where I stand because I have not succeeded in gaining a theoretical understanding of repression and its interplay of forces.' Since, as Freud later stated, 'The theory of repression is the cornerstone on which the whole structure of psycho-analysis rests,'[39] this was by no means a marginal difficulty.

In Toews' radically foreshortened account, which coincides with the 'mythical' version of Freud's theoretical development handed down by Freud to 'the first among his disciples,' Jones[40], '(h)is aim

---

[37] John Toews, 'Historicizing Psychoanalysis: Freud in His Time and for Our Time', *Journal of Modern History* 63, September, 1991: (pp. 504-545), p. 504.

[38] Masson (ed.), pp. 239, 247. Qu. Toews, p. 512.

[39] *SE, II*, p. 157, SE, *XIV*, 16, *SE, XX*, pp. 29-30.

[40] Jones, p. 294.

was now to excavate the inner history of psychosexual desire through an interpretation of the signs – images, gestures, words, symptomatic actions – through which this desire both revealed and hid itself. A true and complete life or case history would therefore no longer describe an externally observable sequence of events but would bring into consciousness – or, more aptly, "make conscious" – the repressed unconscious process of the representation, displacement, and alienation of psychosexual desire.'[41]

The sense of optimism which is undoubtedly expressed in Freud's letter to Fliess, and which Freud himself struggles to explain, may well have more to do with the resolution of the personal crisis triggered by the death of his father, a resolution in part made possible by the decision that his own father would not 'have to be' accused of sexual abuse. In any event, it is clear that the renunciation of the seduction theory, made so emphatically to Fliess, was followed by a protracted period of tortuous indecision and equivocation before it could finally be revealed to the public. The result of a failure rather than a breakthrough, the task of theoretical reconstruction would occupy the rest of Freud's life and many of the theoretical problems generated by it would remain unresolved.

Freud's conception of reality

It must be emphasized that Freud had begun with an extremely rigid and confining notion of reality. As Toews indicates, 'In 1895-6 Freud did not differentiate phenomena of inner and outer experience or the inner and outer reality that made these phenomena possible. There was only one reality worthy of being the object of science.'[42] Freud states

[41] Toews, p. 513.
[42] Toews, p. 542.

explicitly in the Introduction to the unpublished *Project for a Scientific Psychology* (1895), 'The intention is to furnish a psychology that shall be a natural science: that is, to represent psychical processes as quantitatively determinate states of specifiable material particles, thus making those processes perspicuous and free from contradiction.'[43]

The biophysical reductionism of the Helmholtz-Brücke School, as applied by Freud in the *Project*, sought to explain conscious experience in terms of the quantifiable movements of neuronic energy, regulated by the 'constancy principle' borrowed from physics. As Strachey points out in his editorial note to the *Project*, Freud's aim at this stage of his development was to avoid the postulation of unconscious mental events as unobservable gaps disrupting the flow of psychic continuity. Instead, Freud believed it possible to explain this flow in a purely physical causal chain which would be empirically observable. The result would be a psychology which was entirely grounded in neurology.[44] The writings of the Breuer period are, as Strachey notes, all professedly based upon this goal. Breuer himself, however, had firmly disowned this approach in his contribution to the co-authored *Studies in Hysteria*. As Breuer puts it:

> In what follows little mention will be made of the brain and none whatever of molecules. Psychical processes will be dealt with in the language of psychology; and, indeed, it cannot possibly be otherwise. If instead of 'idea' we chose to speak of 'excitation of the cortex', the latter term would only have meaning for us in so far as we recognized an old friend under that cloak and tacitly reinstated the 'idea'. For while ideas are constant objects of our experience and are familiar to us in all

[43] *SE* I, p. 287.
[44] *SE* XIV, pp. 162-163.

> shades of their meaning, 'cortical excitations' are on the contrary in the nature of a postulate, objects which we hope to be able to identify in the future. The substitution of one term for another would seem to be no more than a pointless disguise.[45]

As the *Project* advanced Freud similarly came to realize that the complex psychic processes with which he was concerned could be accounted for only in the language of mental events. For example, Laplanche and Pontalis argue that the theory of seduction put forward in the 'Project' must be regarded as Freud's first systematic attempt to explain repression, significantly already linked to its 'object *par excellence*, sexuality.'[46] The model of hysterical repression set out in the *Project* is the case of 'Emma', in which an initial sexual assault took place in childhood, the memory of which was repressed, but aroused unconsciously, after puberty, by a seemingly minor incident, giving rise to a sexual release, transformed into anxiety. Emma (mis)understood the incident by displacing it to a symbol – her clothing – which associated the earlier with the later incident. Freud concludes, 'Now this case is typical of repression in hysteria. We invariably find that a memory is repressed which has become a trauma only by *deferred action* [nachträglichkeit].'[47] The ego, which is on guard against perceptions that release unpleasure, is taken by surprise by a memory which unexpectedly releases unpleasure, and the ego discovers this too late.[48] Laplanche's interpretation of this case will be discussed at length later.

---

[45] *SE* II, p. 185.
[46] Jean Laplanche and Jean-Bernard Pontalis, *The Language of Psychoanalysis*, trans. Donald Nicholson-Smith, (London: The Hogarth Press, 1973), p. 393.
[47] *SE I*, 356.
[48] *SE 1*, 358.

At a number of points in the *Project* Freud admits the difficulty or impossibility of giving an anatomical or mechanical explanation of the complex psychic events he describes. Rather than presenting a solid, empirical basis in which psychological laws can be grounded, the neurophysiological mechanisms presented by Freud are themselves speculative inferences which are merely sketched in outline. As Ricoeur observes, 'As one enters more deeply into the *Project*, one has the impression that the quantitative framework and the neuronic support recede into the background, until they are no more than a given and convenient language of reference which supplies the necessary constraint for the expression of great discoveries.'[49]

Freud's letters to Fliess indicate his increasing frustration and embarrassment with the *Project*, which remained unfinished, its difficulties unresolved. In the famous seventh chapter of *The Interpretation of Dreams*, however, Freud resumed his struggle with the theoretical problems raised in the *Project*. Strikingly, Freud had now abandoned the attempt to depict the neurophysical foundations of our psychic processes and instead confines himself to the workings of a purely *psychic* apparatus. Nevertheless, Freud appears never to have given up the belief that in principle these neurophysical foundations could be made accessible. As he remarks of the workings of the secondary system, 'The mechanics of these processes are quite unknown to me; anyone who wished to take these ideas seriously would have to look for the physical analogies to them and find a means of picturing the movements that accompany excitation of neurones.'[50]

In his monograph, 'On Aphasia' (1891), Freud had tentatively adopted the theory of psycho-physical parallelism, writing:

---

[49] Paul Ricoeur, *Freud and Philosophy: an Essay on Interpretation*, trans. Denis Savage, (New Haven and London: Yale University Press, 1970).
[50] *SE* V, pp. 509-511.

> It is probable that the chain of physiological events in the nervous system does not stand in a causal connection with the psychical events. The physiological events do not cease as soon as the psychical ones begin; on the contrary, the physiological chain continues. What happens is simply that, after a certain point of time, each (or some) of its links has a psychical phenomenon corresponding to it. Accordingly, the psychical is a process parallel to the physiological – 'a dependent concomitant.[51]

Freud's position is taken directly from Hughlings-Jackson's essay on aphasia, published in 1878, which also embraces a form of psycho-physical parallelism.[52] This view, widely held in the second half of the nineteenth century and developed by Gustav Fechner, rejected Cartesian substance dualism in favour of what Fechner called a 'functional dependence' of mental events upon physical events. It could be stated, as it was by Fechner, in terms of a mathematical function, expressing the quantitative relation between a physical stimulus and a psychical sensation. Avowedly anti-metaphysical, it neither asserted nor denied a causal relation between the 'concomitants', but claimed only to provide a methodological principle governing empirical investigation. By this means, positivistic neurological science was allowed its own domain, while psychology was granted autonomy in its attempts to explain

---

[51] *SE* II, p. 207.

[52] See E. Stengel, 'Hughlings Jackson's Influence in Psychiatry', *British Journal of Psychiatry*, 1963, 109, pp. 348-355. Macmillan, pp. 104-5, 172-3.

phenomenal reality. In both domains an unbroken causal chain could be constructed without embarrassing gaps or intrusions.

As Freud became disillusioned with the *Project*, or, as he had intended to call it, his *Psychology for Neurologists*, it was then easy for him to revert to the language of pure psychology, in which the central ideas of the *Project* had clearly been originally conceived. The language of scientific neurology was to remain as a minor accompaniment, with the *caveat* that, at the present stage of scientific development it was impossible to bring the two discourses into full alignment.

In *An Outline of Psychoanalysis*, which can be regarded as Freud's last word on the topic, he explains that psychoanalysis is based upon the assumption that on the one hand we know of the bodily organ, the brain, and on the other, 'our acts of consciousness, which are immediate data and cannot further be explained by any sort of description. Everything that lies between is unknown to us, and the data do not include any direct relation between these two terminal points of our knowledge. If it existed, it would at the most afford an exact localization of the processes of consciousness and would give us no help towards understanding them.'[53]

Later in the *Outline*, however, Freud claims that the hypothesis of a psychical apparatus, extended in space, which gives rise to the phenomenon of consciousness 'only at one particular point and under certain conditions' is sufficient 'to establish psychology on foundations similar to those of any other science, such, for instance, as physics.'

He continues:

[53] *SE* XXIII, pp. 144-145.

> In our science as in the others, the problem is the same: behind the attributes (qualities) of the object under examination which are presented directly to our perception, we have to discover something else which is more independent of the particular receptive capacity of our sense organs and which approximates more closely to what may be supposed to be the real state of affairs. We have no hope of being able to reach the latter itself, since it is evident that everything new that we have inferred must nevertheless be transferred back into the language of our perceptions, from which it is simply impossible to free ourselves.[54]

Reality, he claims, will always remain unknowable, but psychoanalysis, like other sciences, has discovered technical methods 'of filling up the gaps in the phenomena of our consciousness, and we make use of those methods just as a physicist makes use of experiment.' 'And if, for instance, we say: 'At this point an unconscious memory intervened', what that means is: 'At this point something occurred of which we are totally unable to form a conception, but which, if it had entered our consciousness, could only have been described in such and such a way.''[55]

In *The Interpretation of Dreams*, Freud had begun to elaborate a quite new approach to the problem of psychic continuity by fully embracing the concept of the unconscious. Yet, as he repeatedly makes clear, the theoretical argument of chapter seven is underpinned by the theory of hysteria developed in his clinical practice. In the section of the chapter which deals with regression, Freud draws attention to the *Studies in*

---

[54] *SE* XXIII, p. 196.
[55] p. 197.

Hysteria in which it was argued, 'that when it was possible to bring infantile scenes (whether they were memories or phantasies) into consciousness, they were seen like hallucinations and lost that characteristic only in the process of being reported.' Such infantile scenes function 'as models for the content of dreams,' since 'the transformation of thoughts into visual images may be in part the result of the attraction which memories couched in visual form and eager for revival bring to bear upon thoughts cut off from consciousness and struggling to find expression. On this view a dream might be described as *a substitute for an infantile scene modified by being transferred onto a recent experience*. The infantile scene is unable to bring about its own revival and has to be content with returning as a dream.'[56]

Underlying Freud's view of the quasi-hallucinatory theory of dreams, as Ricoeur points out, is Freud's earlier belief in the reality of the childhood scene of seduction. In this 'topographical regression', the flow of psychic energy which normally begins with the sensory image [*Bild*] of perception and ends by being discharged in motor activity (the structure set out in the *Project*), is reversed. Since the idea [*Vorstellung*] is repressed, the energy flows back towards the perceptual pole and ends in hallucinatory activity.[57] For Ricoeur, whose aim is to rescue Freud's thought from realism or the 'snare of thingness', the childhood seduction theory was an error the effects of which are still present here. He insists, 'There is no doubt that by interpreting the infantile scene as a real memory Freud is forced to confuse fantasies with the mnemic traces of real perceptions, in which case topographical regression is a regression to perception and the proper dimension of the imaginary is lost.'[58] The three forms of

[56] *SE* V, p. 546.
[57] Ricoeur, pp. 105-7.
[58] Ricoeur, p. 96.

regression involved in dream, the return of thought to pictorial representation (formal regression), the return to childhood (temporal regression), and the flow from repressed idea to hallucination (topographical regression), are all to be regarded as aspects of the 'dreamwork' [*Traumwerk*], to be understood not as real but as requiring hermeneutic interpretation.

As Ricoeur makes clear, the childhood seduction theory continued to exert a disrupting influence in *The Interpretation of Dreams* which is by no means marginal to the argument. The hallucinatory theory of wishes, upon which the dream theory is based, derives from the *Project* of 1895 and from the theory of childhood seduction as a real memory. The push-pull theory of regression in chapter seven depends not only upon the resistance of censorship which denies entry to a thought into consciousness, but also upon 'a simultaneous attraction exercised upon the thought by the presence of memories possessing great sensory force.'[59] The *psychical* perception system of the visual organ is activated by a memory, 'a *revival* of a visual excitation which was originally an immediate one.'[60] Insofar as fantasies are allowed a role in the content of dreams it is as the reproduction of infantile experiences. The infantile scene, then, is clearly the scene of seduction under another name.

The idea of a another psychic locality

In Ricoeur's view the mistaken persistence of the perceptual model prevents Freud from breaking completely with natural spatiality and replacing it fully with the idea of a 'psychical locality.' Although Freud states, 'I shall carefully avoid the temptation to determine

[59] *SE* V, p. 547.
[60] *SE* V, p. 546.

psychical locality in any anatomical fashion. I shall remain upon psychological ground...'[61], he nevertheless, as Ricoeur points out, wavers between representing places homologous to physical localities and representing a 'scene of action' that is not in any way part of the world. Freud was here attempting to follow Fechner's claim that '*the scene of action of dreams is different from that of waking ideational life.*'[62] This hypothesis alone, Freud remarks, 'makes the special peculiarities of dream-life intelligible.'

The analogy through which Freud attempts to explain the idea of a psychical locality runs as follows. A psychical locality, he claims, corresponds to a point inside the apparatus of a microscope, camera or telescope at which an image starts to come into being. Such images come into being, he continues, at 'ideal points, regions in which no tangible component of the apparatus is situated.' The mental systems may be thought of as standing in a spatial relation to each other in the same way as the systems of lenses in a telescope are arranged, one behind the other. In fact, he points out, all that is necessary is that the excitation passes through the systems in a temporal sequence, one after the other.

The analogy shows the extent to which Freud continues to ground the psychical in the physical. The 'instrument that carries out our mental functions' is clearly the physical brain, 'also known to us in the form of an anatomical preparation', and the mental systems are the equivalent of physical lenses. Freud's analogy, then, is designed to show how the dream-image is able to come into being at a point which does not correspond to anywhere 'within' the systems of our mental apparatus.

---

[61] *SE* V, p. 536.
[62] *SE* V, p. 536.

Ricoeur argues that Freud's belief in the seduction scene prevents him from freeing himself fully from a certain naturalism in the way he conceives of a psychical locality. Mistaking for perception what was in truth fantasy commits him to a topography in which he cannot fully grasp the idea of a 'scene of action' that is in no way part of the natural world, that derives from no real memory but is the product of 'representability' [*Darstellbarkeit*] in the dreamwork.

Freud introduces the discussion of psychical locality in *The Interpretation of Dreams* by referring to the case of the recently bereaved father, sleeping while his son's coffin has caught fire in an adjoining room, while the servant who was attending him has fallen asleep. In the father's dream, the dead son comes to awaken him with the terrible whisper: *Vater, siehst du denn nicht dass ich verbrenne* ('Father, can't you see that I'm burning?') What is of paramount interest to Freud in this particular dream is that it focuses our attention on 'the essential characteristics that differentiate dreams from waking life and consequently call for explanation.'[63]

Lacan takes this as his starting-point in *The Four Fundamental Concepts of Psychoanalysis* for a discussion of the encounter with 'a real that always eludes us,' an encounter which first presented itself in the form of the trauma and repetition-compulsion [*Wiederholungzwang*]. The trauma is that which makes us aware of the existence of the real, and which forces upon us an encounter. The function of traumatic repetition, it might be said, is that of mastering the trauma, but, as Lacan forcefully questions, 'who masters, where is the master here, to be mastered?' How is it possible for the dream, the bearer of desire, to produce that which makes the trauma repeatedly assert itself? Part of that which belongs to the real must remain within the grip of the pleasure principle, exercising itself as compulsion and

[63] *The Interpretation of Dreams*, p. 654. (Pelican, Vol. IV)

constraint, 'in that non-temporal locus … which forces us to posit what Freud calls, in homage to Fechner, *die Idee einer anderer Lokalität*, the idea of another locality, another space, another scene, *the between perception and consciousness*.'[64]

Lacan goes on to draw our attention to the experience in which we are awakened by a knocking on the door and, at first, interpret the knocking within the context of our dream, only then to reconstitute our representation of this knocking in consciousness as we awake, thereby recovering possession of the representation. The question that concerns Lacan is what there is 'that motivates the emergence of the represented reality, namely the phenomenon, distance, the gap itself that constitutes awakening.'[65]

Lacan here goes further than Freud himself by suggesting that what wakes the father from his sleep is '*in* the dream, another reality,' the reality that the child takes his arm and whispers his reproach. Lacan asks, 'Is there not more reality in this message than in the noise by which the father also identifies the strange reality of what is happening in the room next door. Is not the missed reality that caused the death of the child expressed in these words?'[66] The action of preventing the fire is too late 'in relation to the psychical reality manifested in the words spoken.' 'Is not the dream essentially, one might say, an act of homage to the missed reality – the reality that can no longer produce itself except by repeating itself endlessly, in some never attained awakening?'[67] This psychic reality, which it is impossible either to avoid or to act upon, always comes too late. 'Here, the real is that

[64] Jacques Lacan, *The Four Fundamental Concepts of Psychoanalysis*', trans. Alan Sheridan, (London: Penguin, 1994), p. 56.
[65] p. 57.
[66] p. 58.
[67] p. 58.

which always comes back to the same place where the subject in so far as he thinks, where the *res cogitans*, does not meet it.'[68]

The reality principle, although it retains its ascendancy, does not here have the last word. The real, *qua* trauma, lies in abeyance within the homeostatic functioning of the pleasure principle, asserting its existence while never appearing in person. Hence its ability to figure within dream and phantasy. Lacan even suggests that Freud's obsessive search for the first encounter, the actually experienced primal scene, in the story of the *Wolf Man*, the real that lay behind the phantasy, was itself driven by the 'real' that directed his research.[69]

Laplanche and the general theory of seduction

Jean Laplanche, a former student of Lacan's, in developing his 'new foundations' for psychoanalysis, placed a reworking of Freud's seduction theory at the heart of his project, identifying seduction as 'the major generative factor in psychoanalysis.'[70] Characterizing his project as the shift from Freud's 'special theory of seduction' to his own 'general theory of seduction,' his criticisms of Freud largely overlook the inconsistencies in his formulations of seduction theory and focus instead upon the narrowness of its range. Freud concerns himself only with *pathological* scenes brought about by *perverse* adults. Laplanche is able, therefore, to endorse certain of Freud's self-criticisms in the 1897 letter to Fliess, while still regarding the renunciation of the seduction theory as a 'veritable cataclysm.'[71]

[68] p. 49.
[69] p. 54.
[70] Jean Laplanche, *New Foundations for Psychoanalysis*, trans. David Macey, (Oxford: Basil Blackwell, 1989), p. 104.
[71] Laplanche, *NFP*, pp. 114-118.

Freud *represses* the theory instead of widening its range and when he later revises elements of it he does so in an 'unrecognizable' form.

In *Life and Death in Psychoanalysis* Laplanche returns to the *Project* of 1895 and the case of 'Emma' to develop his reading of the seduction theory or what Laplanche calls the theory of the 'hysterical *proton pseudos* [first lie],'[72] arguing that Freud situates seduction in two different registers; first, as clinical observation, variously affirmed, denied, called into question or reaffirmed throughout Freud's writings, but also as a *theory* 'elaborated on the basis of that observation of the fact(s) of seduction.' In his early studies Freud uncovers memories or 'scenes' and tirelessly pursues some previous 'traumatic' event which gave rise to such 'scenes' – ultimately the 'primal scene' [*Urszene*]. Then, as we have seen, in the September 1897 letter to Fliess, Freud announces his loss of faith in the seduction theory and the impossibility of distinguishing between 'truth and emotionally-charged fiction' since there are no 'indications of reality' in the unconscious. Yet, Laplanche notes, Freud continues, despite the crucial introduction of the category of 'psychical reality', to oscillate between the search for real, lived events and conceiving of such memories as (merely) imaginary.

It is here that Laplanche finds Freud wanting:

> We might say that he failed to render explicit what is, nevertheless, present in the notion of "psychical reality," something which would have all the consistency of the real without, however, being verifiable in external experience, a

[72] Jean Laplanche, *Life and Death in Psychoanalysis*, (Baltimore: Johns Hopkins University Press, 1976), p.30.

> category which might, on first approach, be designated as the "structural."[73]

Freud's term *proton pseudos*, as used in the *Project*, signifies, according to Laplanche, 'a first – specifically: hysterical lie.' Hysterics tend to lie and an example of this would be to present a scene as having occurred in their childhood when it was in fact imaginary. The hysteric takes desire for reality, so that the fantasy of seduction by the father is translated into an actual scene of seduction by the father.

Laplanche continues:

> With the term *proton pseudos*, however, something other than a subjective lie is being invoked; at stake is a transition from the subjective to a grounding – perhaps even to a transcendental dimension: in any event a kind of objective lie inscribed in the facts.... If hysterics lie, they are above all the first victims of a kind of lie or deception. Not that they have been lied to; it is rather as though there existed in the facts themselves a kind of fundamental duplicity for which we would propose the term *deceit* [fallace]. "Primal deceit": perhaps such is our best translation of the *proton pseudos* in its specificity.[74]

This is confusing on a number of levels. First, the term *proton pseudos*, taken from Aristotle's *Prior Analytics* (66a, Ch. 18), signifies a preceding falsity which renders a subsequent statement, based upon it, false. A falsity is not necessarily a lie, subjective or otherwise, and in the logical context of Aristotle's discussion it would be irrelevant

---

[73] *LDP*, p. 33.
[74] p. 34.

whether it was a lie or not. Freud's use of the Aristotelian term itself suggests that the focus of his interest is in the unconscious connections made in the aetiology of hysteria. If hysterics have a tendency to lie, and this is nowhere brought into Freud's argument concerning the *proton pseudos*, where the defining characteristic of hysterics is said to be that they are subject to a compulsion exercised by excessively intense ideas, this does not necessarily have any bearing upon the originating event (if there was one) through which they became hysterics.

Secondly, Laplanche is reading back into the seduction theory of the *Project* Freud's later rejection of the seduction theory in favour of the theory of seduction as fantasy. How could this help explain the term *proton pseudos* which is advanced in order to support the early seduction theory? Since Emma *had* been the victim of a sexual assault as a child the *proton pseudos* could not have been a hysterical lie based upon a sexual fantasy.

Freud argues that analysis reveals that an excessively intense idea (A) which inexplicably forces its way into consciousness with distressing effects, is caused by an idea (B) which 'justifiably' and intelligibly produces such effects. 'A has become a substitute, a *symbol* for B.'[75] Idea A has become persistent and intrusive because idea B has been subject to repression and amnesia. In circumstances which should call forth idea B, idea A is produced instead. This is a causal process operating at an unconscious level which Freud in the *Project* believes can in principle be explained in terms of neuronic displacement.

The hysterical *proton pseudos* is presented as 'a special psychical constellation in the sexual sphere.'[76] Having, prior to analysis, no

[75] *SE* I, p. 349.
[76] p. 353.

recollection of the sexual assault upon her as a child, an incident occurring after puberty which revived the still unconscious memory and produced a sexual release transformed into anxiety which she found impossible to explain. Whereas the original incident had not been repressed, the revival of the memory in the second incident was now associated with guilt and consequently repressed. It is therefore the memory rather than the original event which produces the trauma by '*deferred action*' [nachträglichkeit]. To this extent it could justifiably be claimed that Freud has already identified 'psychic reality' as the site of the traumatic event.[77] The underlying cause, however, is said to be 'the retardation of puberty as compared with the rest of the individual's development.'[78] Freud adds that for this reason every adolescent 'must carry the germ of hysteria within him.'

As Laplanche points out, neither the earlier nor the later event was in itself traumatic. The trauma is, he argues, situated in the play of 'deceit' enacted between the two events. Sexuality, uniquely, is the domain in which 'we find that complex and endlessly repeated interplay – midst a temporal succession of missed occasions – of "too early" and "too late".'[79] Even when the existence of pre-pubescent childhood sexuality is acknowledged, it remains the case that the child lacks the affective and ideational resources to assimilate the sexual messages received from the world of adults. It is this 'earliness' or 'lateness' disrupting sexual maturation which Laplanche believes to be at the core of the Freudian scheme.

The theory of seduction must therefore move beyond the question of the '*circumstantial reality of seduction*' to that of 'the intrusion into

[77] *The Language of Psychoanalysis*, Jean Laplanche and Jean-Bernard Pontalis, trans. Donald Nicholson Smith, (London: The Hogarth Press, 1973), p. 406.
[78] *SE* I, p. 356.
[79] Laplanche, p. 43.

the universe of the child of certain meanings of the adult world which is conveyed by the most ordinary and innocent of acts.'[80] Attention is therefore no longer focused upon the 'abusive father' but upon the primal intersubjective relation, that between mother and child. This, Laplanche maintains, 'is the most profound sense of the theory of seduction', and that which Freud discovered in his later writings.[81]

The Freudian theory of the *proton pseudos*, then, must be shifted into the realm of psychic reality and understood not as a putative event but 'as a kind of implantation of adult sexuality in the child.'[82] This primal, structural intrusion is itself the beginning of 'humanization', so that to speak of a prior 'innocence' on the part of the child is 'to forge a myth exactly symmetrical to the myth of seduction.'

Laplanche suggests, following Freud, that what is attacked and threatened by sexuality is the ego itself. The intrusion of sexuality means that 'the ego is outmanoeuvred, taken from behind as by some ruse of war.' The ego is 'overcome, disarmed, subjected to the drive process, that primary process against which, however, it was in its entirety, *constituted.*'[83]

At the heart of Laplanche's reading of Freud is the thesis that the 'Copernican revolution' begun by Freud is based upon the decentring of the psyche, that 'the other thing (*das Andere*) that is the unconscious is only maintained in its radical alterity by the other person (*der Andere*): in brief, by seduction. When the alterity of the other person is blurred, when it is reintegrated in the form of *my* fantasy of the other,

---

[80] Laplanche, p. 44.
[81] Laplanche, p. 44.
[82] Laplanche, p. 46.
[83] Laplanche, p. 47.

of *my* 'fantasy of seduction', then the alterity of the unconscious is put at risk.'[84]

Freud vacillates, Laplanche argues, between, on the one hand, a subjectivism that reduces the other to the subject's perception of the other, and a naïve realism which seeks to track down some real, historical abusive other.[85] His pre-phenomenological approach fails to grasp the fundamental insight which the seduction theory makes possible, namely, *'the reversal of the problem of access to the other into that of the priority of the other.*'[86] Laplanche also rejects the Lacanian prioritization of language insofar as it tends to efface the alterity of the concrete other in trans-individual structures. The infant is surrounded by messages on all sides which greatly exceed his or her capacity for understanding, but many of them are non-verbal. It is not that the child lacks the linguistic code. 'What is crucial is the fact that the adult world is entirely infiltrated with unconscious and sexual significations to which *adults themselves* do not have the code.'

Laplanche, then, addresses the essential task, never adequately resolved by Freud, of giving a precise meaning to the notion of psychic reality. It is, he claims, a third kind of reality, distinct from external, material reality and from psychological reality, the latter signifying that which is, reducible 'in the last analysis to our subjective lived experience.'[87] As already indicated, Laplanche rejects the identification of psychic reality with the Lacanian Symbolic, which he considers narrowly linguistic and structural. In Laplanche's view, when a signifier passes into the unconscious it loses its referentiality, as a result of repression, and no longer 'presents' anything but itself.

[84] *Essays on Otherness*, Jean Laplanche, (London and New York: Routledge, 1999), p. 71.
[85] *EO*, p. 73.
[86] *EO*, p. 72.
[87] *EO*, p. 91.

The *message* is a 'signifier *to*' which is no longer a 'signifier *of*' (a signified). 'We know *that* it signifies, but not *what* it signifies.'[88] This designified-signifier, acquiring a 'thing-like presentation', is the form of unconscious psychic reality;[89] a 'psychical entity that is as hard as iron, and perhaps stronger than the perceptual fact itself.'[90]

Seduction can be said to have occurred when a certain kind of message has been communicated from an adult to child, a message which, Laplanche contends, 'is opaque to its recipient and its transmitter alike.' Seduction 'is neither more nor less real than a parapraxis, the reality of which is not reducible to its materiality. A slip of the tongue is no more *nor* less real materially than a correctly pronounced word. But a slip also does not boil down to each of the interlocutors' conceptions of it, which are often incomplete and reductive. It conveys a detectable, observable message, which is partly interpretable by psychoanalysis.'[91]

The theory of seduction, in Laplanche's view, helps resolve a major difficulty in Freud's thought, that of the origin of sexuality, which Freud attempts to explain through the concept of 'leaning-on' (*étayage, Anlehnung, anaclisis*), whereby the sexual drive and self-preservation arise from the same source, so that, for example, the erotic breast is substituted for the milk, by a kind of metonymy. Laplanche rejects this impossible 'alchemy' which attempts to found the cultural attribute of sexuality on the endogenous resources of the solitary infant. It is rather the breast as the bearer of unconscious adult messages that stimulates the movements which may lead to auto-erotic

---

[88] *New Foundations for Psychoanalysis*, Jean Laplanche, trans. David Macey, (Oxford: Basil Blackwell, 1989), pp. 44-45.
[89] *EO*, p. 92.
[90] *EO*, p. 153.
[91] *EO*, p. 170.

activity and the repression of enigmatic signifiers introduced by the adult.

In primal repression a primordial unconscious is split off from the psyche which constitutes the first source-objects of the drive. These, at first dormant, enigmatic signifiers are implanted but only later repressed at the stage when they are reactivated and become threatening. Infantile sexual theories attempt to 'bind' these traumatic signifiers, and the partial failure of such symbolization leads to the repression of 'an unmasterable, uncircumscribable remainder.' These are the thing-like presentations, isolated, outside of signification, which form the *id*.[92]

Laplanche, then, insists that seduction is not a fantasy but real, brought about by the intrusion of an adult other, and a key moment in the development of the psychic structure. However, he is also at pains to avoid his argument being 'mistaken for a factual realism.' For this reason, he writes, 'it is essential to put forward a third category of reality that is continually reduced to those of material and psychological reality, i.e. the reality of the message and, more specifically in the framework of analytic theory, the enigmatic message.'[93]

Charting a course between determinism and hermeneutics, between the attempt to recover the subject's 'real' history and creative, hermeneutic 'interpretation' by the analyst, Laplanche argues for a shift from 'event' to 'scene', from 'memories' of uncertain verisimilitude to 'mnemic traces' [*Erinnerungensspuren*] cut off from their origins and access routes. But these 'scenes', the powerfully visual, hallucinatory character of which Freud emphasized, are, for

---

[92] *EO*, pp. 128-129.
[93] *EO*, p. 196.

Laplanche, 'first and foremost messages.'[94] Whereas subjective 'interpretation' does not imply the existence of a prior message, 'translation', in Laplanche's terms, involves a signifier which represents one subject to another. In the case of the 'enigmatic signifier' transmitted unconsciously from adult to child, the child construes the message in whatever imperfect way he or she can, using the resources available. This indeterminacy eliminates the possibility of establishing linear causality. The goal of analysis cannot be a general 'lifting of amnesia,' but is rather 'a deconstruction of old constructions,' opening the way to new translations.[95] In answer to Freud's question as to what kind of material it is that the patient puts before the analyst, Laplanche's reply is clear and decisive:

> Memories or fragments of memories, admittedly distorted and ideologized to a greater or lesser extent, but which it would be futile and hypocritical to place on the same level as fantasies, as this would be to deny that they are intentionally and irreducibly directed towards an actual past. It is within these memories that the major scenes are to be found, scattered and often fragmented or repeated – the scenes that are in effect shot through with enigmatic parental messages.[96]

Seduction as a transcendental structure

As Laplanche and Pontalis point out, whatever degree of prominence Freud at various times attributed to fantasy, behind it he continued to search for the ground of reality on which it was based. The case study

---

[94] *EO*, p. 154.
[95] *EO*, p. 164.
[96] *EO*, p. 161.

of the 'Wolf Man' is the *locus classicus* of this apparent obsession. In 1917, in a new version of this quest, Freud introduced the concept of the *Urphantasien*, primal fantasy. As Laplanche and Pontalis observe, since it had proved impossible to determine whether the primal scene was reality or fantasy, Freud resorted to 'a foundation in something which transcends both individual experience and what is imagined.'[97] In them, Freud speculates, the individual reaches into 'primaeval experience,' in which the material of fantasy - the seduction of children, the observation of parental intercourse and castration - 'were once real occurrences.'[98]

While rejecting Freud's phylogenetic explanation, Laplanche and Pontalis raise the possibility that this 'reality which, as Freud insists, has an autonomous and structural status with regard to the subject who is totally dependent on it,' might be assimilated to the symbolic order of Levi-Strauss or Lacan. They resist this move, however, on the grounds that as 'loaded with elements of imagination,' the contingency of such a structure 'would make it difficult to assimilate to a purely transcendental schema, even if it provides the possibility of experience.'

In the case of seduction theory, however, as indicated earlier, Laplanche, in attempting to distinguish the *proton pseudos* from ordinary subjective experience suggests that it be regarded as 'a kind of objective lie inscribed in the facts,' a 'primal deceit' that may be grounded in a transcendental dimension.

Slavoj Zizek, also rejecting the alternatives of 'brutal empirical realism' or fantasy on the part of the patient in relation to childhood seduction, follows Laplanche in claiming:

---

[97] Jean Laplanche and Jean-Bernard Pontalis, 'Fantasy and the Origins of Sexuality', *International Journal of Psychoanalysis*, 1968, Vol.49, I, p. 9.
[98] *SE* XVI, p. 371. Also *SE* XVII, p. 97.

> Seduction is rather a kind of transcendental structure, the minimal *a priori* formal constellation of the child confronted with the impenetrable acts of the Other which bear witness to the Other's unconscious – and we are never dealing here with simple "facts," but always with facts located in the space of indeterminacy between "too soon" and "too late": the child is originally helpless, thrown into the world where he is unable to take care of himself – that is, his or her survival skills develop too late; at the same time, the encounter with the sexualized Other always, by a structural necessity, comes "too soon," as an unexpected shock which can never be properly symbolized, translated into the universe of meaning. The fact of seduction is thus that of the Kantian transcendental X, a structurally necessary transcendental illusion.[99]

Zizek is here drawing upon the concept of the 'parallax view', developed in Kojin Karatani's reading of Kant. The critical role of the 'parallax view', as explained by Zizek, is that confronted by an antinomy such as that presented in Laplanche's seduction theory, in which seduction can neither be reduced to reality or fantasy, is, like the Lacanian Real, to assert the 'impossible difference' which structures our experience of reality. Kant's 'transcendental turn' opened up this new dimension which, as Karatani puts it, involves 'bracketing the imagined self-evidence of the empirical consciousness in order to reveal the (unconscious) conditions that constitute it.'[100]

---

[99] Slavoj Zizek, *The Parallax View*, (Cambridge Mass: MIT Press), 2006), p. 20.

[100] Kojin Karatani, *Transscritique: On Kant and Marx*, trans. Sabu Kohso, (Cambridge Mass: MIT Press, 2005), p. 82.

If, then, there is 'a kind of objective lie inscribed in the facts,' this is because of shared unconscious structures which determine our understanding of the 'facts'. A transcendental illusion occurs when the subjective necessity functioning within these structures is experienced as an objective necessity in things themselves. As Kant explains:

> This is *an illusion* which can no more be prevented than we can prevent the sea appearing higher at the horizon than at the shore, since we see it through higher light rays; or to cite a still better example, than the astronomer can prevent the moon from appearing larger at its rising, although he is not deceived by this illusion.[101]

Transcendental illusion is not, it should be emphasized, an empirical illusion, but a deceptive extension of understanding beyond the proper limits of its application, 'to seize possession of an entirely new domain.'[102] The paralogisms and antinomies generating transcendental illusion are pseudo-rational inferences which are both 'natural' and 'inevitable'.

Any attempt to apply this concept to the seduction theory must therefore take us away from any explanation in terms of the 'hysterical lie' and towards the necessary but illusory reasoning processes employed by the child to grasp the meaning of enigmatic messages within the constraints of childhood sexual theories, later modified by post-pubescent repression. This form of *nachträglichkeit* may well coincide with what remains of significance in the *proton pseudos* theory of the *Project*.

---

[101] *Immanuel Kant's Critique of Pure Reason*, trans. Norman Kemp Smith, (London: Macmillan, 1950), pp. 299-300, A297, B354.
[102] Kant, p. 299, A296.

Sublimation, the sublime and the superego

Antigone, written in the 5th century BC, is one of the founding texts of Western political thought insofar as it deals with the conflict between ethics and political power, between the old and the young, between male domination and female resistance, and, not least, between reason and madness. It raises these issues with a depth and immediacy which have long disappeared from western political theory. It is impossible for the modern reader of *Antigone* not to see prefigured in her the modern 'terrorist' in mortal conflict with the state. Although Antigone's 'crime' was no greater than that of carrying out traditional burial rights upon her dead brother, she nevertheless embodies a particular and extreme form of rebellion against authority, so uncompromising that it takes on the appearance of madness.

Bernard Stiegler has written that Antigone 'is the figure of *transgression* and *youth* par excellence, of filial *love* and *fidelity*, and also of fidelity to that tradition that grants a burial to the departed, whoever they may be – which she refers to as a divine law.'[1] For Stiegler, Antigone represents the *sublimation* of the tensions between the young and the old, and between the letter of the law and justice. She is 'sublime' because she makes her love for her dead brother Polynices into the love of the city, 'even as its undecidable truth, by exceeding that conflict of the generations from which she nevertheless derives.' Although, as the daughter of Oedipus, afflicted with

---

[1] Bernard Stiegler, *Uncontrollable Societies of Disaffected Individuals*, trans. Daniel Ross, (Cambridge: Polity, 2013), p. 35.

'inherited excess' [*démesure*], she proclaims *aidos*, that is, the shame which restrains a person from doing wrong: 'to leave a corpse unburied is to apply the law *shamelessly* (it is to ignore divine law) and to commit in the name of the law the *worst* of injustices.' She is desperate, representing an insoluble conflict, but filled with an energy that she 'precisely, *sublimates*.'

Her despair 'trans-forms itself into a sacrifice which is itself like the sublimation of that death drive that is called, at times, acting out, the passage to the act, or more specifically, suicide.' She takes death over life [*elle se fait donner la mort contre sa vie*] and over her desire. That is, she *prefers* to die, which is not the same as *wanting* to die, and which 'can appear *in the eyes of those who are without shame* only as a refusal of life, as acting out, as the passage to the act of someone who is desperate, who has lost all reason, and who has sunk into excess.' This *aidos*, which for Stiegler is the action of the superego, is 'very close to Hades, that is, also to the death instinct,' the Hades 'where dead souls wander, like demonic powers, revenant spirits, yet weaving the desires of the living.' 'Everything happens as if [...] it was *spirit* insofar as it is the *return* of the most ancient into the current, but a *demonic* return that, mostly, passes through the transgression of youth.' In our time, Stiegler argues, '(t)he tyrant who seizes the law is [...] no longer Creon; it is the market that no longer knows any limits, having forgotten the meaning of shame.'[2]

The Antigone Complex

The modern-day equivalent of Antigone, in Stiegler's view, is to be found in the debased form of the 'Antigone complex'. In present-day consumer society, ruled by the market and the incitement to enjoy, the

---

[2] *Uncontrollable Societies*, p. 39.

'*desire for the most high*', in the absence of a superego, failing to find the authority that sublimates and socializes desire, 'invents itself *from motives that, departing from the search for the better, lead to the worst.* When desublimation liquidates the superego, desire gives itself new figures [...] But it then becomes the hideous beast [*la bête immonde*] of all abominations, liberating that which takes the form of *negative sublimation*.'[3]

The reign of terror imposed by global financial capitalism produces 'literally intolerable *injustices*' in the eyes of anyone endowed with 'the shame of being human,' resulting in 'the proliferation of irrational, demented and murderous acts, bearing that specific death drive that one calls terrorism, and that will only increase to apocalyptic levels if industrial democracies do not take radical measures in their *own* lands.' Such suicidal passages to the act are lived by their authors as 'a form of *testimony*,' that is, in order to attest before others, 'to confront a legacy by leaving a legacy oneself, and through death given as well as through one's own death – which is always in one way or another a testament, even if only through the fear it inspires. If this is true it means that all these acts tend to evolve towards the figure of the martyr.'

The weakening of primary identification, of parental authority and the superego, in modern society and the proliferation of secondary identifications through the agency of the market and the mass media, produce the '*pathogenic*' form of sublimation which is what Stiegler calls 'negative sublimation.' He continues, 'These secondary identifications can become uncontrollable, giving rise to 'suicidal processes, comprised of all kinds of murderous 'sublimation' processes, an infernal *mimesis* that I call the Antigone complex.'[4] The

---

[3] *Uncontrollable Societies*, p. 48.
[4] *Uncontrollable Societies*, p. 60.

failure of society to provide genuinely socially productive objects of sublimation, the condition of the 'social bond', incites desperation and 'a far greater need for *explosive* compensatory objects,' offering to the young reasons for hope, whatever their provenance, from 'extremist ideologies, religious sects, evangelical churches, clandestine mosques,' etc. The actions which result from this are generally met with repressive policies increasing the general sense of despair.

A great deal turns here upon what is meant by the term 'sublimation'. Since Stiegler does not offer a definition, it seems reasonable to assume that he is using the term in a conventional Freudian sense, insofar as it has been possible to establish what Freud himself meant by it. In general, it refers to the capacity of the sexual drive to divert its aim, without repression, into activities which are deemed socially useful. As Laplanche and Pontalis point out, however, the domain of sublimated activities in Freud's thought is 'badly demarcated' and it is unclear whether Freud believes sublimation to involve *both* a change of aim and of object. With the introduction of the theory of narcissism in Freud's later thought, sublimation is then claimed to take place within an intermediate period in which libido is withdrawn from the external object and directed onto the ego, so that desexualization becomes possible. Laplanche and Pontalis conclude that the theory of sublimation was left in a 'primitive state,' with the unsatisfactory consequence that while the concept is essential to psychoanalytic theory and practice it has been theorized only in an inconsistent and inadequate form.[5]

Paul Ricoeur similarly pointed out that although Freud attributed a crucial role to sublimation in the metapsychology of the superego, insofar as the latter is not based upon identification, it depends entirely

---

[5] Jean Laplanche & J.-B. Pontalis, *The Language of Psychoanalysis*, (New York: W.W. Norton & Co.,1973), pp. 430-433.

upon mysterious 'pathways', such that Freud's theory 'presents only a question regarding sublimation.' In the absence of a grounding notion, 'desexualization, sublimation, and identification are...three enigmas placed end to end.'[6] In particular, the conceptual gap between external authority and the 'solipsism of desire' remains unresolved.

Stiegler claims that Antigone is 'sublime' because she transforms her love for Polynices into love for the city, and thereby 'sublimates' the tensions between the young and the old. In the Freudian sense, this would mean that she redirects the (disruptive and incestuous) libidinal energy she feels in relation to her brother towards the 'higher', socially harmonious goal of justice and the public good. It is unclear whether by the term 'sublime' anything more is meant than that she has achieved this form of sublimation. There is no suggestion in Stiegler's analysis that the term is being used with any aesthetic implication.

Antigone's libidinal energy, 'desperate', inherited as an 'excess', transforms itself into a sacrifice, which is *like* the sublimation of the death drive and *wrongly* regarded by those without shame as acting out or a suicidal passage to the act. Her decision to sacrifice herself is a choice based upon her sense of shame, indicating the action of what Freud calls the superego. This is said to be *very close to* the death instinct and acts *as if* it were the return of the spirits of the dead, of spirit in the form of the demonic, passing through the transgressive character of youth. All of these markers in Stiegler's text prepare the way for the distinction between Antigone's 'sublime' sacrifice and what is presented as its evil double, the 'pathogenic' form of modern terrorism, a manifestation of the death drive, both suicidal and murderous.

---

[6] Paul Ricoeur, *Freud and Philosophy: an Essay on Interpretation*, trans. Denis Savage, (New Haven: Yale University Press, 1970), p. 483.

The argument hinges therefore upon the concept of sublimation and the distinction between 'good' sublimation and 'bad' sublimation, that is, *negative* sublimation, which, rather inconsistently, is said to be the product of *de*sublimation. Desublimation, effected through the agency of modern capitalism, 'liquidates' the superego. Negative sublimation is produced by the sense of 'literally intolerable injustice' in the eyes of anyone 'endowed with the shame of being human', but the sense of injustice and the experience of such a sense of shame have already been identified as the mark of the action of the superego. The first problem, then, is how, as a result of desublimation, any form of sublimation is possible. The 'desire for the most high,' we are told, in the absence of the traditional authorities which are internalized as the superego (notably, parental authority), 'invents itself *from motives that, departing from the search for the better, lead to the worst.*' It is not clear how desire can 'invent itself' unless this is simply a reference to sublimation. The 'new figures of desire' that have emerged, Stiegler suggests, embody motives which do not seek the better and which result in the worst. But if negative sublimation *is* a form of sublimation, then its function is to transform the objects of desire from the base into the higher, even if its actions result in the worst. Otherwise these actions have nothing to with sublimation.

Finally, and most fundamentally, negative sublimation seems to be understood by Stiegler mainly in terms of the production of beliefs and activities which he characterizes as not socially constructive and which threaten the social bond. Whether such an external criterion has a proper place in the definition and application of a psychoanalytic concept has been an issue ever since Freud introduced it. There is also, as Stiegler is well aware, a considerable difference between what is socially approved and what is genuinely socially constructive, as well as obvious cultural and historical variations in both. The hollowing out of all social values and the weakening of all forms of authority in advanced capitalist societies seem to make it impossible to draw any clear lines of the kind that Stiegler proposes.

If the formation of the superego depends upon the existence of an authority that sublimates and socializes desire, and if the dominance of the market and the 'incitement to enjoy' have led to the 'absence of a superego,' then negative sublimation could only be a form of sublimation that occurs in the absence of a superego. Stiegler provides no indications of the psychic agencies which might be involved in this process or how it might be possible. If the concepts of sublimation and the superego are to be usefully applied they must be radically rethought, and to this end, the work of Lacan provides a basis upon which we can advance.

Lacan and the concept of sublimation

First, with regard to Antigone, it is worth noting that Stiegler appears to use the terms 'acting out' and 'passage to the act' as more or less synonymous, while Lacan distinguishes between them in a way which is significant here. Whereas 'acting out' involves the address of a symbolic message to the Other, as for instance when Stiegler, rather patronisingly, describes the French riots of November 2005 as 'a call for help, just like those suicide attempts carried out by adolescents,'[7] 'passage to the act' involves, in Lacan's thought, the dissolution of the subject and an exit from the Symbolic order. Antigone's 'absolute act', as understood by Lacan, is not an appeal to anyone but an 'entry into the Real.' The encounter with the Real is a rupture, a dislocation, which disorders the symbolic universe and creates a void in which a change might take place, dissolving the subject, but allowing the possibility of the birth of a new subject. While Stiegler seems to

[7] *Uncontrollable Societies*, p. 53.

explain Antigone's act in terms of sublimation as conventionally understood, Lacan understands it essentially in terms of this entry into the Real.

Lacan's Seminar VII is extensively concerned with the concept of sublimation [*Sublimierung*] which he considers to be such a problematic term that he avoids using it until the seventh session of the seminar (13.1.60). The problem of sublimation is, as one might expect, to be situated in the field of the drives, in the network of drives which are, in Freud's words, 'extraordinarily plastic' and function like communicating channels in which one can compensate for another. Even so, as Freud conceded, there is a remainder of libidinal demand that cannot be sublimated, the demand for 'a certain dose' of direct satisfaction. The polymorphism of the libido, with its 'world of images', is linked to the sets of drives associated with the different stages from the oral to the anal and the genital. Lacan's first question is, 'Do these erogenous zones, these fundamental points of fixation, open onto rosy possibilities and pastoral optimism? Do we find here a path that leads to freedom? Or to the strictest servitude?'[8]

He goes on to question what it means to speak of the *object* of sublimation. Freud characterizes sublimation as a diversion of the drive involving a change of objects, the original objects of libido being replaced by objects that are socially valorized. He envisages, that is, the possibility of *substitutive satisfaction* by means of a *surrogate object* in which purely individual goals are replaced by ones that are considered collectively desirable. Lacan credits the psychoanalyst Siegfried Bernfeld with having raised the problem that the element of social valorization introduces a criterion into the concept of

[8] Jacques Lacan, *The Ethics of Psychoanalysis 1959-1960: The Seminar of Jacques Lacan, Book VII*, ed. Jacques-Alain Miller, trans. Dennis Porter, (London and New York: Routledge, 2008. pp. 114-115, (13.1.60).

sublimation which is external to the realm of psychology. But, he adds, this will turn out to be less of a problem than at first appears.[9]

This is because it is Lacan's intention to entirely re-frame the concept of sublimation. To this end, Bernfeld's article 'Observations on Sublimation' is subjected to a critique, largely carried out in Pierre Kaufmann's contribution to the Seminar, not included in the English translation. Bernfeld's starting point is that sublimation must be approached through the aims set by the ego, the *Ichziele*. There is sublimation, he argues, only when there is transfer of energy from the object libido to the preexistent *Ichziele*. Bernfeld approaches this through the case of a boy, Robert, who from early childhood aspired to become a poet and began writing verse at an early age. Following puberty his libidinal objects were repressed, but later the sexual drives forced their way into consciousness and thereby became capable of being sublimated. Ultimately, Bernfeld claims, these libidinal energies were integrated into the aims set by the ego. Some of Robert's libidinal energy remained repressed, but another part of it was successfully sublimated, thus maintaining the distinction between repression and sublimation. What is crucial for Bernfeld is the primary role of the *Ichziele*; the introduction of the notion of social value, for him, only confuses the issue. From a psychoanalytic point of view, he states, it is irrelevant whether Robert is writing poetry or collecting postage stamps.

Lacan, however, redirects our attention to a completely different level of the problem, claiming that 'sexuality is there from the beginning' and the problem of sublimation is raised 'long before' the moment when the divisions become clear between libidinal aims and the *Ichziele*. 'What needs to be justified is not simply the secondary benefits that individuals might derive from their works, but the

[9] *Ethics*, p. 177, (10.2.60).

originary possibility of a function like the poetic function in the form of a structure within a social consensus.'[10] The problem of valorization is thereby resituated from the individual to the socio-historical level. Kaufmann, in fact, begins his contribution by pointing out that Freud, in the *Three Essays on Sexuality*, states that he has borrowed the concept of sublimation from sociology. In tracing these sources, Kaufmann draws particular attention to Simmel's *Philosophy of Money,* published in 1900, the first section of which is devoted to an analysis of the formation of value, aesthetic value, and economic value.

Simmel, in Kantian mode, argues that the value of objects, thoughts and events can never be inferred from their natural existence and content, and our scale of values would remain meaningful even if none of its objects ever appeared in reality. An object does not acquire a new quality if we call it valuable. 'It is precisely its whole already determined being that is raised to the sphere of value.'[11] Value is a judgment upon objects which remains inherent in the subject. At the most basic level of our practical activity, however, there is as yet no distinction between subject and object. 'Human enjoyment of an object is a completely undivided act [...] The crude impulse, particularly an impulse of an impersonal, general nature, wants to release itself towards an object and to be satisfied, no matter how; consciousness is entirely concerned with satisfaction and pays no attention to its bearer on one side or its object on the other.'[12] In desiring what we do not yet enjoy, we place the content of our desire outside ourselves. In the practical world, 'the origin of the object itself,

---

[10] *Ethics*, p. 179, (10.2.60).

[11] Georg Simmel, *The Philosophy of Money*, ed. David Frisby, trans. Tom Bottomore and David Frisby, (London and New York: Routledge, 1990), p. 60.

[12] Simmel, p. 65.

and its being desired by the subject, are correlative terms – the two aspects of this process of differentiation which splits the immediate unity of the process of enjoyment.' Just as Kant said that the possibility of experience is the possibility of the objects of experience, so 'the possibility of desire is the possibility of the objects of desire.' Value 'does not originate from the unbroken unity of the moment of enjoyment, but from the separation between the subject and the content of the enjoyment as an object that stands opposed to the subject as something desired and only to be attained by the conquest of distance, obstacles and difficulties.'

In a further step, Simmel argues that the contents that exist in the objective world and in ourselves as subjective representations, 'have, in addition, a peculiar ideal dignity.' When, for instance, we judge others as moral, dignified, strong or beautiful, we believe that they would still have these values even if no-one appreciated them, if they went unrecognized. In this way, we can see that the mind is capable 'of separating itself from the ideas that it conceives and representing these ideas as if they were independent of its own representation.' This relation denies the relation to a 'subject' that is necessary for the existence of an 'object'. 'It is rather a third term, an ideal concept which enters into the duality but is not exhausted by it.' This form, Simmel continues, may be described as a claim or demand, a demand which exists only within ourselves but is not imposed by ourselves and does not merely involve acknowledging a quality of the object, a claim for recognition which loses nothing of its reality if the claim is not fulfilled.

> The ability of a tangible symbol to awaken in us religious feelings; the moral challenge to revolutionize particular conditions of life or to leave them alone, to develop or retard them; the feeling of obligation not to remain indifferent to great

> events, but to respond to them; the right of what is perceived to be interpreted in an aesthetic context – all of these are claims that are experienced or realized exclusively within the Ego and have no counterpart or objective point of departure in the objects themselves, but which, as claims, cannot be traced either to the Ego or to the objects to which they refer. Regarded from a naturalistic point of view such a claim may appear subjective, while from the subject's point of view it appears to be objective; in fact, it is a third category, which cannot be derived from either subject or object, but which stands, so to speak, between us and the objects.[13]

This 'metaphysical sublimation of value' does not play a role in the valuations of everyday life, but belongs in an 'ideal realm'. Simmel writes,

> I showed earlier that this process of the formation of values develops with the increase in distance between the consumer and the cause of his enjoyment. The differences in valuation which have to be distinguished as subjective and objective, originate from such variations in distance, measured not in terms of enjoyment, in which the distance disappears, but in terms of desire, which is engendered by the distance and seeks to overcome it. At least in the case of those objects whose valuation forms the basis of the economy, value is the correlate of demand. Just as the world of being is my representation, so the world of value is my demand. However, in spite of the logical-physical necessity that every demand expects to be satisfied by an object, the psychological structure of demand is

[13] Simmel, p. 68.

> such that in most cases it is focused upon the satisfaction itself, and the object becomes a matter of indifference so long as it satisfies the need [...] the conscious wish cannot always be taken as a sufficient index of the really effective valuation [...] The broader basis from which even the most highly differentiated impulses evolve, and the original diffuseness of need which includes only a drive but not yet a definite single goal, remain as a substratum upon which a consciousness of the individual character of more specific desires for satisfaction develops.

This is followed by a passage quoted in part by Kaufmann in Lacan's Seminar:

> Since the differentiation of need goes hand in hand with the reduction of its elemental power, consciousness becomes more able to accommodate the object. Or regarded from the other aspect: because consciousness is constrained by the refinement and specialization of need to take a greater interest in the object, a certain amount of force is removed from the solipsistic need. Everywhere the weakening of the emotions, that is to say, of the absolute surrender of the Ego to his momentary feelings, is correlated with the objectification of representations, with their appearance in a form of existence that stands over against us. Thus, for instance, talking things over is one of the most powerful means for subduing emotions. The inner process is, as it were, projected by the word into the external world; it now stands over against the individual like a tangible structure, and the intensity of the emotions is diverted. The tranquillization of the passions, and the representation of the objective world as

> existing and significant, are two sides of one and the same basic process.[14]

Simmel's axiology is, at the same time, a theory of sublimation, demonstrating how, from the original *jouissance*, driven, as Kaufmann puts it, from behind, seeking only satisfaction, differentiated drives emerge from a 'broader basis', without, as yet, a definite single goal, but providing a 'substratum' for specific desires for satisfaction. The 'object' emerges through a process of distantiation, in which it is able to become more and more specialized and refined, while the drive, for its part, is gradually weakened. Kaufmann draws attention, in particular, to Simmel's claim that to the degree that such specialization and refinement of conscious needs takes place, 'a certain quantity of forces finds itself withdrawn from *solipsistic need*, that is to say that we have something analogous to to the passage from *narcissistic libido* to *objectal libido*.'[15] We should also note the important passage concerning the externalization of the 'inner process' which, as object [*Gegenstand*] comes to stand over against the subject as a 'tangible structure' through the agency of language.

Not surprisingly, Lacan replies, 'there is in Simmel something of interest to me, since he has the notion not only of distantiation but also of an object that cannot be attained. But it is nevertheless an object. On the other hand, what cannot be attained in the Thing [*la Chose*] is precisely the Thing [*la Chose*] – i.e., it's not an object. And the difference is a radical one that has to do with the appearance between his time and mine of the difference that is the Freudian unconscious.'[16] When Lacan refers to Simmel's view that the object of desire cannot

[14] Simmel, pp. 69-71.
[15] *Ethics*, (2.3.60) (my translation).
[16] *Ethics*, p. 195 (2.3.60).

be attained, something that has not arisen previously in the discussion, he may be referring to the Kantian 'Thing-in-itself' [*Ding-an-sich*] or he may be referring to Simmel's argument that desire is engendered by a distancing of the object it seeks to overcome, since where the object is immediately used and enjoyed it is not an object. The object of desire, by contrast, *resists* our desire and is characterized by its separation from the subject. The more it is withheld the more the object is endowed with a value disproportionate to any possible enjoyment it could ever yield. 'Objects are not difficult to acquire because they are valuable, but we call those objects valuable that resist our desire to possess them.'[17] Lacan's *das Ding*, by contrast, is an *impossible* object, an object which is not an object, a field or space which can never be filled, created by an unconscious structure. Nevertheless, Simmel's reference to 'ideal concepts' states explicitly that these are not 'objects' for a 'subject', but, constitute a Third, possessing an 'ideal dignity' such that they place claims or demands upon us. Simmel's theory of value also acknowledges that the formation of values takes place to a significant degree below the level of consciousness, although he is not, of course, working with the Freudian theory of the unconscious.

Lacan and Kant

The session concludes with Lacan's interesting comment that the area he is concerned with in the Seminar of that year, 'is situated somewhere between a Freudian ethics and a Freudian aesthetics […] I am trying to show you how Freudian aesthetics, in the broadest meaning of the term – which means the whole economy of signifiers

---

[17] Simmel, p. 67.

– reveals that the Thing is inaccessible.'[18] It will, in fact, prove to be a Freudian ethics based upon Kant's *Critique of Practical Reason* and a Freudian aesthetics based upon Kant's *Critique of Judgment*. The Thing is what Lacan will call 'the beyond-of-the-signified. It is as a function of this beyond-of-the-signified and of an emotional relationship to it that the subject keeps its distance, and is constituted in a kind of relationship characterized by primary affect, prior to any repression.'[19] We should recall that for Lacan repression operates on nothing but signifiers.[20] *Das Ding*, on the other hand, is 'dumb reality,' which, nevertheless, 'commands and regulates,' in a manner clearly analogous to Kant's moral law. It does not speak but that does not mean it has nothing to do with words.

The resemblances between Simmel and Lacan are partially explained here when Lacan claims that Kant, 'better than anyone else, glimpsed the function of *das Ding*.' 'In the end, it is conceivable that it is as a pure signifying system, as a universal maxim, as that which is most lacking in a relationship to the individual, that the features of *das Ding* must be presented.' Kant comes closest to showing how an action that is moral presents itself. This seems to imply that the commands originating in *das Ding* have an absolute and categorical form. A 'maxim' in the Kantian sense is a subjective rule, devised by ourselves, which is universalizable in the form of a moral law and allows for no excuses or exceptions. This law acquires its obligatory force not from any external source but from myself; if I believe myself to be obliged by it, then I *am* obliged by it; it has, in Kant's words, 'objective reality'. For Lacan, '*Das Ding* presents itself at the level of

---

[18] *Ethics*, p. 197, (2.3.60).
[19] *Ethics*, p. 65 (9.12.59).
[20] *Ethics*, p. 53 (9.12.59).

unconscious experience as that which already makes the law.'[21] It is, however, 'a capricious and arbitrary law' which offers no guarantees.

Simmel's account of sublimation, described above, provided a basis for distinguishing between the libido of 'solipsistic need' and object libido. Similarly, between the narcissistic libido described in Freud's 'On Narcissism', and *das Ding*, the 'Freudian Thing', there is a difference, Lacan claims, and it is in that difference that the problem of sublimation is situated. Sublimation works by colonizing *das Ding* with imaginary schemes. 'In forms that are historically and socially specific [...] the imaginary elements of the fantasm come to overlay the subject, to delude it, at the very point of *das Ding*.' It is in this structural sense that we are to understood the way in which the products of sublimation are deemed 'constructive' and 'socially approved', rather than their providing compensatory benefits for the loss of more immediate forms of enjoyment.

The sublimation that provides the drive with a satisfaction different from its original aim is that which reveals the true nature of the drive in its relation to the Thing 'insofar as it is distinct from the object.'[22] The object of desire, which is the narcissistic reflection of the subject, must not then be confused with the Thing 'to the extent that the latter is at the heart of the libidinal economy.' The general formula for sublimation is that 'it raises an object [...] to the dignity [*digne*] of the Thing.' It is in this sense therefore that sublimation might be said to involve an 'elevation'. Lacan's use of the word 'dignity' here is worth examination. What we have been told about *das Ding* does not immediately suggest that it possesses or bestows the property of dignity. 'Dignity' is, however, a key term in Kantian ethics in which it is primarily related to duties of respect for the higher aspect of one's

---

[21] *Ethics*, p. 89 (23.12.59).

[22] *Ethics*, p. 137 (20.1.60).

person. As Oliver Sensen explains, 'Dignity expresses that this aspect is higher, ennobled or more important. Kant did not say that this aspect is more important because of a value property adhering to it, but because it is the seat of the moral law, which alone expresses what duty is.'[23] The pure moral motive teaches the human being to feel his own dignity by comparing himself with the moral law. 'This is how the genuine moral incentive of pure practical reason is constituted; it is nothing other than the pure moral law itself insofar as it lets us discover the sublimity [*Erhabenheit*] of our supersensible existence and subjectively effects respect for their higher vocation in human beings.'[24] 'Sublimity', as Sensen points out, is used here as elsewhere by Kant as a synonym for 'dignity', indicating Kant's consistently pre-modern usage of the term 'dignity' to signify not an inherent value property but rank, nobility, or elevated position. It is clear that Lacan is following Kant here in employing the term in his formula for sublimation.

Philosophy in the bedroom

Lacan's differences with Kant emerge in relation to Kant's famous example which, Lacan says, is designed to indicate how duty is able to outweigh desire in determining our actions. To control the excesses of a sensualist, a woman he desires is placed in a bedroom with a gallows standing outside the door by which he will leave. In Kant's view there is no doubt that the latter will act as a deterrent upon his 'inclination'. Kant contrasts this with someone who is offered the choice by a tyrant of being hanged or bearing false witness against a

---

[23] Oliver Sensen, *Kant on Human Dignity*, (Berlin and Boston: de Gruyter, 2011), p. 171.
[24] Sensen, p. 172.

friend. Kant's 'proof' is based upon the experience of how these choices actually present themselves to the individuals in question. The first man, who claims that his desire is 'irresistible', will discover, Kant asserts, that if asked whether he would persist despite the certain threat of the gallows, he would find that he could 'control his inclination,' whereas the second man will discover that he is able, that is *free*, to make the moral choice. That is to say, he may or may not make the moral choice but he would have to 'admit without hesitation that it would be possible for him. He judges, therefore, that he *can* do something because he is aware that he *ought* to do it and cognizes freedom within him, which, without the moral law, would have remained unknown to him.'[25]

What primarily interests Lacan in this argument is that 'the power of proof is here left to reality, to the real behaviour of the individual [...] It is in the real [*dans le réel*] that Kant asks us to examine the impact of the weight of reason, which he identifies here with the weight of duty.'[26] But, Lacan points out, one still has 'to prove how reason may make its weight felt.' Lacan follows him onto this ground – 'the real' – in order to make his criticism. His objection concerns the nature of 'object sublimation' which might, contrary to Kant's argument, lead the first man to 'overvalue' the 'feminine object' through a loving passion or, indeed, through perversion, commit a sexual murder knowing that he will be hanged. *Transgressive* sublimation and perversion, Lacan says, introduce a 'dialectical'

---

[25] Immanuel Kant, *Critique of Practical Reason*, trans. and ed. Mary Gregor,(Cambridge: Cambridge University Press, 1997, pp. 27-28. Italics added.

[26] Porter's English translation, 'the weight of reality' appears to be mistaken here, as the French reads '«*le poids de la raison*» pour autant que Kant les identifie ici au «*poids du devoir*».' Kant's example is also mistakenly located in the *Critique of Pure Reason*.

relation into sublimation, not taken into account by Kant, in which excesses, ranging beyond the pleasure principle, are involved.[27] Once *das Ding* is revealed as the place of the drives, the functioning of Kantian practical reason is disrupted, along with the relation between the pleasure principle and the reality principle.

Kant's examples are intended to support Theorem III in the *Critique* which states that 'If a rational being is to think of his maxims as practical universal laws, he can think of them only as principles that contain the determining ground of the will not by their matter but only by their form.'[28] A free will must find a determining ground in the law but independently of the matter of the law. Thus, the lawgiving form is itself the only thing that constitutes a determining ground of the will. Kant's extremely important argument here is that because experience restricts us to cognition of the law of appearances, it is only with the advent of the moral law, once we draw up maxims of the will for ourselves, that reason presents itself to us independently of sensibility and 'leads directly to the concept of freedom.' The moral law 'forces upon us' the concept of freedom, giving rise to the antinomy of pure reason in which science, seeking to ascend to the unconditioned, was led into confusion and incomprehensibilities.

Kant's two examples are designed to illustrate that experience itself 'confirms this order of concepts in us.' In the first case we see 'mechanical' causality at work turning inclination into what we might call *dis*inclination; in the second case Kant does not tell us what the outcome of moral deliberation is but points to the fact that the man has achieved cognition of the unconditionally practical, of 'a freedom within him, which, without the moral law, would have remained unknown to him.'

---

[27] *Ethics*, pp. 134-135 (20.1.60).
[28] CPrR, p. 24, 5:27.

The question, as Lacan posed it, was to prove how reason *makes its weight felt*. This is the question I believe Zupančič approaches when she writes: 'The crucial question of Kantian ethics is thus not 'how can we eliminate all the pathological elements of will, so that only the pure form of duty remains?' but rather, 'how can the pure form of duty itself function as a pathological element, that is, as an element capable of assuming the role of the driving force or incentive of our actions?'[29] How, in other words, can form become matter; something which does not qualify as a cause, become a cause? In Lacanian terms, the task is, as she puts it, to show how it is possible to found an ethics on the concept of the drive.' For Kant the object-drive involved in ethics is clearly not the same as in any other form of pathological motivation, but, she argues, 'neither is it simply the absence of all motives or incentives. The point rather, is that this very absence must at a certain point begin to function as an incentive. It must attain a certain 'material weight' and 'positivity', otherwise it will never be capable of exerting any influence whatsoever on human conduct.' The subject's separation from the pathological produces a 'remainder' that will constitute the drive of the ethical subject, but this implies the emergence of the 'divided subject'.

In the Kantian universe it is always in principle possible to explain any action in the physical world, that is, to establish its cause or motives that drive the 'mechanism'. This is what Zupančič refers to as 'the postulate of determinism'. Where then do freedom and the moral law come from? The free act must be shown to be, as Zupančič puts it, 'entirely foreign to the subject's inclinations.'[30] Doing what we

---

[29] Alenka Zupančič, *Ethics of the Real: Kant and Lacan,* (London and New York, Verso, 2012), pp. 15-16. 'Pathological' is here used in the Kantian sense.

[30] Zupančič, p. 23.

want does not prove that we are free, since '*it is impossible to prove that we are free in our wanting*.' The defining of a free act 'is precisely that it is entirely foreign to the subject's inclinations.' Although on occasion Kant resorts to the *causa noumenon* to try to establish 'causality through freedom,' Zupančič draws attention to a different argument which presents freedom 'as a kind of fact,' based upon Kant's observation that although the moral subject may claim that a past unethical action was determined by events so as to make it inescapably necessary, this in no way absolves the subject of a sense of guilt. The paradoxical structure of guilt, expressed in the statement '*I couldn't have done anything else, but still, I am guilty*', confirms, for Kant, that 'the possibility of freedom has nothing to do with the question of *what* we feel guilty of.'[31] In spite of the postulate of determinism, Kant insists that, because of the existence of transcendental freedom revealed to us through the moral law, we are responsible for *all* our actions and that no 'necessity' can be taken to justify them. In Lacanian terms, Zupančič argues that this position can be compared with Lacan's claim that there is 'a crack in the Other', a gap in the relation between cause and effect which allows the appearance of the subject as correlative to this lack in the Other, where 'structure fails fully to close in upon itself.'

Kant and Sade

Lacan takes up the 'bedroom' example again later in Seminar VII, for the first time linking it with Sade. Kant's 'error' in the earlier treatment was, as we have seen, unawareness of the possibility of 'excessive object sublimation' in the form of a 'loving passion'. In this later

[31] Zupančič, p. 26. Her argument here is based upon a reading of the Critical Elucidation of the Analytic of Pure Practical Reason, pp. 75-89, *CPrR*.

session (20.3.60) Lacan's argument runs rather differently. The significance of the bedroom and gallows example is now that it is 'paradoxically presented to us as a pleasure that is weighed against a punishment to be undergone; it is an opposition which homogenizes them. There is in terms of pleasure a plus and a minus.'[32] Whereas, in the first treatment, what Kant had failed to grasp was the possibility of 'excessive object sublimation', Lacan now states, 'one only has to make a conceptual shift and move the night spent with the lady from the category of pleasure to that of *jouissance*, given that *jouissance* implies precisely the acceptance of death – and there's no need of sublimation – for the example to be ruined.' Lacan continues; 'it is enough for *jouissance* to be a form of evil, for the whole thing to change its character completely, and for the meaning of the moral law itself to be completely changed. Anyone can see that if the moral law is, in effect, capable of playing some role here, it is precisely as support for the *jouissance* involved; it is so that the sin becomes what Saint Paul calls inordinately sinful. That's what Kant on this occasion simply ignores.'

The role of sublimation in Lacan's first treatment of the example was to draw our attention to a relationship to desire which indicated the possibility of formulating 'a different criterion of another, or even of the same, morality' taking its direction from *das Ding*. It is 'the register that makes the subject hesitate when he is on the point of bearing false witness against *das Ding*, that is to say, the place of desire, whether it be perverse or sublimated.'[33] Once *das Ding* is revealed as the place of the drives, it is clear that the drives 'have nothing at all to do with something that might be satisfied by moderation – that moderation which soberly regulates a human

---

[32] *Ethics*, p. 233.
[33] *Ethics*, p. 135 (20.1.60).

being's relations with his fellow man at the different hierarchical levels of society in an harmonious order, from the couple to the State with a capital S.' The concept of sublimation, now linked with perversion (although not a form of perversion), was thereby *un*linked from its role in pacification and the maintenance of social harmony.

In the second treatment Lacan returns to the idea that Kant is 'weighing' the options, having made them commensurable, but has failed to see that the introduction of *jouissance* 'ruins' that calculation, because of its fundamental incommensurability. *Jouissance* involves the acceptance of death as a way of being true to one's desire, the foundation of Lacanian ethics. *Jouissance* is able to align itself with the Kantian moral law insofar as it involves a motivation based upon an absolute choice, but is also seated in the drives, creating that unique relation to the 'pathological' that was missing in Kant's theory. The moral law may find its pathological content in the 'inordinately sinful', in the *jouissance* of transgression, transgression which is understood primarily in its *enigmatic* relation to the Law. Whereas the moral Law is not itself threatened by the idea of excessive object sublimation, its replacement by *jouissance* opens up the moral Law to evil, already present within *das Ding* as the problem of evil – 'evil may be in the Thing,' as it is an essential element of the Creation myth, to which Freud also directs us. When Freud suggests that there is that which in life that prefers death he comes closer than anyone, Lacan believes, 'to the project of evil as such.'[34]

The link with Sade is, in fact, deferred to the next session. Introducing this perhaps not entirely welcome guest to the Seminar, Lacan tells his students that Sade 'goes beyond the limit' in his theory, if not in his fantasm, in teaching us about 'the laws of one's neighbour's space as such.' If we follow Freud in *Civilization and its*

[34] *Ethics*, p. 128 (20.1.60).

Discontents, Lacan writes, 'we cannot avoid the formula that *jouissance* is an evil. Freud leads us by the hand to this point: it is an evil because it involves suffering for my neighbour.'[35] Lacan cites Freud's dark observation that men are creatures who are instinctually aggressive. 'As a result, their neighbour is for them not only a potential helper or sexual object, but also someone who tempts them to satisfy their aggressiveness on him, to exploit his capacity for work without compensation, to use him sexually without his consent, to seize his possessions, to humiliate him, to cause him pain, to torture and to kill him. *Homo homini lupus* [man is a wolf to man].'[36] As Lacan remarks, this passage could be mistaken for a quotation from Sade.

Lacan's argument at this stage rests heavily upon that advanced by Freud in *Civilization and its Discontents.* In fact, from the first session of Seminar VII, this theme had been present in the background, where Lacan began by emphasizing that psychoanalysis had developed in a quite specific moment in the history of man - 'the one we are living in' - and which Lacan follows Angelo Hesnard in describing as 'the morbid world of guilt [*l'univers morbide de la faute*].'[37] The link between guilt and morbidity, Lacan remarks, 'has not failed in our time to mark with its seal all thought about morals.' The Enlightenment project of 'a naturalist liberation of desire' has failed to alleviate the burden of laws and duties. It is the 'omnipresence of a sense of guilt' [*sentiment de culpabilité*] and, further, 'the attraction of guilt' [*l'attraite de la faute*] that justify the attempt to construct an *ethics* of psychoanalysis.

---

[35] *Ethics*, p. 227 (23.360), translation amended.
[36] *The Standard Edition of the Complete Psychological Works of Sigmund Freud*, Vol. XXI, (London and New York: W. W. Norton, 1961), p. 58.
[37] *Ethics*, p. 2, (18.11.59). A. Hesnard, *L'univers morbide de la faute*, (Paris: PUF, 1949). Misleadingly translated by Porter as 'the universe of transgression'.

Both Hesnard and Lacan are in accord with Freud's intention, in *Civilization and its Discontents*, 'to represent the sense of guilt [*Schuldgefühl*] as the most important problem in the development of our civilization and to show that the price we pay for our advance in civilization is a loss of happiness through the heightening of the sense of guilt.'[38] At bottom, Freud argues, the sense of guilt is a variety of anxiety, which in its later phases coincides completely with fear of the super-ego. 'The fear of this critical agency [...] the need for punishment, is an instinctual manifestation on the part of the ego, which has become masochistic under the influence of a sadistic super-ego; it is a portion, that is to say, of the instinct towards internal destruction present in the ego, employed for forming an erotic attachment to the super-ego.'[39] It is a product 'of the conflict between the need for authority's love and the urge towards instinctual satisfaction, whose inhibition produces the inclination towards aggression.'

The greatest problem that faces civilization is 'the constitutional inclination of human beings to be aggressive towards one another; and for that very reason we are especially interested in what is probably the most recent of the cultural commands of the super-ego, the commandment to love one's neighbour as oneself.' Unfortunately, says Freud, '(t)he commandment is impossible to fulfil; such an enormous inflation of love can only lower its value, not get rid of the difficulty.' The cultural superego has no understanding of, or interest in, the mental constitution of human beings and what is possible for them.

Kant *with* Sade

---

[38] Freud, p. 81.
[39] Freud, p. 83.

The bedroom example is taken up yet again in Lacan's essay, 'Kant with Sade' (1963) in which Lacan's reading of Kantian ethics is developed further in a bold and provocative manner. Having discovered the previously unsuspected eroticism in Kant's ethical writings, Lacan attempts to demonstrate that Sade's *Philosophy in the Bedroom* 'yields the truth' of Kant's *Critique*. The 'shift' that the works of Sade and others represent is, according to Lacan, the theme of 'delight in evil' [*bonheur dans le mal*], that is, 'the notion that it feels good to do evil [*qu'on soit bien dans le mal*] – or, if you will, that the eternal feminine does not elevate us.'[40] The idea that it feels good to do evil disrupts the classical association between 'feeling good' and 'doing good', a link which Kant himself had decisively broken in his insistence that 'doing good' must not be motivated by pathological interests.

The Kantian moral law, as we have seen, is to be found in a field cleared of everything 'pathological', that is to say, connected with feelings or the drives, and is conceived as an ethic based upon duty, that is, the necessity of acting purely from respect for the moral law. This is a law generated by the subject him-or-herself, founded upon a maxim capable of being willed as a universal law, which is then binding upon the subject in the form of a categorical imperative and must be obeyed solely for its own sake. But, Lacan asks, does not the purely formal character of the moral law leave the way open for 'evil' maxims so long as they are not founded upon pathological interests?

Lacan presents us with the following Sadean maxim that 'proposes a rule for *jouissance*: "I have the right to enjoy your body," anyone can say to me, "and I will exercise this right without any limit to the

[40] Jacques Lacan' *Ecrits*, trans. Bruce Fink, (New York and London: W.W.Norton & Co., 2006), p.646/766.

capriciousness of the exactions I may wish to satiate with your body.' Lacan asks us to imagine a society in which everyone's will would be submitted to this rule, which would, in his view, meet Kantian standards for a valid moral law, involving 'the unconditioned practice of reason.' This thought-experiment is designed to reveal the logical consequences of a purely formal practical reason which eliminates all substantial elements, including 'goods, passion, or even compassion.' The 'rigour' and 'severity' of the moral law, which Kant frequently advertises, indicate, for Lacan, not only a monstrous product of sublimation but also its affinity with the cruelty and sadistic enjoyment of the superego in its role of inflicting mental torment in the name of morality. In placing the rule in the mouth of the Other, Lacan believes that Sade's maxim is 'more honest' than Kant's appeal to the voice within, 'since it unmasks the split in the subject that is usually covered up.'

Zizek has spared no effort in making us aware of this dimension of Lacanian ethics, asking us to consider, for example, 'is there a line from Kantian formalist ethics to the cold-blooded Auschwitz killing machine?'[41] More guardedly, he points out that Lacan's purpose in this extraordinary appropriation of Kant is not to show, via the notion of the Freudian unconscious, the impossibility of removing all 'pathological' motivations, but rather that 'acting upon one's desire' – the foundation of the Lacanian ethic – cannot be grounded upon 'pathological' interests or motivations and itself meets the criteria of the Kantian ethical act, constituting a way of 'doing one's duty'. This returns us to the lady waiting in the bedroom. Zizek's point is that for lovers of a certain kind, the act is possible only where there is transgression and danger, requiring "the suspension of even the most

---

[41] Slavoj Zizek, 'Kant and Sade: the Ideal Couple', *lacanian ink* 13, 1998.

elementary "egoistic" interests,' and thereby constituting *stricto sensu* an ethical act.

Lacan himself, in *Kant with Sade*, says it is possible that 'a partisan of passion who would be blind enough to combine it with questions of honour, would make trouble for Kant by forcing him to recognize that no occasion precipitates certain people more surely toward their goal than one that involves defiance of or even contempt for the gallows.'[42] Here then, we have not merely transgressive *jouissance* but also a 'selfless' principle of honour which might provide the ground for a visit to the bedroom. This is followed by Lacan's observation that the gallows is not the Law, that is, there is a difference between the Law and the enforcers of the Law. The gallows is brought in, Lacan states, merely so that the subject is (pathologically) motivated by his love of life. But again, Lacan points out that desire can, through the maxim, 'do not forsake the reasons for living in the interests of staying alive' become, in a moral being, a categorical imperative. Only when Law is truly present does desire not stand up, 'but that is because law and repressed desire are one and the same thing – which is precisely what Freud discovered.' In Kant's examples, Lacan believes, Kant has covertly introduced pathological elements wherever the Law has been presented as the sole motivation of ethical action.

Zizek, following Lacan, makes the point that despite the gap between the moral Law and pathological sentiments, there is one *a priori* sentiment, according to Kant, that the subject necessarily experiences in relation to the moral Law, namely, the pain of humiliation. Kant writes, 'Hence we can see a priori that the moral law, as the determining ground of the will, must, by thwarting all our inclinations produce a feeling that can be called pain; and here we have the first and perhaps the only case in which we can determine a priori

[42] Lacan, *Ecrits*, p. 660/782.

from concepts the relation of a cognition (here the cognition of a pure practical reason) to the feeling of pleasure or displeasure.'[43] The remarkable discovery of a feeling, namely, humiliation, that has an intellectual ground 'is the only one that we can cognize completely a priori and the necessity of which we can have insight into.'

This 'moral feeling' is produced entirely externally by reason (by the Other). 'There is no *antecedent* feeling in the subject that would be attuned to morality: that is impossible, since all feeling is sensible whereas the incentive of the moral disposition must be free from any sensible condition.' These imperatives, Lacan claims, 'are imposed upon us, according to the Sadean paradox, as if upon the Other, and not upon ourselves.' This is not, however, a fundamental difference between Sade and Kant, since the moral law 'latently' commands us as Other. The 'bipolarity upon which the moral law is founded is nothing but the split [*refente*] in the subject brought about by any and every intervention of the signifier: the split between the enunciating subject [*sujet de l'enonciation*] and the subject of the statement [*sujet de l'énoncé*].'[44] Sade's discourse of the right to *jouissance* posits the Other qua free – the Other's freedom – as its enunciating subject', in the same way as every imperative tells us, in its 'lethal depths' [*fonds tuant*] 'you are'. 'But this discourse is no less determinant for the subject of the statement, giving rise to him with each addressing of its equivocal content: since jouissance, shamelessly avowed in its very purpose, becomes one pole in a couple, the other pole being in the hole that jouissance already drills in the Other's locus in order to erect the cross of Sadean experience in it.'

The direction of Lacan's argument is clearly to establish a homology between the Sadean discourse of the right to *jouissance* and

[43] *CPrR*, p. 63, 5:73.

[44] *Ecrits* p. 650/770.

the schism in the subject's symbolic world which produces the agency known as the super-ego. In Zizek's reading, Sade renders visible, in the form of the implacable executioner-torturer, the enunciator of the moral law, invisible in Kant, the agent that takes pleasure in the pain and humiliation of the moral subject. Contrary, however, to what might appear to be Lacan's position here, Zizek claims that the Kantian moral law is not simply to be equated with the superego. As Lacan stated, some years later, in the final pages of *The Four Fundamental Concepts of Psychoanalysis*, 'I have proved that (Kant's) theory of consciousness, when he writes of practical reason, is sustained only by giving a specification of the moral law which, looked at more closely, is simply desire in its pure state, that very desire that culminates in the sacrifice, strictly speaking, of everything that is the object of love in one's human tenderness – I would say, not only in the rejection of the pathological object, but also in its sacrifice and murder. That is why I wrote *Kant avec Sade*.'[45]

Zizek reads this as entailing that 'the guilt sustained by the superego' can only be the result of the subject having *betrayed* his or her desire, and of the superego feeding upon such compromises. 'Sade articulates what happens when the subject betrays the true stringency of the Kantian ethics.' This would certainly correspond to Lacan's famous statement, 'I propose then, that from an analytical point of view, the only thing of which one can be guilty is of having given ground relative to one's desire [*Je propose que la seule chose dont on peut être coupable, au moins dans la perspective analytique, c'est d'*avoir cedé sur son désir.'[46] In the last analysis, then, what a subject

[45] Jacques Lacan, *The Four Fundamental Concepts of Psychoanalysis*, trans. Alan Sheridan, (London: Penguin, 1994), pp. 275-276. (Session of 24.6.64)

[46] *Ethics*, p. 392 (6.7.60).

really feels guilty about when s/he manifests guilt is, whether conscience can admit it or not, having giving ground relative to desire, something which s/he may have done for the best of motives. Lacan writes,

> If analysis has a meaning [*sens*], desire is nothing other than that which supports an unconscious theme, the very articulation of that which roots us in a particular destiny [*destinée*], and that destiny demands insistently that the debt be paid, and desire keeps coming back, keeps returning, and situates us once again in a given track, the track of something that is specifically our business [*proprement notre affaire*].

When Lacan looks for examples of being true to one's desire, he immediately turns to heroes of Sophoclean tragedy, Antigone and Philoctetes. What makes a hero, for Lacan, is that, 'In each of us the path of the hero is traced, and it is precisely as an ordinary man that one follows it to the end.' Philoctetes, for example, is a hero because 'he remains fiercely committed to his hate right to the end.' The reiteration of the phrase 'to the end' [*jusqu'à la fin*] brings us into the presence of death, which is the horizon of Lacanian ethics. It is important to point out here that 'giving ground relative to one's desire' may involve not that the subject betrays him or herself, but that s/he *tolerates* being betrayed in some pact by another, for the sake of some 'good'. Tolerance of this kind, once it crosses the line of 'contempt for the other and oneself' is irreversible. 'It might be possible to do some repair work, but not to undo it.' It is in this way, Lacan declares, that psychoanalysis can provide us with an ethical compass, a compass, one might point out, that always points in the direction of death.

Lacan adds a further proposition; that there is no other good than that which may serve to pay the price for access to desire, where desire is understood as the metonymy of our being. Employing the cryptic expression 'eating the book' [*manger le livre*] to signify sublimation, Lacan argues that in this process through which the book 'became *me* so to speak,' a price had to be paid in *jouissance*, that is to say, a pound of flesh [*livre du chair*]. That is the good one must pay for the satisfaction of desire in this change of aim. But, at a more fundamental level, 'eating the book' also indicates the primordial loss of *jouissance* involved in entering the signifying chain, access to desire, and the metonymy of our being. There may be an implied reference also to the eating of the apple from the tree of knowledge which was the mythical origin of human culpability. The good which is sacrificed for desire, the pound of flesh, 'is precisely the thing that religion undertakes to recuperate.'[47] The price paid in suffering, offered on the altar, is consumed by the priest and the religious community 'who stuff themselves with it.' This distinguishes religion from tragedy and from cathartic purification. The spectator of tragedy learns that 'access to desire necessitates crossing not only all fear but all pity,' instead of seeking the good of the other. In this way the spectator of tragedy 'learns a little more about the deepest level of himself than he knew before.'

It is the concern of *Kant avec Sade* to demonstrate that Sade, in Lacan's words, 'stopped at the point at which desire and the law became bound up with each other.' Although Sade's desire was *transgressive* desire, desire aroused by the law to break the law, this is as far as Sade took the relation between law and desire, as evidenced by his rejection of the death penalty. 'His apology for crime merely impels him to an oblique acceptance of the law.'[48] In Sade also, the Supreme Being is also restored in Evil Action [*la Maléfice*]. He

---

[47] *Ethics*, p. 396 (6.7.60).
[48] *Ecrits*, p. 667/790.

believes, as Lacan puts it, that 'by replacing repentance with reiteration he can be done with the law within.' Lacan's verdict is 'There is thus precious little here – in fact, nothing – by way of a treatise that is truly on desire.' If, as Lacan claims, Sade represents the truth of Kant, then it is clearly only in the restricted sense that the Law excludes any concern with the Good, and does not extend to the relation between the Law and desire. The *submission* of desire to the Law, as expressed in transgressive *jouissance*, is clearly not the foundation of Lacanian ethics.

The sublime and the superego

Zupančič has examined in detail the complex relation between the Kantian moral law and the Freudian superego, as they are brought into a relation by Lacan. If an homology is to be demonstrated it must be shown, given the 'cruel' character of the superego, that Kant's moral law is not entirely free of pathological *affect*. Whereas Zizek singles out 'humiliation' for this role, Zupančič identifies respect [*Achtung*] as the 'practical' but non-pathological a priori feeling that characterizes the subject's relation to the moral law, the conversion of the form of the law into a drive. Respect, in Kant, refers to 'a feeling which indicates that the moral law is 'nearby', it indicates the 'presence' of the moral law, the subject's 'close encounter' with the moral law.'[49] In fact, both Zizek and Zupančič are referring to the same passage in Kant in which, in the order of Kant's exposition, the effect of the moral law is first, negative, insofar as it strikes down self-conceit, but 'since this law is still something in itself positive – namely

[49] Zupančič, p. 140.

the form of an intellectual causality, that is, of freedom – it is at the same time an object of *respect* [...] and so too the ground of a positive feeling that is not of empirical origin and is cognized a priori.'[50]

Zupančič suggests, however, that Kant 'introduces two different feelings linked to two different conceptions of the moral law: respect and humiliation. In the first, respect corresponds to a mode of anxiety – the loss of self-representation which thereby opens up the possibility of becoming a subject; in the second, respect corresponds to a mode of fantasy in which we observe ourselves being humiliated by the moral law. In the second, the moral law 'whose *voice* makes even the boldest sinner tremble and forces him to hide from its *gaze*,' becomes the law of the superego.[51] The moral law which Kant had earlier distinguished from feelings of wonder and awe, of being over-powered, is by the end of the *Critique* linked to them.

As Zupančič emphasizes, the moral law in Kant begins to move towards the law of the superego, the concept of 'respect' becoming gradually degraded until integrated into the logic which governs the dialectic of the sublime [*das Erhabene*] set out in the *Critique of Judgment.* In the first moment the subject experiences powerlessness and displeasure at the overwhelming power of nature, but then, in a second moment, the subject becomes aware that as a rational being s/he is capable of elevating her/himself above natural or phenomenal existence. The first experience gives rise to the second. This is why the feeling of the sublime is described by Kant as a 'negative pleasure', a pleasure that can only be obtained by means of a displeasure. What is essential here is that the feeling of powerlessness and anxiety in the face of this overwhelming force gives rise to the experience of a still greater power within, a power which Kant identifies with the moral

[50] *CPrR*, p. 63, 5:73.
[51] Qu. Zupančič, p. 146, emphasis added.

law and Zupančič identifies with the superego, that is, 'a kind of bodying forth of the cruel, unbridled and menacing superego – the 'real or reverse side' of the moral law (in us), of the superego as the place of *jouissance*.'[52]

The feeling of anxiety is resolved into the feeling of the sublime by a certain disjunction in which our everyday lives appear to us as insignificant in relation to this overwhelming power, but, at the same time, we feel ourselves 'elevated' with a kind of narcissistic satisfaction. Confronted by 'the traumatic proximity of a (threatening) Thing,' the subject responds by distancing him/herself, in what, in Freudian terms, can be described as a shift from the ego to the superego, by means of which the ego can appear tiny and trivial. The inflation of the superego 'plays the crucial role in the strategy of avoiding the Thing [*das Ding*],' even though this 'inflation' can lead to death. In this way 'moral agency emerges in the element of the sublime.' Although aesthetic categories can never achieve the universality of law, aesthetic judgments, in Kant's view, are not merely statements of individual taste but *require* everyone's agreement. In this required predisposition to 'moral feeling', Zupančič detects the 'superegoic face' of the moral law.

Just as the destructive power of natural phenomena gives rise to the feeling of the sublime, so the 'devastating force' of the moral law, Zupančič argues, gives rise to the devastating force within me, that is, the superego. 'The feeling of the sublime develops through this metonymy.' Kant's distinction between the beautiful and the sublime accommodates itself to this reading, insofar as the beautiful, in Kant's view, has the form of purposiveness without actually having a purpose; that is to say, things of beauty are structured *as if* they were purposeful, whereas the sublime is quite clearly a *senseless form*,

---

[52] Zupančič, p. 156.

chaotic, appearing as pure excess, a kind of *jouissance*. In the same way that the sublime involves enjoyment *at a safe distance*, so, Zupančič argues, the sublime involves a 'logic of fantasy', whereby 'the subject *watches* herself being subjected to the law – that she watches herself being humiliated and terrified by it.'[53] It should be pointed out here that although Zupančič finds this hidden figure of the superego in Kant's theory of the sublime, she believes that it is possible to find a moral agency in Kant from which that figure can be eliminated.

Zupančič argues that ethics always has a component of excess. In relation to the smooth operation of the reality principle, ethics always appears as excessive, as a disturbing interruption.[54] The ethics of desire necessarily includes fantasy, thus 'we cannot deny all ethical dignity to someone who is ready to die (and to kill) in order to realize his or her fantasy [...] Those who practice such an ethics today are called terrorists, fanatics, fundamentalists, madmen ...'[55] Most of us would prefer to die rather than to realize our desire, in flight from 'the infinite that pursues us in this world.' The infinite pursues us in the form of *jouissance*, a *jouissance* which can kill us by compelling us to act in a way that threatens our well-being and survival. This is the death drive against which we, paradoxically, try to protect ourselves through some kind of self-mortification. The death drive does not aim at death; rather it is indifferent to either death or life. Antigone is a sublime figure but she does not experience the feeling of the sublime, that is to say, she does not observe 'through the window (of fantasy) the spectacle of her own death; she enters, so to speak, into her fantasy.' That is to say, she *acts*. Zupančič writes, 'We do not see the

---

[53] Zupančič, p. 158.
[54] Zupančič pp. 4-5.
[55] Zupančič, p. 254.

infinite; we see only the effect it has on the figure of Antigone, who functions as its screen. This explains the sublime splendour of her figure, which is the result of the Thing which she hides and announces at the same time.'

Lacan and the super-ego

If we are to avoid simply confusing the Kantian moral law with the super-ego, we need to be clear about what Lacan means by the super-ego. In the 'Overture' to Seminar I, in 1953, Lacan already states that the super-ego is 'a law deprived of meaning, but one which nevertheless only sustains itself by language.'[56] Some explanation of this is later provided where Lacan states that the super-ego is an imperative 'essentially located within the symbolic plane of speech.' On the one hand, it is consonant 'with the register and the idea of law, that is to say with the totality of the system of language,' but, on the other hand, 'one should emphasize as a counter to this, its senseless, blind character, of pure imperativeness and simple tyranny.'[57]

He continues:

> The super-ego is at one and the same time the law and its destruction. As such, it is speech itself [*la parole même*], the commandment of law, in so far as nothing more than its root remains. The law is entirely reduced to something, which cannot even be expressed, like the *You must* [tu dois], which is speech deprived of all its meaning [*une parole privée de tous*

[56] *Freud's Papers on Technique 1953-1954: The Seminar of Jacques Lacan, Book I*, ed. Jacques-Alain Miller, trans. John Forrester, (New York and London: W. W. Norton & Co.,1991), p. 3.
[57] *Seminar I*, p. 102 (10.3.54).

> *ses sens*]. It is in this sense that the super-ego ends up by being identified with only what is most devastating, most fascinating, in the primitive experiences of the subject. It ends up by being identified with what I call *the ferocious figure*, with the figures which we can link to primitive traumas the child has suffered, whatever these are.

Lacan's remarks here are made clearer if examined in the context of this session of the Seminar in which the analyst Rosine Lefort had described the case of her patient Robert, a little boy of three and a half years who had suffered devastating abuse and neglect. Robert knew only two words, 'Miss' and 'Wolf', and would scream and howl the latter word all day long. He had attempted to cut off his own penis and to strangle other children in the unit. In Madame Lefort's analysis she expresses the belief that he had 'sunk under the real, that at the beginning of the treatment there was no symbolic function in him, still less an imaginary function.' Asked from where he had acquired the word 'Wolf', she explained, 'In children's homes, you often see nurses scaring them with the wolf. In the home where I had him in treatment, one day when the children were impossible to deal with, they were shut in the children's garden, and a nurse went outside to howl like a wolf so as to make them be good.' In Madame Lefort's view, Robert's 'wolf' was, at least in part, 'the devouring mother'.

Just as Freud had insisted that the superego was composed of 'word-presentations', rather than identifications, Lacan places all the emphasis here upon the word 'Wolf', Robert's sole connection to the symbolic order of the community, through which alone the possibility of a dialogue existed, although there was no way of understanding its meaning for the child. The 'ferocious figure', then, in Lacan's account, is reducible to a *word*, or, as one might say, to a figure of speech. Madame Lefort goes on to describe the significant change in Robert's condition when he began to project onto her all the bad things that had happened to him and she became 'the Wolf'. This 'exorcism' through transference marked a decisive improvement, a transformation which Lacan sums up as follows:

> What is remarkable in this case is the moment when, after a scene which you described, the use of the word *Wolf!* disappeared. It is around this pivot of language, of the relationship to this word, which for Robert is the summary of a law, that the turning-point from the first to the second phase occurs. There then follows this extraordinary elaboration, brought to a close by this touching self-baptism, when he utters his own Christian name. At that point we come close to the fundamental relation, in its most reduced form, of man to language. It is extraordinarily moving.

In the name of the Law

In Lacan the superego is strongly identified with the symbolic order via the Law. Law is the 'concrete discourse' which dominates the human world, but, in Lacan's view, although the Law presents itself as full and coherent, 'there can never be any relation with the law in its entirety, since the law is never made completely one's own.' At the level of the Real, 'no one grasps where the very fact of the interdiction is located.' There is 'a final, unexplained, inexplicable mainspring upon which the existence of the law hangs.' What can 'never be completely brought to completion in the discourse of the law [...] is this final term which explains that there is one.' As Lacan explains, if God does not exist, it by no means follows that everything is permitted. The law has no need of an Other to guarantee it; it draws its power over us from elsewhere. But this also constitutes its weakness, since 'at the same time there is something irreducibly discordant about it, in every one of its parts. It takes very little, very little at all, being locked up in the toilets, or having a father falsely accused of Lord knows what crime, for the law all of a sudden to appear to you in a lacerating form.'[58] If the Law is ultimately reducible to a *You must* regardless of any particular content, so opposition to the Law is, at root, equally 'senseless,' driven by a desire that cannot be expressed. In any specific case, the hold of a particular prescription upon the subject or of a sudden revelation that the law is not lawful will be explicable in relation to former 'inadmissible, conflictual, symptomatic unconscious expressions'. It is when 'the traumatic elements – grounded in an image that has never been integrated – draw near that holes, points of fracture appear in the unification, the synthesis of the subject's history.' From these the subject 'can re-align himself within the different symbolic determinations which make him a subject with a history.'[59]

The function of the Thing

In Seminar VII, Lacan proposes to demonstrate the function of 'the Thing' at work in the sublimation of 'the feminine object' in courtly love, an object 'invented' for a special purpose that society can esteem and valorize. 'In analysis the object is a point of imaginary fixation which gives satisfaction to a drive in any register whatsoever,' and any object, Lacan claims, can be elevated in this way. He gives as an example a collection of matchboxes connected together at the home of

[58] *The Seminar of Jacques Lacan: the Ego in Freud's Theory and in the Technique of Psychoanalysis 1954-1955, Book II*, ed. Jacques-Alain Miller, trans. Sylvana Tomaselli, (New York and London: W. W. Norton & Co. 1991), pp. 128-130 (16.2.55).
[59] *Seminar I*, pp. 196-197 (19.5.54).

his friend Jacques Prévert. 'The wholly gratuitous, proliferating, superfluous, and quasi absurd character of this collection pointed to its thingness as match box. Thus the collector found his motive in this form of apprehension that concerns less the match box than the Thing that subsists in a match box.'

Insofar as the example is intended to be taken seriously, it indicates how freely Lacan feels able to employ this term, to extend its field, in trying to grasp what is most primordial. The match box came to be endowed with a dignity it did not formerly possess, but it is not itself the Thing, which remains veiled and which obliges us to spend the whole of our psychic life passing around it. The Thing is 'that which in the real, the primordial real [...] suffers from the signifier,' that upon which the signifier imposes itself. It is in the field of the Thing that the Freudian original 'lost object', forever inaccessible to the 'speaking being', is situated as represented by something else. Lacan here takes over the Heideggerian idea of the making of a vase which creates the void around which the vase is constructed, and thereby the possibility of filling it. Creation, in other words, involves not only the creation of objects but of voids or spaces from which something is *lacking*. This fabricated signifier – 'the Thing' - signifies nothing but the possibility of signification as such. The fashioning of this signifier, a creation *ex nihilo*, is identical with the introduction of a gap or a hole in the Real.

It should be noted that this is Lacan's introduction to a discussion of the theological problem of evil – 'the central problem of ethics'. Evil 'may be in the Thing', insofar as the myth of creation maintains the presence of 'the human factor' – for which 'original sin' is another name. Evil, Lacan argues, can only be thought in creationist terms. 'The Thing is, in effect, involved insofar as it is defined by the fact that it defines the human factor – although, as we know, the human factor escapes us.' The human factor is to be defined in the same way as the Thing, that is, as that which in the Real suffers from the signifier.[60] The issue here is not that of whether man is fundamentally good or bad, but the wider question of our relation to the Real.

The problem of sublimation, as it presents itself to Lacan - and we should take note of this - is that of how the signifier comes to be fashioned in the image of the Thing when the Thing is unimaginable. Sublimation understood in this fundamental way is not so much concerned with energetics, of how 'sublimated energy' might be produced, but rather with how signification is raised to the level of the Thing in an attempt to represent the unrepresentable – that is to say, precisely the problem of the sublime. This is both an aesthetic *and* an ethical problem, hence Lacan's persistent fascination with the ethics of tragedy, where the ethical issues of human life are subject to their most intense questioning. Lacan's approach also marks a break with the traditional idea of sublimation insofar as it is based upon the transformation of the 'bad' sexual drives, especially those of a 'polymorphous perverse' character, into activities which aim at the general Good. The Thing demands that the relation between good and evil be thought in a completely new way.

Courtly love and the Thing

Lacan's investigation of courtly love in the age of chivalry is a case study indicating how 'the feminine object' came to have the value of representing the unrepresentable Thing. This does not mean, Lacan tells us, that sublimation is centred upon the man-woman relation. Rather, he emphasizes, everything must begin with *emptiness*. 'This Thing, all forms of which belong to the sphere of sublimation, this Thing will always be represented by emptiness, precisely because it

---

[60] *Ethics*, p. 154 (27.1.60).

cannot be represented by anything else – or, more exactly, because it can only be represented by something else. But in every form of sublimation, emptiness is determinative.'[61] The Thing is a 'vacuole'. This includes all forms of art, religion and science. While art is based upon repression [*Verdrängung*] and religion upon displacement [*Verschiebung*], Lacan argues that science is centred upon unbelief [*Unglauben*], that is, the repudiation or foreclosure [*Verwerfung*] of the Thing, insofar as science embraces the ideal of absolute knowledge, thus positing the Thing while paying no attention to it and falling foul of the Lacanian formula that what is foreclosed in the symbolic reappears in the Real.

In the poetry of courtly love the feminine object is introduced as inaccessible, but also emptied of all real substance. This is in accord with the general formula that what is aimed at in sublimation, 'what man demands, what he cannot help but demand, is to be deprived of something real.'[62] Desire, as we know, thrives upon inaccessibility. The poetry of courtly love, in fact, posits an object Lacan describes as 'terrifying, an inhuman partner.' The object is not merely inaccessible but separated from the one who longs to reach it 'by all kinds of evil powers.' The sexual object, Lacan insists, contrary to the general belief, does not necessarily disappear in sublimation, but can appear in all its crudity as a cruel, unattainable, emptiness, humiliating those who seek to obtain it. Here we catch a glimpse of the 'cruel' superego at work in the process of sublimation, drawing its energy from the aggression the subject turns back upon itself. The superego 'seems to find in itself its own exacerbation, as the result of a kind of malfunctioning of the brakes which should limit its own authority. It

---

[61] *Ethics*, p. 160 (3.2.60).
[62] *Ethics*, p. 184 (10.2.60).

remains to be seen how within this breakdown in the depths of the psychic life the instincts may find their proper sublimation.'[63]

In Freud, as in Sade, 'the notion of the death drive is a creationist sublimation, and is linked to that structural element which implies that, as soon as we have to deal with anything in the world appearing in the form of the signifying chain, there is somewhere – though certainly outside of the natural world – which is the beyond of that chain, the *ex nihilo* on which it is founded and is articulated as such.'[64] The death drive is 'a will to create from zero, a will to begin again.' Contrary to a certain reading of Freud, therefore, the death drive is not to be explained by the 'Nirvana principle', seeking a return to absolute rest or equilibrium. What matters more for Lacan is that Freud's discovery of the death drive led us to a problematic place which reveals the structure of the field, the site of the Thing. 'Freud evokes there his sublimation concerning the death instinct insofar as that sublimation is fundamentally creationist.' The creation *ex nihilo* is what gives birth to the historical dimension of the drive, a birth which required the signifier. 'In the beginning was the Word.' In the annihilation of the world, language is born *ex nihilo*.

This creationist perspective is, paradoxically, the only one that 'allows one to glimpse the possibility of the radical elimination of God.' It is only by grasping an absolute beginning which is the origin of the signifying chain, 'which isolates in their own specific dimension the memorable and the remembered, that we do not find Being [*l'être*] always implied in being [*l'étant*], the implication that is at the core of evolutionist thought.' In the place of the Thing doubt is cast on all that is the place of being, the chosen place where sublimation occurs. If in courtly love woman is placed in this beyond, this 'has nothing to do

[63] *Ethics*, p. 177 (10.2.60).

[64] *Ethics*, p. 262 (4.5.60)

with her as a woman but as an object of desire.' The being to whom it is addressed 'is nothing other than a being as signifier [*un être de signifiant*]. The *inhuman* character of the object of courtly love is plainly visible. This love that led some people to acts close to madness was addressed at living beings, people with names, but who were not present in their fleshly and historical reality - there's perhaps a distinction to be made there. They were in any case in their being as reason, as signifier [*dans leur être de raison – du signifiant*].'[65]

The good and the beautiful both serve as barriers to 'the unspeakable field of radical desire that is the field of absolute destruction, of destruction beyond putrefaction.'[66] The relation between beauty and desire has traditionally been thought in terms of beauty suspending or disarming desire, in the form of 'beauty that mustn't be touched.'[67] This limit that must not be crossed is what Lacan calls 'the phenomenon of the beautiful,' which is also 'the limit of the second death'. In Sadean crime the victim is not dismembered and destroyed but is 'doubled' in a form inaccessible of destruction. The space thus provided for the play of pain is, Lacan claims, the same as that space of freedom generated by the aesthetic. In this sublimated form, Sade's victims are always adorned with beauty and grace in a way that 'leaves man speechless at the prospect of the image that is silhouetted behind it and threatens it. But what precisely is the threat, since it isn't the threat of destruction?'[68]

---

[65] *Ethics*, p. 265 (4.5.60). Translation modified.
[66] *Ethics*, pp. 267-268.
[67] *Ethics*, p. 295 (18.5.60).
[68] *Ethics*, p. 321 (1.6.60).

The beauty effect

It is at this point that Lacan refers his students to the 'extraordinarily precise' passages in Kant's *Critique of Judgment* that deal with beauty, telling them that there the object itself plays only a minor role in the phenomenon of beauty in the same way as in the Sadean fantasm, 'since the object there is no more than the power to support a form of suffering, which is in itself nothing else but the signifier of a limit. Suffering is conceived of as a stasis which affirms that that which is cannot return to the void from which it emerged.' The image of the crucified Christ similarly signifies a fantasmic limit to suffering which 'attracts to itself all the threads of our desire', an image which similarly 'poisons' our desire. The alternative to this stasis can be found only 'by means of a concept that moreover represents the disqualification of all concepts, that is, the concept of *ex nihilo*.'

The 'beauty effect', the 'violent illumination', in *Antigone* 'coincides with the moment of transgression or of realization of Antigone's *Atè*.' It simultaneously establishes a certain relation to the beyond and 'prevents us from seeing its true nature, that which dazzles us and separates us from its true function. The moving side of beauty causes all critical judgment to vacillate, stops analysis, and plunges the different forms involves into a certain confusion or, rather, an essential blindness.'[69] The beauty effect blinds us to the fact that this is an illustration of the death instinct. Antigone appears as *autonomos* but 'she pushes to the limit the realization of something that might be called the pure and simple desire of death as such.' Everything goes back to the desire of Jocasta, the mother/wife of Oedipus who brought these children into the world, whose desire was a criminal desire, of 'a radically destructive character.' Antigone chooses 'to be purely and

[69] *Ethics*, p. 346 (15.6.60).

simply the guardian of the being of the criminal as such.' She is required to sacrifice her own being 'to maintain that essential being which is the family *Atè* [...] Antigone perpetuates, eternalizes, immortalizes that *Atè*.' This is what Lacan calls 'the second death', the zone where death encroaches upon life, imposing a stasis in which everything that concerns transformation comes to a halt and the debt must be settled. The 'beauty effect' is integral to *catharsis* which Lacan understands not so much in the Aristotelian sense of an emotional purgation but rather as ritual purification. From Aristotle, however, he retains the idea of catharsis as a pleasurable calm to which one returns after 'a crisis that occurs in another dimension,' a crisis that threatens pleasure.[70]

The beautiful and the sublime

This brings us directly to Kant's theory of the beautiful and the sublime as set out in the exposition by Pierre Kaufmann (15.6.60) which again is unfortunately omitted from the English translation of Lacan's Seminar. Rather strangely, given that Lacan has discussed sublimation at length, the concept of the sublime has not been referred to explicitly in the analysis up to this point. Not until the end of the seminar of 22.6.60 does Lacan remark, as if it had just occurred to him, 'That, then, is what I wanted to remind you of today, so as to indicate to you the direction taken by our research on the subject of the beautiful and, I would add, the sublime. We haven't yet extracted from the Kantian definitions of the sublime all the substance we might. The conjunction of this term with that of sublimation is probably not simply an accident nor simply homonymic.' Although he promises to

[70] *Ethics*, pp. 302-303 (25.5.60).

make good this omission there is no further discussion of this association in Seminar VII.

In fact, although Lacan had acknowledged his debt to Kant's *Critique of Judgment* earlier in Seminar VII, his re-framing of the concept of sublimation had clearly been almost entirely governed by the logic of the sublime. The relation between sublimation and the sublime remains therefore unclarified. Zizek, in *The Sublime Object of Ideology*, feels able to refer to Lacan's definition of 'the sublime object' in Seminar VII as 'an object raised to the level of the (impossible-real) Thing,' when the latter is Lacan's definition not of the 'sublime object' but of sublimation.[71] Lacan's argument in the passage cited by Zizek is that sublimation, in providing the drive with a satisfaction different from its aim, reveals 'the Thing insofar as it is distinct from the object.' Lacan does not say that sublimation involves the creation of a 'sublime object.' His emphasis is upon the drive as 'an absolutely fundamental ontological notion,' which obtains satisfaction by endowing an object with 'the value of representing the Thing.'

The 'sublime object,' with which Zizek is so centrally concerned, makes its first appearance in Zizek's attempt to solve a problem which, he says, Marx left unsolved, namely, 'that of the *material* character of money: not of the empirical, material stuff money is made of, but of the *sublime* material, of that other 'indestructible and immutable' body which persists beyond the corruption of the body physical – this other body of money is like the corpse of the Sadean victim which endures all torments and survives with its beauty immaculate. This immaterial corporality of the 'body within the body' gives us a precise definition

[71] Zizek, *The Sublime Object of Ideology*, (London and New York: Verso, 1989), pp. 202-203, Lacan, p. 138.

of the sublime object...'[72] Zizek's attempt to explain '*sublime* material' as 'immaterial corporality' through a comparison of money with the enduring beauty of the body of a Sadean torture victim, I would suggest, provides us with anything but a precise definition of sublimity.

When Zizek later returns to 'the logic of sublimity,' although he provides a more considered account of the sublime in Kant's *Critique of Judgment*, his persistent attempt to centre sublimity upon the 'sublime object' leads him to say that 'with Kant the Sublime designates the relation of an inner-worldly, empirical sensuous object to *Ding an sich*, to the transcendent, trans-phenomenal, unattainable Thing-in-itself.'[73] If this were so, however, the sublime could have been fully incorporated within the problematic of the *Critique of Pure Reason*. Zizek continues, 'the Sublime is an object in which we can experience this very impossibility, this permanent failure of the representation to reach after the Thing.' The sublime, however, is not experienced 'in' thc object. As Kant puts it, 'all we are entitled to say is that the object is suitable for exhibiting a sublimity that can be found in the mind.'[74] Zizek's emphasis upon 'the sublime object' draws attention away from Kant's location of sublimity in formlessness and the failure of representation.

Sublimation and the sublime

'The sublime', named as such in the sixteenth-century Latin translation of Longinus' *Peri tou hupsou*, *De Sublimitate*, derives from

[72] Zizek, p. 18.
[73] Zizek, p. 203.
[74] Immanuel Kant, *Critique of Judgment*, trans. Werner S. Pluhar, (Indianapolis: Hackett Publishing Company, 1987) , p. 99/246, §23.

the term *sub limen*, meaning 'up to the lintel', indicating metaphorically the upper limit of the earthly sphere as it touches heaven. Implying both a separation from and a proximity to the divine, it refers originally to the use of elevated language producing an overpowering effect on the hearer, which 'falls on our ears like the voice of a god.' The sublime combines a grandeur of thought with a vigorous and spirited treatment of the passions, a 'fine madness' such as to raise the hearer or spectator as close as possible to the gods. With Edmund Burke's *A Philosophical Enquiry into the Origin of our Ideas of the Beautiful and Sublime* (1757), however, the scope of the sublime is widened from the rhetorical to include the experience of overpowering natural phenomena, their physiological effects upon the senses and the reactions produced in the mind. As in Longinus, the overwhelming power of the sublime is linked to the divine, and to feelings of terror and awe giving way to 'delight' (i.e. 'the sensation which accompanies the removal of pain or danger') on the part of those observing the sublime from a position of safety. The decisive change in the concept of the sublime, however, occurs in the philosophy of Kant in which, for the first time, the sublime is entirely *subjectivized.*

Pierre Kaufmann's contribution to Lacan's Seminar begins by relating Kant's argument in the *Critique of Judgment* (1790) to the publication of Goethe's *The Sorrows of Young Werther* (1787). In Goethe's epistolary novel, Werther describes the transition from the experience of the beautiful to that of the sublime, taking on the form of death anxiety [*l'angoisse de mort*]. The progression from the former to the latter in Kant's analysis is, Kaufmann states, 'a sublimation of Werther's experience. All in all, one can say that the 'Critique of Judgment' is, quite precisely, Werther sublimated [*sublimé*].' From the marvellous serenity of the beautiful, Werther passes to a sense of the presence of the Almighty, an 'infinite dilation' which manifests itself as a demand for poetic invention, in which the abyss of the infinite tortures him 'like an eternally open tomb'. Kant's treatment seeks, in Kaufmann's words, to provide the experience of Werther with a positive sense, endowing it with universality and a kind of pleasure. It is, in a general sense, the universalization of human finitude in the feeling of the sublime, 'universalizing pure pleasure, and universalizing the conflict between our attachment to the natural world and the awareness of our supra-sensible destination.'

Kant rejects all empiricist accounts of both the beautiful and the sublime, including that of Burke. The sublime, like the beautiful, is produced by an object of our liking, giving us a feeling of pleasure, and judgments about both are aesthetic, reflective and disinterested. The feeling of the beautiful brings a direct feeling of life being furthered and imagination at play, whereas the feeling of the sublime 'is a pleasure that arises only indirectly: it is produced by the feeling of a momentary inhibition of the vital forces followed immediately by an outpouring of them that it is all the stronger.'[75] The liking for the sublime is therefore what Kant calls 'a negative pleasure'. It is not the object, he repeatedly emphasizes, which is sublime, 'for what is sublime, in the proper meaning of the term, cannot be contained in any sensible form but concerns only ideas of reason, which though they cannot be exhibited adequately, are aroused and called to mind by this very inadequacy, which can be exhibited in sensibility.' It is mistaken to call the vast ocean raised up by storms sublime; it is what is already in one's mind that makes the sight sublime.

Although Kant himself does not use the term 'sublimation,' Goethe and Novalis had begun to conjugate 'sublime' as a noun or verb, signifying a mental construct rather than a natural or supernatural property. For Goethe, human feeling and events had to be 'sublimated'

---

[75] *Critique of Judgment,* Part I, §23, p. 98.

in order to be represented artistically, a form of elevated transmutation which can be considered homologous to alchemical sublimation in which base metals were supposed to obtain spiritual and salutary properties. Kaufmann takes this a step further insofar as Goethe's autobiographical experiences, having been 'sublimated' artistically are 'sublimated' once more in Kantian philosophy, in a theory of the 'sublime'.

Kaufmann emphasizes the role of judgments of taste and aesthetic pleasure in overcoming the opposition, established in the *Critique of Pure Reason* between 'the thing' [*la chose, das Ding*] and 'appearance' [*l'apparence, Erscheinung*]. The thing as object of a judgment of taste is assimilated into its appearance as a form of representation through disinterested aesthetic pleasure. Aesthetic pleasure takes a universal form as the free play between the transcendental imagination (the capacity of the mind to form images without posing the question of their adequacy to anything which actually exists) and the understanding (which categorizes and unifies the multiplicity of images). The feeling of aesthetic pleasure is that of the free relation between unity and diversity. The necessary character of judgments of taste is therefore built into the very structure of subjectivity. Besides being universal the judgment of taste, as a judgment of beauty, bears upon a fixed, determined form, whereas the experience of the sublime is at first an experience of the formless or unformed. In the sublime the imagination is divested of its power and must be 'sacrificed'. 'We sacrifice in the feeling of the sublime this beautiful harmony which rules in the feeling of beauty between our subjectivity and the experience.' In the sublime our subjectivity recognizes that it is powerless to unify the diversity of sensible impressions and must sacrifice its claim to grasp the sensible. However, this feeling of powerlessness awakens in us the feeling of another power which is the power of the infinite, of which *reason* is the faculty.

The sublime is divided into two domains. One is what Kant calls 'the mathematical' which is the domain of quantity [*grandeur*], the other 'the dynamic' which is the domain of causality. In the sublime we are stripped of all power to determine its measure, which would involve a seemingly endless pursuit, but this in turn gives us a sense of the infinite power of reason. Kant is undoubtedly here referring to the discovery of the infinitesmal calculus. It is this faculty of 'resistance' that provides us with a place of safety from which to admire and enjoy the spectacle of the sublime and, Kant adds, the courage to measure ourselves against the overwhelming power that confronts us. It is in the face of this menace that we discover a sense of freedom, that is, of our *autonomy* – that we discover the law inside ourselves, the law given to us by reason.

In Lyotard's words,

> The *Geistesgefühl*, the sentiment of the mind, signifies that the mind is lacking in nature, that nature is lacking for it. It feels only itself. In this way the sublime is none other than the sacrificial announcement of the ethical in the aesthetic field. Sacrificial in that it requires that imaginative nature (inside and outside the mind) must be sacrificed in the interests of practical reason […] This heralds the end of an aesthetics, that of the beautiful, in the name of the final destination of the mind, which is freedom.[76]

[76] Jean-François Lyotard, *The Inhuman: Reflections on Time*, trans. Geoffrey Bennington and Rachel Bowlby, (Cambridge: Polity Press, 1991), p.137.

From the beautiful to the sublime

As Jean-Luc Nancy argues, despite the order of Kant's argument, one can only fully understand beauty by way of the sublime. It reveals the beautiful, beneath its apparent accord with subjectivity, as an unstable, intermediate category, preparing the passage from the aesthetic to the ethical, or, as one might say, its *sublimation*. The sublime is not simply a presentation of the infinite, but is rather the *movement of the unlimited*, of the 'unlimitation' [*die Unbegrenztheit*] that takes place on the border of the limit, and thus of presentation.[77] The unlimited is that 'which sets itself on the border of the limit, that which detaches itself and subtracts itself from limitation (and hence from beauty) by an unlimitation that is coextensive with the external border of limitation.' It is 'the gesture by which all (finite) form gets carried away into the absence of form. It is the gesture of formation, of figuration itself (of *Ein-bildung*), but only insofar as the formless itself too stands out – without itself taking on any form – along the form that traces itself, joins itself to itself, and presents itself.' It is what Kant refers to as 'indirect' or 'negative' presentation, but Nancy points out that these terms fail to disturb the logic of re-presentation. 'The sublime is: *that* there is an image, hence a limit, along whose edge unlimitation makes itself felt.' There is nothing to present 'but merely that it [*ça*] presents itself.' The sublime is also, as Nancy emphasizes, an emotion, 'the emotion of a subject at the limit,' and an emotion which cannot be fully analyzed either within the philosophy of subjectivity or the notion of aesthetic pleasure. 'This (e)motion is without complacency and without satisfaction: it is not a pleasure

[77] Jean-Luc Nancy, 'The Sublime Offering' in *Of the Sublime: Presence in Question*, ed. Rodolphe Gasché and Mark C. Taylor, trans. Jeffrey S. Librett, (New York: SUNY Press, 1993), p. 35.

without being at the same time a pain. But its ambivalence does not make it any less sensible, does not render it less effectively sensible: *it is the sensibility of the fading of the sensible.*'[78]

Lyotard, like Nancy, seeks to bring out the special temporality of the sublime, in that 'the inexpressible does not reside in an over there, in another word, or another time, but in this: in that (something) happens.'[79] The sublime presents itself as a 'happening' in the face of which all concepts of the understanding are disarmed. This dislocation of the faculties gives rise to the feeling of agitation which is the pathos of the sublime, as opposed to the sense of calmness induced by beauty. The art-object attempts 'to present the fact that there is an unpresentable,' often in the form of shock, the evidence of something happening, coupled with suspended cognitive privation and the defeat of the controlling will. Not surprisingly, this disruption of the sensory and intellectual order leads Lyotard to suggest that the sublime brings us into proximity with 'the Thing'. 'The Thing is not waiting to be destined, it is not waiting for anything, it does not call on the mind. How can the mind situate itself, get in touch with something that withdraws from every relationship?'[80] While the sublime is clearly linked with modernism and, by Leotard, with the concept of the *avant-garde*, he acknowledges that its relation to capitalism is ambivalent, since, although it disrupts established patterns of thought and sensibility, there is something of the sublime in the capitalist economy itself in its excessive dynamism, regulated only by the Idea of infinite wealth and power.

Formlessness

---

[78] Nancy, p. 45.
[79] 'The Sublime and the Avant-Garde', in *The Inhuman*, p. 93.
[80] *The Inhuman*, p. 142.

The Kantian sublime closely resembles 'formlessness' in the thought of Georges Bataille, which Paul Hegarty refers to as 'a new way of (dis)ordering categories of modern art.' From this perspective 'form' is seen as a way to conceptualize the world, 'bringing it into language, meaning, and hierarchies of suitability, moral goodness, truthfulness.' In Bataille's words, 'it is a matter of giving a frock-coat to what is.'[81] Formlessness [*l'informe*], on the other hand, is understood as an active movement, 'like a spider or an earth-worm'. Against the Platonic tradition, formlessness reveals that form has nothing to do with resemblance or design. Hegarty writes, 'As with chaos mathematics, it is a mistake to think that the 'formless' is the site or process of the loss of forms – rather it is a new way of looking at how form coalesces – a way that entails thinking the continual movement between something and nothing, form and lack of form. In short, all form 'contains' *formlessness* and the formless cannot be brought out.'[82] It is both 'inside' and 'outside'. Bataille presents formlessness as a way of 'bringing down' art from its elevated position, that is, as a *desublimation*, related to the sense in which, for example, Goethe understood art as necessarily involving sublimation. Bataille writes instead from a position of 'base materialism', demanding that art be 'brought down' to the drives which sustain it and from which creativity is drawn.

It is from this position that Bataille criticizes André Breton's advocacy of 'dialectical' sublimation in the *Second Manifesto of Surrealism* (1929) and other writings. Breton writes that those who are

[81] Georges Bataille, 'Formlessness', in *Visions of Excess: Selected Writings 1927-1939*, ed. and trans. Allan Stoekl, (Minneapolis: University of Minnesota Press, 1985), p. 31.

[82] Paul Hegarty, *Georges Bataille: Core Cultural Theorist*, (London: Sage Publications, 2000), p. 143.

drawn to surrealism 'are especially interested in the Freudian concept which affects the greater part of their deep concerns as men – the concern to create, to destroy artistically – I mean the definition of the phenomenon known as "sublimation".' What this means for Breton is that the process known as 'inspiration' be stripped of its associations with the 'sacred' and be understood as flowing from the deeper sources of the human psyche:

> We can easily recognize it by that total possession of our mind which, at rare intervals, prevents our being, for every problem posed, the plaything of one rational solution rather than some other equally rational solution, by that sort of short circuit it creates between a given idea and a respondent idea (written for example). Just as in the physical world, a short circuit occurs when the two "poles" of a machine are joined by a conductor of little or no resistance. In poetry and in painting, Surrealism has done everything it can and more to increase these short circuits. It believes, and it will never believe in anything more wholeheartedly, in reproducing artificially this ideal moment when man, in the grip of a particular emotion, is suddenly seized by this "something stronger than himself" which projects him, in self-defence, into immortality. If he were lucid, awake, he would be terrified as he wriggled out of this tight situation. The whole point for him is not to be free of it, for him to go on talking the entire time this ringing lasts: it is, in fact, the point at which he ceases to belong to himself that he belongs to us. These products of psychic activity, as far removed as possible from the desire to make sense, as free as possible of any ideas of responsibility which are always prone to act as brakes, as independent as possible of everything which is not 'the passive life of the intelligence' – these products which automatic

> writing and the description of dreams represent offer at one and the same time the advantage of being unique in providing elements of appreciation of great style to a body of criticism which, in the realm of art, reveals itself to be strangely helpless, of permitting a general reclassification of lyrical values, and of proposing a key capable of opening indefinitely that box of many bottoms called man, a key that dissuades him from turning back, for reasons of self-preservation, when in the darkness he bumps into doors, locked from the outside, of the "beyond," of reality, of genius, and of love.[83]

There is evidently much less distance here between Breton and Bataille than the intensity of their quarrel might suggest. This may be partially explained by the fact that both are drawing upon the thought of Nietzsche in which the concepts of the 'sublime' and 'sublimation' came into proximity in a complex and sometimes confusing manner, a relation which changes in the course of his writings. Nietzsche *both* demands that we purify ourselves of the desire for the sublime which is an investment in an imaginary world, *and* seeks to discover an understanding of the sublime which would open up new possibilities. Nietzsche in part follows the traditional concept of the sublime as the elevated and lofty, but it is also bound up for him with practices of purification and sublimation that involve the overcoming of traditional conceptions of what is possible in experience. The purification demanded by Nietzsche is, however, precisely a purification of the imaginary, deluded, 'higher feelings' traditionally associated with the sublime, that must now be abandoned in the name of truth. The

[83] André Breton, *Manifestoes of Surrealism*, trans. Richard Seaver and Helen R. Lane, University of Michigan Press, 1972, pp. 161-162.

'sublime' and 'sublimation' are brought together within the project of 'self-overcoming'

The relation between Breton and Bataille is not the relation between sublimation and desublimation. In the *Second Manifesto* Breton invokes the Nietzschean idea of sublimation as the production of a new consciousness [*une* conscience *nouvelle*]. Breton's idea of sublimation, as indicated above, involves both (aesthetic) destruction and construction, unlike Freudian sublimation which produces only the socially valorized. Klem James has argued that what he calls the notion of 'transgressive sublimation' to be found in Lacan's *Ethics of Psychoanalysis* reveals that there is no binary opposition between sublimation and desublimation and there is therefore common ground between Breton and Bataille. Lacan's concept of sublimation, as developed in the *Ethics*, argues that instead of a re-direction of libido towards a non-sexual object, sublimation is 'a change in the position of the love object within the structure of the subject's fantasy life.'[84] The love object (*das Ding*) is transfigured metaphorically within the mind, a propensity to exalt the other which necessarily increases against a background of prohibition. Courtly love, as indicated earlier, flourished alongside what Lacan describes as 'uninhibited fucking.' Characteristic of sublimation is that the symbolic representation is elevated while the woman herself is described in the crudest terms. Temptation is integral to desire and the sustaining of desire. For Bataille, eroticism involves both sensitivity towards the anguish which is the basis of the interdiction *and* the desire to violate it. The sacred requires the diabolical as its other. Sublimation can therefore be said to contain the seeds of desublimation.

[84] Klem James, 'Breton, Bataille and Lacan's Notion of "Transgressive" Sublimation', *Episteme*, Vol. 2 (1), 2009.

The articulation of ethics and aesthetics

In order to grasp fully the nature of the sublime it is necessary to take into account why Kant believed it necessary to write the third *Critique* in order to complete his critical system. By the term 'judgment', Kant means 'the ability to think the particular as contained under the universal.' As *transcendental* judgment it states a priori the conditions for subsuming the particular under the universal. It is the role of judgment to bring about a transition from the pure cognitive power, that is, 'from the domain of the concepts of nature, to the domain of the concept of freedom.'[85] This relation which establishes the possibility of linking purely conceptual discourse to an empirically determined discourse is what Kant calls the *aesthetic*. Judgment's application of the concept of purposiveness [*Zwechmässigkeit*] to objects of nature or art gives rise to pleasure or displeasure. The spontaneous, harmonious play of the faculties makes the concept of purposiveness suitable for mediating the concept of nature with the concept of freedom, as regards freedom's consequences, 'inasmuch as this harmony also promotes the mind's receptivity to moral feeling.'[86] The aesthetic is therefore where Kant brings together what he calls the transcendental and the metaphysical, where a 'metaphysical' concept is one that implies an empirical moment external to the concept, taking the existence of their object for granted. As Paul de Man points out, the section in the *Critique of Judgment* where this articulation of the transcendental with the metaphysical takes place is precisely the section on the sublime.[87]

---

[85] *Critique of Judgment*, p. 18/179.
[86] *Critique of Judgment*, p. 38/197.
[87] Paul de Man, 'Phenomenality and Materiality in Kant', in *Aesthetic Ideology*, ed. Andrzej Warminski, (Minneapolis: University of Minnesota Press, 1996), p. 73.

The object of an aesthetic judgment is understood as 'purposive without purpose', that is to say, it necessarily appears to us as if it served some purpose or design, but this purpose is indeterminate. It manifests an order or regularity, but not an order which is determinate, such as would allow us to subsume an intuition under a concept. The subject takes pleasure in this indeterminate harmony between the imagination and the understanding as a form of free play without the constraints of normal cognition. In the case of the sublime, an aesthetic judgment which is reflexive, disinterested and claims universal validity, there is however a certain crisis in the power of judgment, in which the object of the sublime experience appears 'contrapurposive for our power of judgment, incommensurate with our power of exhibition [*Darstellung*], and as it were violent to our imagination, and yet we judge it all the more sublime for that.'[88] This dramatic turn in the argument means that although Kant begins by describing the sublime as a 'mere appendix' to the theory of the beautiful,[89] it turns out to be crucially important for what it tells us about the operation of our own faculties, as the mind is forced to resort to 'ideas containing a *higher* purposiveness.'[90]

De Man writes:

> Contrary to the beautiful, which at least appears to be all of a piece, the sublime is shot through with dialectical complication. It is, in some respects, infinitely attractive but, at the same time, thoroughly repellent; it gives a peculiar kind of pleasure (*Lust*), yet it is also consistently painful; in less subjective, more structural terms, it is equally baffling: it knows of no limits or

---

[88] *Critique of Judgment*, p. 99/245, §23.
[89] *Critique of Judgment*, p. 100/246, §23.
[90] My italics.

> borders, yet it has to appear as a determined totality; in a philosophical sense, it is something of a monster, or, rather, a ghost: it is not a property of nature (there are no such things as sublime objects in nature) but a purely inward experience of consciousness (*Gemütsbestimmung*), yet Kant insists, time and again, that this noumenal entity has to be phenomenally represented (*dargestellt*); this is indeed an integral part, the crux, in fact, of the analytics of the sublime.[91]

He continues, 'Out of the pain of the failure to constitute the sublime by making the infinite apparent (*anschaulich*) is born the pleasure of the imagination, which discovers, in this very failure, the congruity of its own law (which is a law of failure) with the law of our suprasensory being. Its failure to connect with the sensory would also elevate it above it. This law does not reside in nature but defines man in opposition to nature…' De Man questions whether in Kant's argument, 'the sublime surreptitiously posits itself by claiming to exist by dint of the impossibility of its own existence.'

It is at this point that de Man refers to the same quotation from Kant that we saw cited earlier by Zizek, which Zizek took to be an anticipation of Lacan's definition of 'the sublime object.' In Barnard's translation, slightly modified by de Man, Kant defines the sublime as 'an object (of nature) the representation [*Vorstellung*] of which determines consciousness [*Gemüt*] to *think* the unattainability of nature as a sensory representation [*Darstellung*] of ideas.'[92] The key word here for de Man is *denken*, indicating for Kant the contrast

[91] De Man, p. 74.

[92] *Critique of Judgment,* §29. Quoted de Man, p. 76, (emphasis added by de Man). Zizek quotes Meredith's (1964) translation of the *Critique* in which the word 'think' does not appear.

between thinking and knowing [*erkennen*]. By the way of knowledge, de Man suggests, it has been impossible to establish the existence of the sublime as an intelligible concept, but there may be a way of thinking, possibly indebted to Heidegger, that would allow us to *think* the sublime in its being. This would again bring us back to the Lacanian Thing, the being of which was explained by means of Heidegger's vase as *das Ding*.

As was the case with the moral law, the emphasis on the inward, noumenal nature of the sublime can obscure the fact that it takes on a phenomenal manifestation. Kant insists in his theory of the faculties that the feeling for the sublime cannot be thought without 'a mood of *consciousness* which is akin to the moral.' Although the feeling for the sublime has been prepared through culture, allowing us to experience it as the dominance of practical reason over sensibility, which experiences the infinite only as an abyss, it is founded in human nature. Moral feeling is something we presuppose in human beings and the basis for the *necessity* we attribute to aesthetic judgments. It is this presupposed necessity 'that reveals an a priori principle in them and lifts them out of [the reach of] empirical psychology,' and into the realm of the transcendental.[93] Otherwise they could be mistaken simply for refinement. In the beautiful the moral is felt in a much weaker form than in the sublime, where it is experienced not as play but as 'law-directed labour' [*gesetzliches Geschäft*]. As de Man puts it, 'The only restriction that keeps the sublime from passing entirely into the camp of morality is that the faculty involved in it is not reason, or at least not an unmediated manifestation of reason, but that the sublime is represented by the imagination itself, as a tool of reason.'[94]

[93] *Critique*, p. 125.
[94] De Man, p. 84.

The need for this incarnation of practical reason in the aesthetic is a result of the fallen condition of man. Although we speak of intellectual beauty or sublimity, Kant states, these expressions are incorrect, since if we were pure intelligences we would not present things in this way at all. The might of the moral law 'actually reveals itself aesthetically only through sacrifice (which is a deprivation – though one that serves our inner freedom – in return for which it reveals in us an unfathomable depth of this supersensible power, whose consequences extend beyond what we can foresee.'[95] In relation to sensibility the liking is negative, but from the intellectual side it is positive. To judge aesthetically the moral good we must present it as sublime, so as to arouse a feeling of respect rather than love and affection. 'For human nature does not of itself harmonize with that good; it [can be made to harmonize with it] only through the dominance that reason exerts over sensibility.'

The inferiority of the aesthetic, as de Man points out, as symptomatic of our inherent shortcoming, becomes evident only in relation to moral judgment. Morality and aesthetics are both disinterested but 'this disinterestedness becomes polluted in aesthetic representation,' by being linked to 'positively valorized sensory experiences.' De Man adds, 'The moral lesson of the aesthetic has to be conveyed by seductive means which, as we know, can reach far enough to make it necessary to read "Kant avec Sade" rather than the reverse.'[96]

Sublimation and the logic of the sublime

[95] *Critique*, p. 131/271.
[96] De Man, p. 84.

The problem of sublimation is, as we have seen, how the signifier comes to represent the Thing when the Thing is unimaginable. The structure of Lacan's argument here, as Zupančič demonstrates, is similar to that of Kant's analysis of the sublime. The instability of the beautiful, of the 'beauty effect', shields but can also give way to what lies beyond it, the overpowering of the imagination by the unimaginable, formless Thing. In *Antigone*, 'a certain beyond of the central field is established for us, but it is also that which prevents us from seeing its true nature, that which dazzles us and separates us from its true function. The moving side of beauty causes all critical judgment to vacillate, stops analysis, and plunges the different forms involved into a certain confusion or, rather, an essential blindness.' The beauty effect blinds us. 'Something else is going on on the other side that cannot be observed.'[97]

Kant's treatment of the concepts of the beautiful and the sublime provides Lacan with a means of reframing the concept of sublimation, linking it to an essential 'emptiness' upon which art, religion and science are projected, an aesthetic and ethical beyond which demands sacrifice as the price of entry and involves no clear break between sexual and desexualized desire, between law and transgression, between creation and destruction, and between good and evil. Sublimation is no longer a transformation in which the higher disowns the lower from which it originated. The purification demanded by Lacanian ethics is of a different order, namely, the purification of desire by its remaining true to itself.

The 'world of guilt' with which Lacan's ethical inquiry began is not simply to be revealed as a realm of illusion; the omnipresence of guilt is admitted and traced back to what Lacan believes to be its true source, the betrayal of one's own desire. It is this betrayal which turns

---

[97] Lacan, *Ethics*, p. 346.

desire against itself and gives rise to its Sadean, punitive form as the superego. It is an understanding of the superego already anticipated in Freud's later writings where, in order to explain the punitive and *excessive* character of the superego, Freud increasingly emphasized its origins in the energies of the lawless and disruptive id and its connections with the death drive.

Whereas Stiegler counterposes the role of sublimation and the socially constructive superego to the market's shameless 'incitement to enjoy,' Lacan in his later writings identifies the incitement to enjoy [*Jouis!*] as precisely the imperative issued to the ego by the superego itself.[98] The *jouissance* demanded in this way both *forces* us to enjoy and punishes us severely for our failure to enjoy as much as it tells us we should.

In explanation of the differences between Freud and Lacan, Adrian Johnston has observed that whereas Freud regarded the superego as 'the direct heir of the Oedipus complex,' Lacan claims that the earliest prototypes of the superego are not the parental figures of the Oedipus complex but '*the drive-sources as internal dictators from which the nascent subject-to-be cannot flee.*'[99]

Johnston continues,

> Consequently, prior to the traditional version of the Freudian prohibitive super-ego, the drive-sources function as a Lacanian super-ego. Their imperative is invariably the same: "Obtain enjoyment by always recovering the same form of satisfaction! Or "Endlessly re-find the initial object-choices.

---

[98] *The Seminar of Jacques Lacan: On Feminine Sexuality, the Limits of Love and Knowledge Book XX 1972-1973 Encore*, trans. Bruce Fink, (London: W. W. Norton & Co, 1999), Session of 21.11.1972.

[99] Adrian Johnston, *Time Driven: Metapsychology and the Splitting of the Drive*, (Evanston, Illinois: Northwestern University Press, 2005), p. 296.

While the imperatives transmitted by parental and other authority figures are historical and contingent, those of the superego, considered as the expression of the drive-sources are not.

Johnston argues, however, that the ferocious demands of this 'primordial' superego, impossible to satisfy, if left unchecked would lead to the complete destruction of the ego. Hence, jouissance encodes itself in fantasies functioning as unconscious defensive strategies. The inability to gratify the drives is shifted onto impediments beyond one's control. It is this process that 'actually transforms the super-ego' into its Freudian form as an agent of interdiction:

> The Lacanian super-ego demands *jouissance* so long as this enjoyment remains expected and not obtained – with Lacan, in his seventh seminar, observing that the prohibitory super-ego of *Civilization and its Discontents* preserves *jouissance* by keeping it a distance, on the hither side of the ethico-moral limits defining transgression.

The unfortunate consequence of this is that the subject then finds itself at the mercy of 'two masters'; on one side the Freudian superego which 'inevitable spoils the subject's enjoyment by inflicting penalties in the form of negative effects,' on the other, 'the Lacanian super-ego tirelessly punishes the subject for its futile attempts to cede to its inclinations, regardless of whether this ceding is motivated by the pleasure principle or by moral sentiments.'[100]

The understanding of the 'dark side' of the superego is founded, especially in Zizek's reading of Lacan, upon an analysis of Law itself as containing a secret, 'obscene' supplement, solicited by the big

[100] Johnston, pp. 335-336.

Other, which incites us to a transgressive *jouissance* and which, rather than the explicit, public face of the Law as presented in liberal-democratic societies, is the ultimate means of binding us into collective conformity: 'we' who have 'broken' the law together forming a social bond that cannot be publicly acknowledged and is ultimately founded upon shared guilt.

In Zizek's words:

> What 'holds together' a community most deeply is not so much identification with the Law that regulates the community's 'normal' everyday circuit, but rather *identification with a specific form of transgression of the Law, of the Law's suspension* (in psychoanalytic terms, with a specific form of enjoyment.[101]

It is in this way that toxic currents of racist and sexist ideology continue to circulate undisturbed or tacitly encouraged by the official face of the Law, and that those who take a stand against them may be ostracized by their own communities. When sublimation and the superego are rethought in this way, it is clear that Stiegler's prescriptions for overcoming the pathological maladies of contemporary society can have potentially disastrous outcomes.

---

[101] Slavoj Zizek, *The Metastases of Enjoyment*, (London: Verso, 1994), p.54.

Trauma and Class in Literary Modernity

Baudelaire and the Crowd: poetic form and the modern urban experience

In *Le Peintre de la Vie Moderne*, Baudelaire draws attention to Poe's short story, 'The Man of the Crowd', in which a convalescent, sitting in the window of a London coffee house, becomes absorbed in the movement of the crowd outside and, after observing the various urban types and 'tribes' to be seen there, becomes fascinated by one particular individual, and is drawn to follow him back and forth through the bustling streets of the city. This sinister and elusive figure, the narrator concludes at the end of the tale, is 'the type and genius of deep crime. He refuses to be alone. *He is the man of the crowd.* It will be in vain to follow; for I shall learn no more of him, nor of his deeds.'[1]

The artist Constantin Guys, the eponymous 'painter of modern life,' was, Baudelaire tells us, a '*Grand amoureux de la foule et de l'incognito*' (great lover of the crowd and of the incognito), and, similarly, '*toujours, spirituellement, à l'état du convalescent,*' (always, spiritually, in a state of convalescence)[2] seeing everything with the freshness and intensity of a child. The crowd is his *domain*:

---

[1] Edgar Allen Poe, 'The Man of the Crowd', in *Poe's Tales of Mystery and Imagination* (London: Dent & Sons, 1975), pp. 101-109 (p. 109).

[2] Charles Baudelaire, *Oeuvres complètes*, ed. by Claude Pichois, Bibliothèque de la Pléiade, 2 vols (Paris: NRF, Gallimard, 1975-6), II, p. 690. All quotations from this edition. Hereafter OC. *The Painter of Modern Life and Other Essays*, trans. Jonathan Mayne (London: Phaidon Press, 1995), p. 7.

his passion is *d'épouser la foule* (to be wedded to the crowd). Guys, as the model of the modern artist, is not, Baudelaire tells us, to be mistaken for a dandy, since the dandy is *blasé* whereas Guys is dominated by an insatiable passion for seeing and feeling that draws him to the crowd. Not a dandy, then, but a *flâneur*:

> For the perfect flâneur, for the passionate spectator, it is an immense joy to set up house in the heart of the multitude, amid the ebb and flow of movement, in the midst of the fugitive and infinite. To be away from home and yet to feel oneself everywhere at home; to see the world, to be at the centre of the world, and yet to remain hidden from the world – such are a few of the slightest pleasures of those independent, passionate, impartial natures which the tongue can but clumsily define. The spectator is a *prince* who everywhere rejoices in his incognito.

The crowd, for Baudelaire, is the form of universal life, coursing with energy and becoming conscious through the artist who acts as its mirror, '*un kaleïdoscope doué de conscience* (a kaleidoscope gifted with consciousness).' Sovereign in the realm of consciousness, the artist's task is not to judge but first to immerse himself passionately, '*un* moi *insatiable du* non-moi,' delighting in the rich detail of urban life and the pursuit of nocturnal pleasures; then, through his powers of expression, to transform life into art.

'The phantasmagoria has been distilled from nature. All the raw materials with which the memory has loaded itself are put in order, ranged and harmonized, and undergo that forced idealization which is the result of a childlike perceptiveness – that is to say, a perceptiveness acute and magical by reason of its innocence.'

The significance of Poe's tale for Baudelaire, which he had earlier translated in the *Nouvelles Histoires Extraordinaires*, is here confined entirely to the state of mind of the observer-narrator who, '*Revenu récemment des ombres de la mort*', (lately returned from the shadows of death)' breathes in with pleasure 'all the odours and essences of life.' Baudelaire adds, 'as he has been on the brink of total oblivion, he remembers, and fervently desires to remember, everything.' It may be noted that Baudelaire is here elaborating rather freely upon Poe's text, which makes no mention either of death or of the role of memory. Instead Poe's convalescent observer-narrator describes himself as 'in one of those happy moods which are so precisely the converse of *ennui* – moods of the keenest appetency, when the film from the mental vision departs [...] and the intellect, electrified, surpasses as greatly its everyday condition, as does the vivid yet candid reason of Leibnitz, the mad and flimsy rhetoric of Gorgias [...] I felt a calm but inquisitive interest in everything.'

While Baudelaire's claim that Poe's observer-narrator is driven by curiosity is certainly valid, it may be questioned whether he has accurately described the state of mind from which that curiosity springs. Convalescence, according to Baudelaire, is like a return towards childhood...The child sees everything in a state of newness; he is always drunk. This intoxication is in turn held to resemble closely the state of artistic inspiration. From here Baudelaire is led to conclude that 'genius is nothing more than *childhood recovered* at will'. But this recovery of the sensuous intoxication of childhood by the rational will of the adult artist clearly has nothing in common with the 'Leibnitzian' ratiocination of Poe's convalescent, which is perhaps closer to the reflective intellect of his prototype detective, Auguste Dupin.

Benjamin and the *flâneur*

Walter Benjamin, in *Das Paris des Second Empire bei Baudelaire*, had indeed observed that Poe's tale is like an X-ray of a detective story with the details of the crime removed. 'Only the armature remains...[3] But Benjamin goes on to claim, mistakenly, that the *inconnu* at the centre of Poe's tale is the *flâneur*, both for Poe and Baudelaire. This misidentification may be in part caused by the strange tack of Baudelaire's argument which, having drawn a direct parallel between the state of mind of Poe's narrator and the form of Guys' artistic inspiration, goes on to develop what can best be described as a quasi-phenomenological investigation of the *flâneur*'s experience of the urban crowd, the relation of which to Poe's tale is highly problematic. The second element in this misidentification is Benjamin's determination to analyse the position of the *flâneur* in terms of the commodity form, a reading that leads him further and further astray.

In the first version of his essay, '*Edgar Allen Poe, sa vie et ses ouvrages*', Baudelaire summarizes for his readers the story of *L'Homme des Foules*, describing the man of the crowd's frantic searches as follows: 'To the degree that the circle of light and life shrinks, he searches for the centre of it anxiously; like the men of the flood he clings desperately to the last focal points of public agitation. And that is all. Is he a criminal horrified by solitude? Is he an imbecile who cannot stand himself?'

---

[3] Walter Benjamin, *Gesammelte Schriften*, Band 1 – 2 (Frankfurt-am-Main: Suhrkamp, 1991), p. 550. The *Writer of Modern Life: Essays on Charles Baudelaire*, ed. by Michael W. Jennings, trans. by Howard Eiland, Edmund Jephcott, Rodney Livingston, and Harry Zohn (Cambridge MA and London: The Belknap Press of Harvard University Press, 2006), p. 79. Hereafter *WML*.

It is clear from this alone that Baudelaire could not have identified the man of the crowd with the strolling *flâneur*. Benjamin, however, states categorically, 'This unknown man is the *flâneur*. That is how Baudelaire understood him when, in his essay on Guys, he called the *flâneur* "*l'homme des foules*".) (*GS* 1-2, 550, *WML*, 79.)

Martina Lauster, in a root and branch assault upon Benjamin's concept of the *flâneur*, makes the point forcefully that 'to see the *object* of the narrator's vision, 'the man of the crowd,' as a *flâneur* is absolute nonsense; if anything, it is the observing narrator who could be labelled thus.'[4] Benjamin was, I believe, drawn into this misidentification by the following line of thought:

> The crowd is not only the newest asylum of outlaws; it is the latest narcotic for people who have been abandoned. The *flâneur* is someone abandoned in the crowd. He is thus in the same situation as the commodity. He is unaware of this special situation, but this does not diminish its effect on him; it permeates him blissfully, like a narcotic that can compensate him for many humiliations. The intoxication to which the *flâneur* surrenders is the intoxication of the commodity immersed in a surging stream of customers.[5]

Rather than having 'been abandoned,' Benjamin clearly means those who are in a state of abandonment or loss of self, but it is difficult to see how the demonic energy of Poe's man of the crowd can be described as a state of blissful intoxication. Benjamin remarks that if the commodity had a soul, ‚it would be the most empathetic ever

---

[4] Martina Lauster, 'Benjamin's Myth of the 'Flâneur'', *MLR*, 102 (2007), 139-56, p. 144.
[5] *WML*, p. 85.

encountered in the realm of souls, for it would be bound to see every individual as a buyer in whose hand it wants to nestle. Empathy is the nature of the intoxication to which the *flâneur* abandons himself in the crowd.[6] Behind the voice of the poet-*flâneur* Benjamin claims to detect that of the fetishized commodity as the poet-prostitute is obliged to trade his wares in the marketplace.

So far as Poe's 'Man of the Crowd' is concerned, it must be said that Benjamin's attempt here to integrate the tale into his reading of Baudelaire is unsuccessful. Poe's man of the crowd, as Benjamin notes, enters a large and busy bazaar with which he seems well acquainted, leading Benjamin to infer that this is the *flâneur* who 'roamed through the labyrinth of commodities as he had once roamed through the labyrinth of the city.' When the clock strikes eleven and the shops begin to close, he shudders violently and runs into the street. But this is not the behaviour of a crazed shopper in amorous communion with the souls of commodities.

Poe writes, 'He entered shop after shop, priced nothing, spoke no word, and looked at all objects with a wild and vacant stare.' If the key to Poe's tale is the quotation from La Bruyère with which it begins: '*Ce grand malheur, de ne pouvoir être seul*' (this great misfortune of not being able to be alone), then the man of the crowd, far from being an embodiment of empathy, is surely one who is desperate to avoid being alone, who follows the crowd with demonic energy, but who can never cease to be alone because he can never surmount his own egotism. The crowd is the element in which he moves and from which he draws his energy, but this is because he is incapable of empathy with another human being. It is in this sense that he may represent, as Poe's narrator puts it, 'the essence of all crime,' and why Benjamin

---

[6] *WML*, pp. 85-86.

perceptively describes 'The Man of the Crowd' as the X-ray of a detective story.

Lauster states that Benjamin corrected his error in his later essay, '*Über einige Motive bei Baudelaire*', where, returning to Poe's tale, he states, 'The man of the crowd is no *flâneur*. In him composure has given way to manic behaviour. He exemplifies, rather, what had to become of the *flâneur* after the latter was deprived of the milieu to which he belonged.[7]

But how much of a correction is this? Benjamin's position now appears to be that Poe's man of the crowd corresponds to the changed role of the *flâneur*, once Paris, the natural habitat of the *flâneur*, had become as hectic and feverish as London. Yet these differences were already pointed up in the earlier essay, where Benjamin remarks of London, 'In a mass of this nature, flânerie could never flourish.' Paris, on the other hand, at that time still provided elbow room for the strolling *flâneur* (and his turtle). Yet, nevertheless Benjamin still insists in the earlier essay that the 'man of the crowd' is a *flâneur*.

The dialectic of *flânerie*

Lauster also notes that Benjamin left statements corresponding to his earlier view unchanged in the *Passagen-Werk*, citing as an example, his reference to a dialectic of *flânerie*: 'on the one side, the man who feels himself viewed by all and sundry as a true suspect and, on the other side, the man who is utterly undiscoverable, the hidden man.' Presumably, it is this dialectic that is developed in "The Man of the Crowd.'[8] It seems likely that Benjamin has in mind here Baudelaire's

[7] *WML*, p. 188.

[8] *Gesammelte Schriften* V-1, (Frankfurt am Main, Suhrkamp, 1991), Band V-1, 529. *The Arcades Project*, tr. by H. Eiland & K. McLaughlin

characterisation of the *flâneur* as an incognito, the reflective observer moving within the crowd, and, on the other side, Poe's man of the crowd, prowling the urban jungle of Sue's *Les Mystères de Paris* or Balzac's stories in which scenes from the American woods of Fenimore Cooper are transposed into Parisian life.

In the *Arcades Project* Benjamin also states, 'The case in which the *flâneur* completely distances himself from the type of the philosophical promenader, and takes on the features of the werewolf restlessly roaming a social wilderness, was fixed for the first time and forever afterward by Poe in his story "The Man of the Crowd."'[9]

We begin now to see the shape of a more complex argument in Benjamin which recognizes that his earlier identification of Poe's man of the crowd with the *flâneur* was mistaken. The misconceived reliance on the commodity form to explain both *flânerie* and Poe's tale has been sidelined and the basis of a dialectical interpretation sketched out. The dialectic of *flânerie* would now seem to function as follows. On one side is the *flâneur* as incognito, the hidden observer, the philosophical promenader who brings the urban crowd to the level of reflective consciousness. This would correspond to the role of the narrator-observer in Poe's story.

In a further passage in the *Passagen-Werk*, Benjamin writes,

> Preformed in the figure of the flâneur is that of the detective. The flâneur required a social legitimation of his habitus. It suited him very well to see his indolence presented as a plausible front, behind which, in reality, hides the riveted

(Cambridge, Mass & London: The Bellknap Press of Harvard University Press 1999), p. 420.

[9] *AP*, pp. 417-418.

> attention of an observer who will not let the unsuspecting malefactor out of his sight.[10]

This can only be a reference to Poe's story and establishes a clear connection between the *flâneur* and the observer-detective. On the other side is the *flâneur* as bohemian social outcast, the poet-ragpicker, poet-prostitute, poet-pariah of *Les Fleurs du Mal*, 'the werewolf roaming a social wilderness,' which might apply equally to the man of the crowd and to Baudelaire (in his own imagination at least.)

At the core of Poe's tale is the relation of observer and observed, a drama of interpretation, between, in terms of Benjamin's dialectic, *incognito* and *inconnu*, moving within the anonymity of the crowd. The story, as Benjamin points out, shows a purposely distorting imagination at work, played out under the gas lamps as an urban phantasmagoria in an alienated landscape. The man of the crowd remains unaware throughout that he is being observed, so that any dialectic is enacted entirely within the consciousness or the imagination of the observer. The narrator is an anonymous reader just as we are, struggling and ultimately failing to make sense of what he sees, to grasp the nature of this rapidly moving, elusive and ever-changing fugitive. There are some books, the narrator tells us, at the beginning of the story, which do not permit themselves to be read.

As the tale comes to an end the observer stands in front of the man of the crowd and looks directly at him but the man fails to notice him, suggesting that he may exist only in the mind of the observer himself, as a distorting mirror or a Hoffmanesque 'double'. The narrator concludes that the man 'is the type and genius of deep crime,' but we were warned at the beginning of the story that some secrets are so horrific that they are they are taken to the grave, 'And thus the essence

---

[10] *AP*, p. 442.

of all crime is undivulged.' Nevertheless, the deeper bearing of the text is to establish the urban crowd as a phenomenon in which evil [*le mal*] moves, an insight which gives itself to the artist-observer, himself implicated in that evil, and which, seen through the prism of Baudelaire's poetics, takes its place at the heart of modernity. The defining characteristic of evil in this narrative is that it is a text that does not permit itself to be read.

Between multitude and solitude in the modern city

The '*moi* insatiable du *non-moi*' of *Le Peintre de la Vie Moderne* is an echo of '*Ce grand malheur, de ne pouvoir être seul,*' but we touch here upon the dynamic which drives much of Baudelaire's poetry. In the prose-poem, '*Les Foules*', he writes:

> Multitude, solitude : terms equivalent and interchangeable for the active and fertile poet.The man who is unable to people his solitude is equally unable to be alone in a bustling crowd. The poet enjoys the incomparable privilege of being able to be himself or someone else, just as he chooses. Like those wandering souls who go looking for a body, he enters as he likes into each man's personality. For him alone everything is vacant; and if certain places seem closed to him, it is only because in his eyes they are not worth visiting.

In the *lettre-dédicace* of *Le Spleen de Paris* which precedes the prose-poems, Baudelaire directly links this new poetic form, 'supple enough and rugged enough to adapt itself to the lyrical impulses of the soul, the undulations of reverie, the jolts of consciousness.)' with the experience of the modern city. 'It is above all out of the frequenting of great cities, from the intersecting of their innumerable relations that this haunting ideal was born.'

These multiple intersections are reflected in a splitting of the lyric subject, ironic displacement, and the disintegration of univocity. Whereas over twenty of the prose-poems which compose *Le Spleen de Paris* are written in the first person, '*Les Foules*', surprisingly, since it makes the splitting of the lyric persona thematic, is discursive, univocal, and written entirely from the point of view of an impersonal narrator, seemingly 'the poet'.

This form is however, subtly undermined from within, beginning with the opening statement, 'It is not given to everyone to take a bath in the multitude: to enjoy the crowd is an art.' The narrator proclaims the ironic self-elevation of the poet and his 'incomparable privilège,' freely choosing whether to be himself or another; yet Baudelaire persistently suggests to us through the use of erotic metaphors that the poet's involvement with the crowd is illicit and transgressive, the counterpart of solitary, onanistic fantasy. 'Whoever weds himself easily to the crowd knows feverish delights...What men call love is something very small, restricted and feeble compared with this sacred prostitution of the soul which gives itself entire, its poetry and its charity, to the unexpected as it reveals itself, to the stranger who passes.'

Victor Brombert, in his essay, '*Baudelaire: Claustration et Infini*' examines Baudelaire's poetry in terms of what he calls '*la dialectique du solipsisme baudelairien*' revealed in the opening statement of '*Mon Coeur Mis à Nu*': '*De la vaporisation et de la centralisation du Moi. Tout est là*. (*OC*, I, 676) These two poles of Baudelairean anguish, Brombert observes, recur with their numerous synonyms, throughout his writings.[11] In the privileged moment of poetic insight there is a feeling of spatial and temporal expansion, a sense of the infinite, but, in its negative form, this is experienced as dissipation, evaporation, and self-loss. This is why the experience of the crowd cannot simply be the *jouissance* in which the poetic soul enters the flesh of anonymous others. The 'moi *insatiable du* non-moi' signifies, as Brombert points out, 'searching for the fugitive, the non-self, and, beyond this fluctuating and unstable non-self, yearning for the infinite.'[12]

The movement outwards into the other is by no means a simple expression of desire, but rather a tension between two polarities that can never be stabilized. 'The polarity opposing contact and claustration, opening and enclosure, is established in the usual way: Baudelaire emphasizes the horror of solitude and extols its virtues.' The dandy must never lose himself: 'he must live and sleep in front of a mirror', and, as Baudelaire puts it: 'To fuck is to try to enter another, and the artist never leaves himself.'

This is a much more plausible account, I believe, than that of Georges Poulet, in whose phenomenology of reading Baudelaire plays an exemplary role. In contrast to Rousseau, for whom nothing is more moving than to feel himself in communion with a crowd, Baudelaire's thought, Poulet argues, 'tends to identify not with the crowd, but with the thought of individuals situated within the crowd.'[13] 'All identification remains between one individual and another, between one interiority and another. While emphasizing in Baudelaire's case

---

[11] Victor Brombert, 'Baudelaire: Claustration et Infini', in *La Prison Romantique*: *Essai sur l'imaginaire* (Paris: Librairie José Corti, 1975), p. 140.

[12] *BCI*, p. 142.

[13] Georges Poulet, *La Conscience Critique* (Paris : Librairie José Corti, 1974), p. 28.

the tortured origins of this struggle 'to go outside yourself in order to forget yourself in the other', Poulet insists that the kind of identification required, in his view, by the act of poetic imagination is precisely a '*prostitution de l'âme*' (a prostitution of the soul) in that it is easier to identify with a stranger than a person known and loved. 'It is perhaps that love, precisely because it supposes a choice, a previous knowledge, prevents this kind of plunge into the unknown that assumes contact with a thinking which is entirely different. There is identification only when starting from a clean slate, from total ignorance.'[14] Although this is clearly intended as a space within which imagination moves, it is nevertheless grounded, according to Poulet, in Baudelaire's endorsement of Poe's version of the theory of correspondences; 'the law according to which the exterior and the interior are in harmony and mutually determined.'

The man of the crowd, however, in Poe's tale could be considered a limiting case of this theory, since the narrator-observer strikingly fails to establish any kind of contact with the man of the crowd's 'interiority'. On examining his countenance, the narrator tells us, 'there arose confusedly and paradoxically within my mind, the ideas of vast mental power, of caution, of penuriousness, of avarice, of coolness, of malice, of blood-thirstiness, of triumph of merriment, of excessive terror, of intense - of supreme despair. I felt singularly aroused, startled, fascinated. "How wild a history," I said to myself, "is written within that bosom!"'[15] Would it not be justified to say here that the 'law of correspondences' has here reached its limit and that Poe's text from the beginning undermines itself in its attempt to read the book that cannot be read and to tell the secret that cannot be told?

---

[14] *LCC*, p. 30.
[15] Poe, p. 105.

Paul de Man has suggested that we read Baudelaire's self-forgetting and the 'moi *insatiable du* non-moi' in terms of literary modernity and its forever unfulfilled desire to achieve an absolute grasp of the present by means of a *tabula rasa* in which the immediacy of perception is untarnished by any memories of the past. Employing Constantin Guys 'as a kind of emblem for the poetic mind', Baudelaire argues that the perfect form for the modern work of art is the sketch, which, as de Man puts it, 'remains steadfastly in motion and exists in the open, improvised manner [...] of a constant new beginning,' covering up the duration of its own production.[16] The temptation of modern art is to move outside itself and outside language in order to make contact with the facticity of entities in the present moment. As regards the 'moi *insatiable du* non-moi' of Baudelaire, de Man writes, 'If one remembers that this '*moi*' designates, in the metaphor of a subject, the specificity of literature, then this specificity is defined by its inability to remain constant to its own specificity.' This is the first move 'of a certain mode of being, called literature,' a moment of flight which in Baudelaire is directed towards 'the most anonymous and shapeless "theme" of all, that of the crowd.' The crowd – anonymous, ever-changing, kaleidoscopic – is the perfect theme in which literary modernity can take on a shape that appears to sever all links with the past and lose itself in the immediacy of its object.

This move away from itself is followed by a move in which literature must return to itself. 'All that remains of the theme is a mere outline, less than a sketch, a time-arabesque rather than a figure.' (*BI*, 160) The movement of the literary work, which parallels the development of Baudelaire's own poetry, is compelled to return to 'a literary mode of being, as a form of language that knows itself to be

[16] Paul de Man, *Blindness and Insight*: *Essays in the Rhetoric of Contemporary Criticism* (London: Routledge, 1983), p. 156.

mere repetition, mere fiction and allegory, forever unable to participate in the spontaneity of action or modernity.' (*BI*, 161) Applying this to Poe's tale, we see that the narrator finally ceases to follow his quarry and remains 'absorbed in contemplation,' concluding that he will learn no more and that this 'worst heart of the world' is a book that will not let itself be read. The failure to find a writing that can be deciphered within the world itself impels a withdrawal from the world *into* literature, the failed desire to penetrate the (rotten) heart of the world prompting the return into the ambivalence of allegory, in which the object itself disappears.

Baudelaire and the revolutionary crowd

Those readings of Baudelaire which have sought to explain his conception of the crowd in terms of his political involvements have done little therefore to illuminate the role of the crowd as a figure in his poetic imagination, and much to obscure it. While Burton's account of Baudelaire's political formation and his role in the revolutions of 1848 sheds considerable light on some of his poetic themes, it simply assumes an identity between the figure of the crowd in Baudelaire's writings and the revolutionary crowd. For example, Burton claims that the revolution of February 1848:

> marked his first real encounter with 'la foule' whose ambiguous appeal he was to explore so profoundly in his later writing. It was on the February barricades that he first experienced what he called 'l'ivresse des foules (*Mon coeur mis à nu* (*OC* I, 693), here that he first knew the rapturous deliverance from self that fusion with the crowd affords: 'Ivresse religieuse des grandes villes. – Panthéisme. Moi, c'est tous; tous, c'est moi (*Fusées* (*OC* I, 651). Merging with the delirious throng in the streets,

> Baudelaire derived, as he says in 'Les Foules', 'une singulière ivresse de cette universelle communion' (a singular intoxication from this universal communion.) (*OC* I, 291).[17]

This would suggest that the meaning of the figure of the crowd derives essentially from Baudelaire's experience of political participation in the revolutionary events of February and June, 1848. Certainly, in *Mon coeur mis à nu* Baudelaire writes of '*Mon ivresse en 1848'*, but from a perspective of de Maistrean post-revolutionary disillusionment in which he goes on to explain that intoxication as '*Goût de la vengeance. Plaisir naturel de la démolition*' (Taste for vengeance. Natural pleasure in destruction.) The '*universelle communion*' he describes in 'Les Foules' is not that of the revolutionary street-fighter, but that of '*Le promeneur solitaire et pensif.*' Michel Butor similarly claims, '*C'est l'insurrection de 1848 elle-même qui lui avait découvrir dans le foule ce miroir instructeur dont il avait besoin.'* (It was the insurrection of 1848 itself that revealed to him the crowd as the instructive mirror that he needed.)[18] He goes on to claim that in Baudelaire's 1852 summary of 'The Man of the Crowd' (cited above) he reads Poe's essay in the light of the *coup d'état* of December 2, 1851, identifying himself with the man of the crowd, clinging desperately '*aux dernier points culminants de l'agitation politique'* (the last culminating points of political agitation). (*HE*, 104) Butor notes that the expression '*agitation politique*' is not to be found in Poe, but neither is it to be found in Baudelaire, since Baudelaire's text in fact reads '*agitation publique*', referring only to the desultory

[17] R. D. E. Burton, *Baudelaire and the Second Republic* (Oxford, Clarendon Press, 1991), pp. 101-102.
[18] Michel Butor, *Histoire Extraordinaire: essai sur un rêve de Baudelaire* (Paris, Gallimard, 1961), p. 103.

movements of late-night revellers. More significant here perhaps is the comparison with the passage in *Le Peintre de la Vie Moderne* in which Baudelaire describes Constantin Guys' activities in the Parisian night: '*M. G. restera le dernier partout où peut resplendir la lumière, retentir la poèsie, fourmiller la vie, vibrer la musique…*' (Monsieur G. will be the last to linger wherever there can be a glow of light, and echo of poetry, a quiver of life or a chord of music). (*OC* II, 693)

If Baudelaire's idea of the crowd were based upon the revolutionary crowd, then it seems highly unlikely that he would have chosen Guys' work as exemplary, since Guys' depictions of Parisian bourgeois taking the air are a world away from popular insurrection. Indeed, Marshall Berman, while hailing Baudelaire as an artist of the people, berates his 'pathetic' admiration of Guys' second-rate art, which, he claims, for Baudelaire constitutes 'not merely a lapse in taste but a profound rejection of himself,' and accuses him of embracing an intoxicated vision of *la vie élégante* as shallow and empty as Guys' own inferior illustrations.[19] If Baudelaire's idea of the crowd had been determined by his participation in the events of 1848, the choice of Guys would be perplexing, but it is clear that the considerations which led him to extol Guys as the model of the modern artist were not political but aesthetic.

Lyric poetry and urban trauma

Benjamin himself makes the point that 'The masses had become so much a part of Baudelaire that is rare to find a description of them in his works. His most important subjects are hardly ever encountered in

[19] Marshall Berman, *All that is Solid Melts into Air: the experience of modernity* (London, Verso, 1983), p. 138.

descriptive form.'[20] In striking contrast to Victor Hugo, Baudelaire describes neither the Parisians nor their city. Yet, in the *Tableaux Parisiens*, for example, Benjamin claims, the 'secret presence' of a crowd is demonstrable almost everywhere. 'The masses were an agitated veil, and Baudelaire views Paris through this veil.' In the deserted streets at dawn in *Le Crepuscule du Matin*, according to Benjamin, the crowd makes itself present by its absence. In *Le Squelette Laboureur*, browsing the illustrations in anatomy books being sold on the banks of the Seine, Baudelaire sees these skeletons as '*Manants résignés et funèbres*' (peasants, resigned and funereal) at work, digging the land. *Les Sept Vieillards* begins: '*Fourmillante cité, cité pleine de rêves, / Où le spectre, en plein jour, raccroche le passant*!' (Swarming city, city full of dreams,/ where ghosts by day accost the passer-by.) And *A Une Passante* begins, '*La rue assourdissante autour de moi hurlait.*' (The deafening street howled around me.)

Benjamin writes, 'Fear, revulsion, and horror were the emotions which the big-city crowd aroused in those who first observed it. For Poe, it has something barbaric about it'. The shock experience [*Chockerlebnis*] experienced by the passer-by in the crowd, the central motif in Benjamin's account of modernity, found in both Poe's 'The Man of the Crowd' and in Baudelaire, has been interpreted in terms of 'trauma', as Benjamin himself anticipated in *Über einige Motive bei Baudelaire*, characterizing Baudelaire as a 'traumatophile' type.[21] Drawing upon Freud's *Beyond the Pleasure Principle* and upon the writings of Proust, Benjamin sets out the view that one of the functions of consciousness is to protect the organism against stimuli, acting as a shield against potentially traumatic shocks from external sources.

---

20 *WML*, p. 183.
21 *WML*, p. 178.

Consciousness as such stores no memory traces, and the most powerful and enduring vestiges of memory are those that were never directly registered by consciousness at all, as in the Proustian *mémoire involuntaire*. The problem then posed by Benjamin is that of how lyric poetry can be grounded in experience in which exposure to shock has become the norm, since consciousness is permanently on guard, filtering out the material required for deep, authentic experience.

Freud, in the passage in question, distinguishes between 'fright' [*Schreck*], 'fear' [*Furcht*] and 'anxiety' [*Angst*]. His argument is that *Furcht* has a definite object, while *Angst* is the state of preparing for a danger even though its nature is as yet unknown. *Schreck* occurs when we encounter a danger for which we are unprepared and against which, therefore, we have no defence. It is Freud's admittedly speculative thesis that trauma occurs therefore only when the subject is not protected by *Angst*.[22] Having once penetrated the unconscious, the experience exists in a timeless form, in contrast to the experience caught in the screen of consciousness which, as Benjamin puts it, is assigned an exact point in time, '*auf Kosten der Integrität seines Inhalts*' (at the cost of the integrity of its contents) (*GS* 1-2, 615, *WML*, 178) Of particular interest to Freud is the role of repeated dreams which bring the subject back into the situation of his original trauma and from which he wakes in renewed fright. These dreams, Freud maintains, 'are endeavouring to master the stimulus retrospectively, by developing the anxiety whose omission was the cause of the traumatic neurosis'. (*BPP*, 304, qu. Benjamin, *WML*, 176)

The abrupt transition from dream or reverie to a brutal awakening, from *idéal* to *spleen*, is a recurring theme in Baudelaire's poetry,

---

[22] Sigmund Freud, 'Beyond the Pleasure Principle', in *The Penguin Freud Library*, vol 11, On Metapsychology', trans. by J. Strachey (London: Penguin, 1984), pp. 281-282.

perhaps most notably in '*La Chambre Double'*, in which the poet is woken from his blissful state by a knock on the door: 'a terrible, heavy, knock resounded on the door, and, as in infernal dreams, I seemed to feel a pitchfork being stuck into my stomach.' (*OC* II, 281) It should be recalled from the *lettre-dédicace* of *Le Spleen de Paris* that Baudelaire demands of the new poetic form that it be capable of rendering not only the sudden jolts of consciousness to which we are exposed in modern urban life, but also the '*mouvements lyriques de l'âme*' and the '*ondolations de la rêverie'* which city life also produces. Both the conflicting elements which combine in trauma are directly associated with the urban crowd.

Benjamin places the struggle to build shock defences at the centre of Baudelaire's poetic production, attributing to him a high degree of self-consciousness in creating a new kind of poetry in keeping with the modern need for the human sensorium to be 'trained' to cope with the incessant shocks to which it is subject. 'Baudelaire's poetic production is assigned a mission. Blank spaces hovered before him, and into these he inserted his poems. His work cannot be categorized merely as historical, like anyone else's, but it intended to be so and understood itself as such.'

Chockerlebnis understood as trauma raises difficult epistemological problems. In what sense can we speak of an experience that bypasses consciousness and is not accessible either to representation or conscious recollection? As Sanyal observes, 'Trauma cannot be located since the experience was missed in its occurrence and only emerges through its delayed, symptomatic replay in the psyche, the product of a 'missed encounter'. The *Nachträglichkeit* quality – or 'afterwardness' – of the trauma's manifestation thus foils attempts at locating its origins.'[23]

The traumatic nature of Baudelaire's encounter with the crowd is clearly what Benjamin has in mind when claiming that the experience of the crowd became so internalized in Baudelaire that the crowd figures in his poems only as an absence. As Sanyal remarks, this produces a precarious balance in Benjamin's reading between historical and structural explanation. Once trauma is understood as 'missed experience' its historical basis can be explained only as a series of blind spots that *resist representation.* On some accounts it would be this break with history that would mark Baudelaire as the first truly modern poet, and lead to a notion of 'textual history', as in de Man's view that the literary work attempts to express the trauma of history in an endless repetition that must forever miss its mark.

As an example of Baudelaire's 'traumatophile' nature, Benjamin claims in his reading of '*À Une Passante*' that what makes the poet shake and twitch, is when 'an imperious desire suddenly overcomes a lonely man.' Benjamin remarks of these verses that their inner form is revealed in the fact that they depict love itself as being stigmatized by the big city. The crowd both brings this apparition to the poet and is the refuge into which it disappears. Benjamin wishes us to understand this in terms of the general tendency of the big city to erase the traces of private life and the 'bourgeois' struggle to retain such traces. However, if the original traumatic event is in principle inaccessible to representation or conscious recollection then it seems inappropriate to analyse this putative event in terms of cause and effect. Rather, we must understand the retrospective investigation of the trauma as a question of interpretation, which in this case can proceed only from

[23] Debarati Sanyal, *The Violence of Modernity: Baudelaire, Irony, and the Politics of Form* (Baltimore: Johns Hopkins University Press, 2006), p. 23.

the text itself. The shock articulated in '*À Une Passante*' takes the form, I would suggest, of a poetic encounter with beauty itself in the form determined by modern urban existence:

Un éclair...puis la nuit! – Fugitive beauté
Dont le regard m'a fait soudainement renaître,
Ne te verrai-je plus que dans l'éternité? (*OC* 1, 93)
(A flash of lightning…then the night – Fugitive beauty/ Whose glance has suddenly brought me back to life,/ Will I see you again only in eternity ?)

This is the same beauty as that evoked in '*Le Confiteor de l'Artiste*', in which, '*L'étude du beau est un duel où l'artiste crie de frayeur avant d'être vaincu.*' (The study of beauty is a duel in which the artist cries out in terror before being vanquished.) (*OC* I, 279) The task of the artist in relation to the modern age, as outlined in *Le Peintre de la Vie Moderne*, is 'to devote oneself to distilling the mysterious beauty that it may contain, however slight or minimal it might be. Modernity is the transitory, the fugitive, the contingent, the half of art of which the other half is the eternal and immutable.' (*OC* II, 694) In this 'self-consuming actuality,' as Habermas has characterized it, 'Actuality can be constituted only as the point where time and eternity intersect […]; in Baudelaire's understanding, it is so disposed that the transitory moment will find confirmation as the authentic past of a future present.'[24] Because the work of art is conceived as radically bound to the moment of its production and therefore consuming itself in actuality 'it can bring the steady flow of trivialities to a standstill,

[24] Jürgen Habermas, *The Philosophical Discourse of Modernity: Twelve Lectures*, trans. by Frederick G. Lawrence (Cambridge: Polity Press, 1987), pp. 8-9.

break through normality, and satisfy for a moment the immortal longing for beauty – a moment in which the eternal comes into contact with the actual.' This lightning flash, which will become the basis for Benjamin's concept of the dialectical image, is revealed only to those who are open to it, 'with the optics of the idler, the genius, and the child.' But this fails to grasp the traumatic nature of this encounter in which the poet whose desire is heightened to an unbearable intensity finds himself suddenly caught in the gaze of the infinite or the eternal, transfixed by beauty.

The figure of the crowd is then closely allied to the presencing of beauty under the conditions of modernity. Beauty makes its appearance in the transient, the ephemeral, the aleatory and the unexpected, in the moment captured by the artwork when normal time and eternity intersect. The crowd is, as the essay on Guys makes clear, not an object to be represented, but the modern artist's '*domaine, comme l'air est celui de l'oiseau, comme l'eau celui du poisson.*' (*OC* II, 691) As Benjamin at times seems to suggest, the crowd is not to be understood as a physical entity but as both an aesthetic *field* and a rhetorical figure which functions so as to dissolve the material reality of the object and to produce phantasmagoric effects. Usually evoked in the opening lines, the figure of the crowd resonates through the poem as rhythmic disturbance and as a prismatic dispersal of images. If the crowd does not *appear* it is because its rhetorical function is to desubstantialize the material world and to dissolve the normal sense of space and time.

Être hors de chez soi, et pourtant se sentir partout chez soi; voir le monde, être au centre du monde et rester caché au monde (To be away from home, and yet to feel oneself everywhere at home; to see the world, to be at the centre of the world and yet to remain hidden from the world). If these were the sentiments which drove the younger Baudelaire into the embrace of the crowd and in which they found their adequate object, in his later writings they give way to melancholy and a deepening sense of exile, expressed in the form of allegory and irony. Although, as de Man points out, the experience of the crowd was itself one of the key experiences that allowed the *dédoublement* in which his ironic consciousness and diction developed, his increasing deployment of irony took him further and further away from any positive, creative identification with the crowd.[25] In the final entry in *Fusées* he wrote, '*Perdu dans ce vilain monde, coudoyé par les foules, je suis comme un homme lassé dont l'oeil ne voit en arrière, dans les années profondes, que désabusement et amertume, et, devant lui, qu'un orage où rien de neuf n'est contenu, ni enseignement ni douleur.*' (Lost in this base world, jostled by the crowd, I am like a weary man whose eye, looking backwards into the depth of the years, sees only disenchantment and bitterness, and ahead of him only a storm which contains nothing new, neither instruction nor pain.) (*OC* II, 667).

Benjamin concludes:

> Of all the experiences which made his life what it was, Baudelaire singled out being jostled by the crowd as the decisive, unmistakable experience. The semblance of a crowd with a soul and movement all its own, the lustre that had dazzled the flâneur, had faded for him.

Benjamin claims that, betrayed by his last allies, Baudelaire fought the crowd as one might battle against the wind or the rain. 'This is the nature of the immediate experience to which Baudelaire has given the

[25] Paul de Man, 'Allegory and Irony in Baudelaire', in *Romanticism and Contemporary Criticism: the Gauss Seminar and Other Papers* (Baltimore: Johns Hopkins University Press, 1993), p. 111.

weight of long experience. He named the price for which the sensation of modernity could be had: the disintegration of the aura in immediate shock experience.'

The crowd, no longer a field of electrical energy and source of *jouissance*, has instead become, as Baudelaire puts it in the prose-poem '*Perte d'auréole*', '*ce chaos mouvant, où la mort arrive au galop de tous les côtes à la fois,*' (this seething chaos, in which death arrives at the gallop from all sides at once), a presentiment of death and disintegration, in which the poet, reeling from the shock, stumbles, and the halo slips from his head into the street. (*OC* II, 352) But now he no longer cares, since '*la dignité m'ennuie*', and, from a position of ironic detachment he can laugh at any poet who presumes to pick up the halo. Still *incognito* but no longer a prince, he has become indistinguishable from the crowd. '*Et me voici, tout semblable à vous, comme vous voyez!*' (And here I am, just like you, as you see!)

Class and Shame: D. H. Lawrence and the General Strike

In September 1926, in the latter stages of the six-month long strike which the miners had continued alone after the capitulation of the TUC brought the General Strike to an end, D. H. Lawrence visited the mining village where he had grown up. Lawrence, wandering around the village, was shocked to see miners, who had got up before dawn, collecting blackberries. What so disturbed him was not that the miners and their families had been living for months on 'bread, margarine and potatoes,' but that they were collecting blackberries to sell at fourpence a pound. When he had been a boy, it would have been 'utterly *infra dig*' for a miner to pick blackberries. A miner would never have 'demeaned himself to such an unmanly occupation,' and walked home with them in a little basket. 'But nowadays, their pride is in their pocket, and the pocket has a hole in it.'[1]

The police, who occupy the countryside in their thousands, are 'great big strangers,' perhaps brought from Scotland or Ireland, 'for they are no Englishmen.' The people call them 'blue-bottles' and 'meat-flies,' which, Lawrence tells us, would have been unthinkable in his day when the village policeman was properly respected. Worst of all, is the behaviour of the women, 'who have no respect for anything.'

---

[1] D. H. Lawrence, 'Return to Bestwood', in *Late Essays and Articles*, ed. James T. Boulton, (Cambridge: Cambridge University Press, 2004), pp. 15-24.

> There was a scene in the market-place yesterday, a Mrs Hafton and a Mrs Rowley being taken off to court to be tried for insulting and obstructing the police. The police had been escorting the black-legs from the mines, after a so-called day's work, and the women had made the usual row. They were two women from decent homes. In the past they would have died of shame, at having to go to court. But now, not at all.
>
> They had a little gang of women with them in the market-place, waving red flags and laughing loudly and using occasional bad language. There was one, the decent wife of the post-man. I had known her and played with her as a girl. But she was waving her red flag, and cheering as the motor-bus rolled up.
>
> The two culprits got up, hilariously, into the bus.
>
> "Good luck, old girl! Let 'em have it! Give it the blue-bottles in the neck! Tell'em what for! Three cheers for Bestwood. Strike while the iron's hot, girls!"
>
> "So long! So long, girls! See you soon! Merry home-coming, what, eh?"
>
> "Have a good time, now! Have a good time! Stick a pin in their fat backsides, if you can't move 'em any other road. We s'll be thinking of you!"'

Lawrence sees all this through the eyes of his dead mother, who he now addresses: 'Oh my dear and virtuous mother, who believed in a Utopia of goodness, so that your own people were never quite good enough for you – not even the spoiled delicate boy, myself! […] Nothing was good enough! We must all rise into the upper classes! Upper! Upper! Upper!' Although his judgments of the miners' wives are made entirely from her viewpoint, the tone is ironic, partly because she was 'tragic' at a time 'when there was nothing to be tragic about', partly because of her naïve belief 'in the ultimate benevolence of all the masters, of all the upper classes.'

While mocking his mother's belief in "getting on", he is, at the same time, eager to prove to her that he has "got on," living in his cinquecento Italian villa, having published his writings, and living longer than she had expected, despite his poor health. In a passage that would have excited Freud's attention, Lawrence imagines his mother's ghost returning to see his sister's 'lovely house':

> Would she then say: It is reached! Consummatum est!
>
> When Jesus gave up the ghost, he cried: It is finished! Consummatum est! But was it? And if so, what? What was it that was consummate?
>
> Likewise, before the war in Germany I used to see advertised in the newspapers a moustache-lifter, which you tied on at night and it would make your moustache stay turned up, like the immortal moustache of Kaiser Wilhelm II, whose moustache alone is immortal. This moustache-lifter was called: Es ist erreicht! In other words: It is reached! Consummatum est!'
>
> Was it? Was it reached? With the moustache lifter? [...]
>
> Do say we've got on! Do say, we've arrived. Do say, it is reached, es ist erreicht, consummatum est.

In this fantasy, however, 'the little ghost turns aside, she knows I am teasing her. She says nothing but her gaze says, "I shan't tell you, so you can't laugh at me. You must find out for yourself." And she steals away to her place, wherever it may be.'

Having completed this possibly incestuous encounter with the ghost of his mother, Lawrence is able to continue his tour of the mining village. At the end of the paths leading from the pits, along the road, the two sides are gathered: the colliers squatted on their heels, silent and watchful. 'Their faces are clean, white and all the months of the strike have given them no colour and no tan. They are pit-bleached. They squat in silent remoteness, as if in the upper galleries of hell. And the policemen, alien, stand in a group near the stile. Each lot pretends not to be aware of the others.'

At three o'clock the scabs, 'the dirty ones', leave the pit, escorted by the police. 'No voice is raised: nobody seems aware of anybody else. But there is the silent, hellish registering in the consciousness of all three groups, clean ones, dirty ones, and the blue-bottles.'

> So it is now all the way into Chesterfield, whose crooked spire lies below. The men who have gone back to work – they seem few, indeed – are lurching and slinking in quiet groups, home down the high-road, the police at their heels. And the pickets, with bleached faces, squat and lean and stand, in silent groups, with a certain pale fatality, like Hell, upon them.'

Lawrence contrasts the ranks of these silent, 'hellish' figures with the colliers as he remembers them from his boyhood, with the 'ringing of the feet, the red mouths and the quick whites of the eyes, the swinging pit-bottles, and the strange voices of men from the underworld, calling back and forth, strong and, it seems to me, gay with the queer, absolved gaiety of miners – I shiver, and feel I turn into a ghost myself. The colliers were noisy, lively, with strong underworld voices such as I have never heard in any other men, when I was a boy.'

After 1920, 'the strange power of life in them, something wild and urgent, that one could hear in their voices,' went silent. 'These are the men of my own generation, who went to the board school with me. And they are almost voiceless. They go to the welfare clubs, and drink with a sort of hopelessness [...] they have got a new kind of shallow consciousness, all newspaper and cinema, which I am not in touch with.'

Lawrence's commentary now moves into a different register. Instead of identifying with the mother who taught him to look down upon his father, and feeling the shame that *she* would have felt at the insurrectionary *jouissance* of the women, Lawrence evokes the world of his father and his father's mates, the powerful voices from below that still resonate in his memory. Lawrence's father worked down the pit from the age of twelve until he was seventy. He had little education and was almost illiterate, but lived within the solidarity of a working-class community to which Lawrence never sought or gained admission. That generation is dead and gone, replaced by a 'shallower', voiceless generation, which Lawrence confesses he hardly recognizes. But he continues:

> At the same time, they have, I think an underneath ache and heaviness very much like my own. It must be so, because when I see them I feel it so strongly.
>
> They are the only people who move me strongly, and with whom I feel myself connected in deeper destiny. It is they who are, in some peculiar way, "home" to me. I shrink away from them, and I have an acute nostalgia for them.
>
> And now, this last time, I feel a doom over the country, and a shadow of despair over the hearts of the men, which leaves me no rest. Because the same doom is over me, wherever I go, and the same despair touches my heart.'

He now feels that, 'at home', the miners are very much like himself and want the same things. The miner doesn't want poverty and hardship, he wants to earn enough money to be free, and he wants to earn it without humiliation. 'I know that most decent people feel very much the same in this respect: and the indecent people must, in their indecency, be subordinated to the decent.' Ahead, there is 'a mortal struggle for property [...] I know we are on the brink of a class war.' What matters, for Lawrence, is that the struggle for true democracy be fought in the right spirit, a spirit which overcomes the morbidity which has taken hold in England, and which is based upon a new idea of what it is *to live*.

The reference to 'decency' as the line of division in the class war re-introduces the viewpoint of what we might call the *imaginary* and *symbolic* mother, since this is not a matter of Lawrence's actual mother, but of the mother in Lawrence's mind, the mother who was clearly both source and object of his libidinal attachments, and the mother who provided him with the cultural and aesthetic resources both to become a great writer and to feel ashamed of his own people. The division between the 'decent' and the 'indecent' is here not, of course a division between classes, but a division within the working-class itself, the division represented by Lawrence's mother, that is, the division between the 'respectable', aspiring, working-class and, to use E. M. Forster's term, 'the people of the abyss.' This is the division which has traditionally preoccupied working-class consciousness far more than the division between the working-class and the middle or owning classes.

Lawrence's presentation of the *shameless* behaviour of the termagant wives who attacked policemen is one of mock horror – 'What *would* my mother say! – but there is no doubt that, despite this ironic distancing effect, his own understanding of working-class life is centred upon questions of honour, respect, decency, and, what necessarily accompanies them, a sense of shame. The coming struggle is, he hopes, to be between those who possess these attributes and those who do not. The suggestion is, however, that those values have been eroded in the mining community.

The positive values which govern Lawrence's understanding of working-class life are located in what he takes to be the ethical code of a previous generation of miners and their wives. Men who were 'manly' and disciplined in their conduct, but also full of life; women with a strong sense of moral and civil propriety. The impact of mechanized, industrial civilization based upon unrestricted profit-making has, he believes, led to the decay of all values, including those of the working-class. The age of the philanthropic capitalist has passed. The miners are on strike, which Lawrence considers to be itself something terrible, based upon self-interest and portending all kinds of irresponsible behaviour and violent social division. His description of the 'hellish' silence of the pale, voiceless pickets indicates that the 'morbidity' of English society has invaded their once vital way of life. Lawrence can sympathize with them as they are 'in their homes,' with what they want for themselves, but not with their industrial militancy.

The essay, 'Which Class I Belong To', probably written in the spring of 1927, gives us further indications as to Lawrence's troubled state of mind. It was already being argued that the expanding European middle class had assimilated both the former upper class and the working-class, so that the latter had become merely the lower stratum of the middle class. Everyone was now said to be striving for the same material goals. Lawrence remarks that, 'Seen from the outside this is true. Seen from the inside, it is a great fallacy.'[2]

But from where on the 'inside' does Lawrence see this? In a brief autobiographical sketch, he describes the way in which, as a scholarship boy at Nottingham High School, the 'better-class boys' treated him in a kindly, usually respectful manner, but 'there was a peculiar, indefinable difference. It was as if, boys of the same race, the same locality, the same everything, still we were, in some way,

[2] 'Which Class I belong To', in *Late Essays and Articles*, pp. 35-40.

different *animals*.' At Nottingham University also, there was 'the indefinable gulf.' 'It was something in the very way the heart beat.' The professors, 'had that other peculiar vibration which caused them to be uninteresting, and in some curious way, *outside* one's own life.' The middle class was open, willing to accept those who sought to 'climb into it,' but 'one turned away, ungratefully.'

When he broke into the world of publishing with *The White Peacock*, he was told by his editor, 'Your book has got every fault that the English novel can have, but you have genius.' As Lawrence acutely observes, 'They never seem to grudge me genius, because, perhaps, it is something that can be legitimately patronised.' Despite his literary success and the generally kind treatment he had always received in the world of the masters, he concludes, 'Yet here I am, nowhere, as it were, and infinitely an outsider. And of my own choice.' He has left the working-class and has refused adoption into the middle class.

This brings us to the point of Lawrence's self-questioning. 'What is the obstacle? I have looked for it in myself, as a clue to this dangerous cleavage between the classes.' He reads himself as a symptom of the class war and finds that the 'deep obstacle' lies in 'the manner of contact.' The manner of contact 'between man and man' is more physical among the lower classes. 'The middle class can be far more *intimate*, yet never so *near* to one another.' What links the middle class together is the intensification in modern society of the acquisitive and possessive instinct. The working man, however, 'like my father, for example, is far too vague to be really acquisitive.' He demands only enough money to go drinking down the pub with his mates, 'in that queer physical contact which is the affinity of the blood, and is, in the long run, more deeply necessary to men than the affinity of the mind, but which, none the less, can be a prison either to man or woman who is confined to it. So that I could never go back into the working class, to the blindness, the obtuseness, the prejudice, the mass-emotions. But neither can I adapt myself to the middle-class, to sacrifice the old, deep blood-affinity between myself and my fellows.'

Not surprisingly, this conflict remains unresolved for Lawrence. One *could*, he speculates, have both affinities, but one of them must predominate. 'And the mental affinity, in its insistence on predominating, insists on the destruction and the sacrifice of the physical affinity.' 'To enter the middle class, a man has to sacrifice something that is very deep and necessary to him, his natural physical affinity with other men and women. That is, *if he's got it*. If he hasn't got it, he is bastard middle-class already.'

The vehemence of these last remarks indicate the anxiety at work throughout the essay. The unspoken question is: *does he himself have it* or did his mother steal it from him? Has he therefore become an illegitimate child of the middle class, who can never be at peace? Unlike Hamlet, Lawrence enters into a dialogue with the ghost not of his father but of his mother. The wrong that it falls to him to put right, besides the rift which tore apart the relation between his mother and his father, is, as he sees very clearly, the destructive effects of the class system, played out in his own inner conflicts.

The references to *race* and *blood* here, as elsewhere in Lawrence's writings indicate, rather than any orientation towards fascism, that he is trying to think, on the level of the *animal* and the *physical*, what belongs properly on the plane of the social and the psychoanalytical. The bond that unites the miners has nothing to do with blood, but with the experience of working together in the appalling conditions of the privately-owned pits of the early twentieth century. The image of 'vague' and 'obtuse' working men, spending their hard-earned money in the pub, discussing their ill-formed visions of the world produced from undigested scraps of knowledge, sounds very much like the complaints Lawrence would have heard as a boy from his mother, and not subjected to further examination. But these were also miners who financed educational institutions and libraries from their own pockets.

Despite the fear that causes him now to 'shrink' from their company, Lawrence undoubtedly feels a deep affinity with the miners at a largely unconscious level, recalling from his childhood the 'strong underworld voices' such as he had never heard in other men, the voices of men used to 'calling out to each other in the dark.' It is a wonderful image of a lost communion that, for Lawrence, remained the key to what was missing in his life of exile.

Human Dignity and the Political Order

Proletarianization in the thought of Marx and Bernard Stiegler

There are two senses in which the term 'proletarianization' can be understood. The first, its standard sociological usage, for which the classical source is *The Communist Manifesto*, denotes a process of downward social mobility in which, 'the lower strata of the middle class – the small tradespeople, shopkeepers, and retired tradesmen generally, the handicraftsmen and peasants,' gradually 'sink' into the proletariat because they possess insufficient capital to compete in the age of Modern Industry.[1] Put crudely, those who possess only small amounts of capital fall into the class of those who possess no capital and who live only through the sale of their labour-power. A second, more fundamental sense, logically and historically presupposed by the first, denotes the proletarianization which produced the proletariat itself; that is, the process through which, in Marx's account, the bourgeoisie 'called forth' what he also refers to as 'the modern working class.' Stiegler's usage of the term 'proletarianization,' for reasons which will become evident, does not distinguish between these two senses.

It is worth pausing to reflect why Marx should have coined this term at all. Why not simply refer to 'the modern working class?' What is added by the term 'proletariat?' And why renovate an obscure and antiquated term to refer to what Marx emphasizes is a very modern

---

[1] K. Marx & F. Engels, *The Communist Manifesto*, (Moscow: Progress Publishers, n.d., p. 18.

phenomenon? This should draw our attention to the fact that its function is by no means that of merely empirical description. On the contrary, it would be difficult to imagine a more theory-laden and rhetorical appellation. Žižek, in the context of an exposition of Alain Badiou's distinction between Knowledge and Truth, has written:

> although Marx himself used 'proletariat' as synonymous with 'the working class', normally one can none the less discern in his work a clear tendency to conceive 'the working class' as a descriptive term belonging to the domain of Knowledge (the object of 'neutral' sociological study, a social stratum subdivided into components, etc.); whereas 'proletariat' designates the operator of Truth, that is, the engaged agent of the revolutionary struggle.[2]

This, although it echoes the practice of the post-war Stalinist Communist parties, is entirely misleading, since 'the working class' is first and foremost the way the working class designates itself, based upon the material fact that it lives by its *work,* rather than a sociological term. 'Proletariat', on the other hand, is a term devised entirely within the 'scientific Knowledge' which became the theory of dialectical materialism.

The text within which 'proletariat' first acquires its significance is Marx's *A Contribution to the Critique of Hegel's Philosophy of Right. Introduction*, written in 1843-1844, which includes a sustained tirade against German backwardness and the failure of the German bourgeoisie to make a revolution. Adapting Hegel's idea of the

---

[2] Slavoj Žižek, *The Ticklish Subject:The Absent Centre of Political Ontology*, (London and New York: Verso, 2008), p. 158.

'universal class' [*der allgemeine Stand*] – for Hegel, the bureaucracy - which makes itself the representative of the general interest, it is only at the climax of his argument that the much-delayed annunciation takes place and Marx *names* the proletariat as the class that will free the whole of German society:

> So where is the *positive* possibility of German emancipation? *This is our answer.* In the formation of a class with *radical chains*, a class [*Klasse*] of civil society which is not a class of civil society, a class [*Stand*] which is the dissolution [*Auflösung*] of all classes [*aller Stände*], a sphere [*Sphäre*] which has a universal character because of its universal suffering and which lays claim to no *particular right* because the wrong it suffers is not a *particular wrong* but *wrong in general*; a sphere of society which can no longer lay claim to a *historical* title, but merely to a *human* one, which does not stand in one-sided opposition to the consequences but in all-sided opposition to the premises of the German political system; and finally a sphere which cannot emancipate itself without emancipating itself from – and thereby emancipating – all the other spheres of society, which is, in a word, the *total loss* of humanity and which can therefore redeem itself only through the *total redemption of humanity*. This dissolution of society as a particular class is the *proletariat*.[3]

In a single sentence, the signifier 'proletariat' is said to signify variously, a *Klasse*, a *Stand* [estate], and a *Sphäre*, but none of these as a concrete particular which could be said to *exist* in the normal

---

[3] K. Marx, *Early Writings*, trans. Rodney Livingstone and Gregor Benton, London: Penguin Books, 1975), p. 256.

sense. As Avineri points out, 'It is not the proletarians' concrete conditions of life but their relation to an anthropological determination of man which primarily interests Marx.'[4] The proletariat *represents* society's '*acute disintegration*,' the suffering body of man; it *universalizes* not its own particular interests but its own lack. Its total loss of humanity is *converted* into the imperative *need* that humanity must be completely redeemed. Clearly, such a concept could not have been developed within the working class itself. The 'secret' disclosed *to* the working class is that it *is* the proletariat. For the proletariat is the passive element, the material basis through which philosophy will realize itself; 'once the lightning of thought has struck deeply into this virgin soil of the people [*diesen naiven Volksboden*].'

In *The Holy Family*, (1844) Marx spells this out:

> It is not a question of what this or that proletarian, or even the whole proletariat, at the moment *regards* as its aim. It is a question of what the proletariat *is*, and what, in accordance with this *being*, it will historically be compelled to do. Its aim and its historical action is visibly and irrevocably foreshadowed in its own life situation as well as in the whole organization of bourgeois society today.[5]

It could hardly be clearer that *what the proletariat is* is by no means for the proletariat to determine. The 'secret' of its historical mission has been discovered by philosophy and assigned to it. Even the *entire* proletariat can be mistaken as to what it is until it sees itself reflected in the mirror held up to it by philosophy. By a peculiar irony, any idea

---

[4] Shlomo Avineri, *The Social and Political Thought of Karl Marx*, (Cambridge: Cambridge University Press, 1970), p. 52.
[5] K. Marx, *The Holy Family*, (Moscow: Progress Publishers, 1975), p. 44.

of self-determination has been removed from the class whose appointed task is to emancipate the whole of mankind. All that is left to the proletariat is to become conscious of its predetermined mission and to fulfil it.

Marx had brought the word 'proletariat' with him from his studies of Roman law, indicating specifically those who are propertyless and therefore excluded from political society. The lack of property traditionally implies a lack of social and political *substance*, a position which Marx takes over to help define proletarianization as a process of ontological displacement, denaturalization and dehumanization. But this is dehumanization in a very specific sense. One might have thought that no social group could be more propertyless and dehumanized than the *lumpenproletariat*, the ancestor of the modern 'under-class,' characterized in *The Communist Manifesto* as 'that social scum, the passively rotting mass thrown off by the lowest layers of the old society,'[6] but the dehumanization Marx is interested in is inseparably involved with a metaphysics of labour, derived from Hegel, in which the worker is claimed to realize him/herself in the productive act. It is because, in the capitalist mode of production, the worker, dispossessed of the means of production, now owned by capital, is no longer able to appropriate his/her self-identity through labour, that the worker's labour-power is alienated and dehumanized. It is only on this account that the dehumanization of the proletariat qualifies it to become the redeemer of humanity.

Having determined that the revolution must be carried out by the emergence from the working class of a revolutionary *subject*, it is worth reflecting also for a moment on why this revolutionary subject had to emerge from a social *class*. In the absence of a revolutionary bourgeois class in Germany, on the French model, Marx constructs the

[6] *CM*, p. 20.

idea of a quite different revolutionary class with a much more radical mission. The working class is a class, that much is sure; but the proletariat, as Marx conceives it, is a class that both is and is not a class: it is a class whose mission is to abolish class. His argument here is conducted on two distinct levels, one empirical and one metaphysical. The proletariat is not recognized as a class by the bourgeoisie, and does not therefore 'count as a class.' Also the proletariat is not *like other classes* in that its conditions of existence, he claims, do not allow its members ever to achieve upward social mobility. Its conditions therefore make it impossible for it to have a particular interest or ever to have a stake or foundation in existing society. But, more fundamentally, Marx wishes to establish that the proletariat is a class but not a class in the sense that is a class which, beyond any empirical claims, is the *negation* of the existing class system. It does not, therefore, *exist* as a class in the fullest sense. The social ontology of the proletariat is such that it exists as a *hole* in the social being; it is this *lack* from which is inferred its revolutionary character and its readiness to become the receptacle of revolutionary philosophy.

Marx's concept of class identity

We are provided with some idea of what it means to *be* a proletarian in *The German Ideology* (1845-1846), where Marx elaborates a new and important theory of social class. Historically, he argues, in the mediaeval estates system, the entire *being* of an individual was considered to be determined by his or her social position. The bourgeoisie then emerges as the first social *class*, properly speaking, which means that for the first time individuals are recognized as formally equal and their socio-economic status is deemed 'accidental'. With this generalized demystification of social status there now appears for the first time a division in the life of each individual between the part which is personal and the part which is class-determined. Individuals appear to be freer under bourgeois rule, but, Marx warns, 'they are less free because they are to a greater extent governed by material forces.'[7] That is, instead of being under the domination of their 'masters,' they are now entirely subjected to the laws of political economy and commodity production, the manifestation of a new and brutal form of necessity. This structural division applies, of course, to *all* individuals in a class society.

When, however, with the development of the productive forces, 'the contradiction appears on the scene,' the historically determined social conditions of individuals, already understood as contingent, will be *seen* to act as an 'accidental fetter [*eine zufällige Fessel*],' holding back possible individual development and the creation of genuinely free communal life. That is to say, for the first time, the division becomes a contradiction which is *lived*. The possibility of a completely free life appears. Marx's position, as stated here, is clearly not that of technological determinism. On the contrary, technical development is conceived entirely within an anthropological framework. Because of the fundamental identity of human productive *powers* and technological productive *forces* [*Produktivkräfte*], the productive forces will come to appear as an alien force which, instead of furthering human life, has wrested away the productive powers of proletarians, who are thereby 'robbed of all life-content,' and have become 'abstract individuals.' They will therefore be impelled to appropriate the totality of productive forces, not only to achieve 'self-activity [*Selbsbetätigung*],' but to safeguard their very existence. At

[7] K. Marx & F. Engels, *Collected Works, Vol.5, (London:* Lawrence and Wishart, 1975), p. 79.

this stage human life will finally be delivered from the realm of necessity into the realm of freedom.

The proletariat and the working class

Marx's concept of the proletariat is, as we have seen, integrated into a theory of class and into a rudimentary theory of individuation which will be discussed later in relation to the thought of Simondon and Stiegler. At this point, however, I wish to emphasize the discursive conditions within which Marx's concept of the proletariat was framed. The 'proletariat,' a nomination directed towards the class of direct producers, occupying a crucial site within the capitalist mode of production, is, most particularly in *The Communist Manifesto*, a discursive entity *interpellated* as the revolutionary subject of modern industry. As such it must be understood as something quite distinct from the actual, historical working class. When, therefore, Stiegler states that, 'The proletariat is not the working class. All of Marxism has misinterpreted Marx in confusing the two,' he is, to that extent, quite correct.[8] The concept of 'proletarianization' should be understood in relation to the formation of the 'proletariat' as a theoretical entity within the Marxian discourse. Once disengaged from any essential identification with the actually existing working class, recognizing the gap between revolutionary theory and the actual working class which is suppressed by the term 'proletariat,' and that, in an important sense, it was Marx, rather than capital, who 'proletarianized' the working class, the question would then be whether concrete, non-metaphysical, criteria of 'proletarianization' can be meaningfully applied to contemporary social phenomena in

---

[8] Bernard Stiegler, *For a New Critique of Political Economy*, (Cambridge: Polity Press, 2010), p. 40.

order to compare them with, or to establish any continuity with, the experiences of the nineteenth-century industrial working class.

Stiegler's concept of proletarianization

Proletarianization as Stiegler defines it, following Simondon, 'is a process of losing knowledge [*savoir*] – that is, also a loss of savour [*saveur*] and of existence – which is engendered by grammatization insofar as it short-circuits the processes of transindividuation through which, by becoming individuated through work, that is, through learning something, the worker individuates the milieu of their work.'[9] This is said to be what Marx and Engels were describing in *The Communist Manifesto* in their comments upon the deskilling of labour brought about by modern industrial methods. 'Grammatization' here refers to the concept developed by Sylvain Auroux which designates the transformation of a temporal continuum into discrete spatial units, a process of coding/decoding, initially transforming speech into writing, the precondition of the development of both grammar and logic.[10] More generally, it has been extended to signify the exteriorization of memory by means of breaking down 'gestures' [*gestes*][11] or operational sequences into discrete units, including both writing and mechanical reproduction. The history of human memory, as Stiegler understands it, is that of grammatization, the process through which human memory is exteriorized in the form of what

---

[9] *For a New Critique*, p. 38.

[10] Sylvain Auroux, *La révolution technologique de la grammatisation*, Liège: Mardaga, 1994).

[11] 'Gesture' is used here to translate the French *geste*, in the sense given to the term by André Leroi-Gourhan in *Le Geste et la parole*, (Paris: Albin Michel, 1964-65), where it signifies material action, linked to the creation of an exteriorized material culture.

Plato, opposing 'living' memory to 'dead' memory, called *hypomnemata*, external aids to memory which, at the same time, constitute an inevitable *loss* of memory proper.

It is this grammatization which, with the advent of the industrial revolution, transforms the labour process, discretizing the activity of workers through automatic reproduction, that 'was the basis of what Marx described as the process of proletarianization, that is, as *loss of savoir-faire*, (which) is then pursued with the development of electronic and digital devices to the point that *all* forms of knowledge become grammatized via cognitive and cultural mnemotechnologies [....] it will also include *savoir-vivre*, that is, behaviour in general, from user profiling to the grammatization of affects, all of which will lead to the "cognitive" and "cultural" capitalism of hyperindustrial *service* economies.'[12] This is because, once technologically exteriorized, memory can become the object of sociopolitical and biopolitical controls, of the kind analyzed by Foucault, capable of rearranging memory in all its forms, both corporeal and psychic.

The historical proletariat, then, appears as the original victim of this process, 'insofar as it is true that the proletariat are those economic actors who are without knowledge because they are without memory: their memory has passed into the machine that reproduces gestures that the proletariat no longer needs to know – they must simply serve the reproductive machine and thus, once again, they become serfs.'[13] On this basis, 'the truth of Plato would then be found in Marx,' except that Marx 'fails to think the hypomnesic character of technics and human existence.' A new critique of political economy is therefore necessary '*in which technics becomes the central stake*,' in which grammatization is the dynamic process.

---

[12] *For a New Critique*, p. 33.
[13] *For a New Critique*, p. 35.

Since Stiegler returns again and again in his writings to the theme of proletarianization, it is clear that in some ways he wishes to anchor his theory in elements of Marx's thought, while at other times establishing a clear distance from it. He readily concedes that throughout Marx's writings the proletariat is always presented as being comprised of the working class. 'But that this is so is due to a state of historical fact, tied to an *archaic* stage (archaic in all senses of the term) of the development of capitalism and industry*, that is, of grammatization*, and which is destined to evolve appreciably by bringing into the process of proletarianization all those whose knowledge is absorbed by hypomnesic processes consisting not only in machines, but in apparatuses, expert systems, services, networks, and technological objects and systems of all kinds.'[14]

Remarkably, Stiegler's disidentification of the proletariat with the working class means not only that the worker [*ouvrier*] is transformed into a proletarian, but that 'the proletarian *ceases to be* a worker,' on the grounds that workers operated with their *work*-hands [*mains d'*oeuvres], producing *work* upon the world, which ceased to be the case when they became proletarians.[15] Work, as Stiegler understands it, is action which transforms the world on the basis of the knowledge one has of it.[16] If the proletarian ceases to work, and to be a worker, it seems to follow that, in Stiegler's terms, s/he ceases to be working-class.

Since all middle-class technical workers and all consumers are also subjected to 'proletarianization,' it would also seem to follow that proletarianization, paradoxically, brings about the dissolution of class

[14] p. 39.
[15] Bernard Stiegler, *The Decadence of Industrial Societies*, tr. Daniel Ross and Suzanne Arnold, (Cambridge: Polity, 2011), p. 62.
[16] Bernard Stiegler, *La Télécratie contre la démocracies*, (Paris: Flammarion, 2006), p. 244.

society, as, in Stiegler's words, 'the total proletarian emerges.' Proletarianization is 'a condition from which it has become nearly impossible to escape.'[17] The negativity inherent in the concept of the proletariat, the class which is not a class, appears, instead of having produced a revolutionary subject, to have extended, along with 'proletarianization,' potentially to swallow up the whole of class society and to have eliminated, along with classes, the possibility of class struggle. Either we understand 'proletarianization' as proletarianization without a proletariat or we accept the possibility that the whole of society becomes the proletariat. In either case any grounding in Marx appears to be lost along with any logical coherence. If 'proletarianization' *de*classes both the working-class worker and the middle-class worker then it is clear that what we are dealing with is not 'proletarianization' but '*massification*.'[18] This raises again the question of why we need either the concept of the proletariat or of proletarianization, when the cultural and psychic phenomena which Stiegler very capably analyzes might be adequately theorized without the use of these concepts, from either inside or outside Marxist thought.

Worker and machine in Marx

Having looked at the concept of the proletariat developed in Marx's early writings, in the 'revolutionary' period, I want to turn to the account of 'proletarianization' in *Capital*, in which, as is generally the

---

[17] *Decadence*, p. 35.

[18] See for example, *Decadence*, p. 150

case in Marx's later writings, the term 'proletariat' rarely appears. By the 1860s the English working class would have had much more difficulty recognizing itself in the figure of the 'proletariat' developed by Marx than in the revolutionary 1840s. In particular, I want to examine Marx's account of the relation between workers and machines, in order to compare it with that presented by Simondon and Stiegler.

In the guild system, Marx argues, the worker remained closely united with his means of production, usually working with his own tools. The transition from the guild system to capitalist manufacture came about with 'the autonomy of the means of production, as capital *vis-à-vis* the worker.'[19] The fundamental relation between capital and labour is thus established by Marx independently of and prior to the process of mechanization. Capitalist manufacture began in the form of handicraft production, with a preponderance of skilled workers, cooperating in the workshop under the control of a master. The fundamental antagonism in the productive process is that between the worker and the instrument of labour, an antagonism which is later intensified when machinery is introduced in competition with handicrafts.[20] At that point the capitalist mode of production is able to proceed to develop total control over the productive process.

The advantages of the division of labour, Marx observes, were well understood in the ancient world, but concerned only use-values; that is to say, the specialization of skills produced goods of a better quality. The division of labour in the manufacturing workshop, however, constituted 'an entirely specific creation of the capitalist mode of production,' in which 'the collective working organism is a form of

[19] K. Marx *Capital Vol. I*, trans. Ben Fowkes, (London: Penguin Books, 1976), p. 480.
[20] *Capital*, p. 559.

the existence of capital.'[21] This system 'seizes labour-power by its roots,' and 'converts the worker into a crippled monstrosity, by furthering his particular skill, as in a forcing-house, through the suppression of a whole world of productive drives and inclinations [...] Not only is the specialized work distributed among the different individuals, but the individual himself is divided up, and transformed into the automatic motor of a detail operation, thus realizing the absurd fable of Menenius Agrippa, which presents man as a mere fragment of his own body.'

The knowledge, judgement and will [*Die Kenntnisse, die Einsicht und der Wille*] which, even though to a small extent, are exercised by the independent peasant or handicraftsman, in the same way as the savage makes the whole art of war consist in the exercise of his personal cunning, are faculties now required only for the workshop as a whole. The possibility of an intelligent direction of production expands in one direction, because it vanishes in many others. What is lost by the specialized workers is concentrated in the capital which confronts them. It is the result of the division of labour in manufacture that the worker is brought face to face with the intellectual potentialities of the material process of production as the property of another and as a power which rules over him [*Es ist ein Produkt der manufakturmaßigen Teilung der Arbeit, ihnen die geistigen Potenzen des materiellen Produktionsprozesses als fremdes Eigentum und sie beherrenschende Machtgegenüberzustellen*]. This process of separation starts in simple cooperation, where the capitalist represents to the individual workers the unity and will of the whole body of social labour. It is developed in manufacture, which mutilates the worker, turning him into a fragment of himself. It is completed in large-scale

[21] *Capital*, pp. 480-481.

industry, which makes science [*Wissenschaft*], a potentiality for production which is distinct from labour and presses into the service of capital. [22]

This passage tells us a great deal about the theoretical infrastructure of *Capita*l, which is still dominated by the schema which directs Marx's thought from his earliest writings, revealing capital as the alienated Other of subjective human powers. In this process of alienation [*Entfremdung*], everything which has accrued to capital is to be understood as originating in labour. Central here is the transfer, resulting from the division of labour, of the intelligence which directs production. Marx specifies the kind of intelligence which the traditional craftworker possessed – *Kenntnisse, Einsicht, Wille* – emphasizing its character as skill, know-how and discernment, coupled with shrewdness and cunning. This is very close to what the Greeks signified by the term *metis*, as examined by Marcel Detienne and Jean-Pierre Vernant, 'a term applied to situations which are transient, shifting, disconcerting and ambiguous, situations which do not lend themselves to precise measurement, exact calculation or rigorous logic.'[23] Which is exactly why, for Plato, it belonged to 'a type of cognition which is alien to truth and quite separate from *epistēmē*, knowledge.' Embraced, however, by the Sophists, it denoted the kind of intelligence associated with politics, the art of war, healing, and artisanal skills. It involved multiple skills, craft secrets, the use of philtres and herbs, and resourcefulness of every kind. The authors point out the remarkable silence among Greek scholars on this kind of intelligence, arising mainly from the dominance of the Platonic

[22] *Capital*, p. 482.

[23] Marcal Detienne and Jean-Pierre Vernant, *Cunning Intelligence in Greek Culture and Society*, [Les ruses d'intelligences: la metis de Grecs], (Chicago: University of Chicago Press, 1991), pp. 3-4.

heritage which haunts Western metaphysical thought.[24] What Marx rather understates, in his desire to present the transfer of intelligent direction as an alienation of the worker's powers to capital, is that 'know-how' is being subordinated to a quite different kind of knowledge, which will result in the systematic 'rationality' of 'scientific management.'

Marx presents the conversion of the worker into 'a crippled monstrosity,' 'a fragment of himself,' as a result, not of mechanization in the factory, but as a result of the reorganization of the form of cooperation, in accordance with the division of labour, in the manufacturing workshop. This is not, strictly speaking, deskilling, but the fragmentation and specialization of skills with the goal of increased productivity, in which 'the collective working organism is a form of the existence of capital.' This is certainly consistent with a process of 'grammatization,' in which a continuous operational sequence is discretized and systematized, but involves the 'exteriorization' of living memory into 'dead' external forms or *hypomnemata* only in the form of an emerging body of writings on 'scientific management.' It is clear, however, that what Marx would have called 'proletarianization,' if he had restricted it to the process of 'losing knowledge' (which he did not), would have referred to the transformation of the worker in the establishment of the capitalist mode of production through the division of labour in the manufacturing workshop, a process only intensified and brought to completion by the large-scale introduction of machinery and automation.

This is not in any way to diminish the significance of mechanization and automation. In manufacture, Marx states, labour-power is the starting-point, whereas in 'large-scale industry,' the instruments of

---

[24] p. 318.

labour are the starting-point. The latter are converted from tools into machines. On this important distinction, Marx believes that the manner in which motor power is imparted is not the essential factor; '(f)rom the moment that the tool proper is taken from man and fitted into a mechanism, a machine takes the place of a mere implement.' [25] Whereas a worker is naturally restricted as to the number of tools that can be used simultaneously, a machine is not. A real machine *system* is established only when a number of independent machines are replaced by 'a connected set of graduated processes carried out by a chain of mutually complementary machines of various kinds.' [26] This division of labour among machines replaces the division of labour in manufacture. There is, however, an essential difference:

> In manufacture, it is the workers who, either singly or in groups, must carry on each particular process with their manual implements. The worker has been appropriated by the process; but the process had previously to be adapted to the worker. This subjective principle of the division of labour no longer exists in production by machinery. Here the total process is examined objectively, viewed in and for itself, and analysed into its constitutive phases.

Once driven by a self-acting prime mover, the factory, in Ure's words, becomes 'a vast automaton, composed of various mechanical and intellectual organs, acting in uninterrupted concert for the production of a common object, all of them being subordinate to a self-regulated moving force.'[27] The disciplinary advantages of such a system were

[25] *Capital*, p. 495.
[26] *Capital*, p. 501.
[27] Ure, *Philosophy of Manufactures*', p. 18. Qu. Marx, p. 544.

quickly appreciated. Ure, whom Marx describes as the Pindar of the automatic factory, observes in relation to the self-acting mule, that it is, '(a) creation destined to restore order among the industrious classes [...] This invention confirms the great doctrine already propounded, that when capital enlists science into her service, the refractory hand of labour will always be taught docility.' [28]

At a corporeal level, in manufacture the worker makes use of a tool; in the factory, the machine makes use of the worker. In the former, 'the movements of the instrument of labour proceed from him, here it is the movements of the machine that he must follow.' In the factory 'we have a lifeless mechanism which is independent of the workers, who are incorporated into it as its living appendages.'[29] The worker is both subordinate to the machine and in direct competition with it for his or her subsistence. Marx is quite clear that this opens up a new phase in the conflict between labour and capital in which workers embark upon a struggle against the instrument of labour itself:

> The struggle between the capitalist and the wage-labourer starts with the existence of the capital-relation itself. It rages throughout the period of manufacture. But only since the introduction of machinery has the worker fought against the instrument of labour itself, capital's material mode of existence. He is in revolt against this particular form of the means of production because it is the material foundation of the capitalist mode of production. [30]

Simondon on man and machine

---

[28] Ure, pp. 367-370. Qu. Marx, pp. 562-563.
[29] *Capital*, p. 548.
[30] *Capital*, pp. 553-554.

Simondon's project, like that of Marx, involves overcoming the alienation between man and machine, and demonstrating that 'in technical reality there is a human reality,' but the two understand this conflict in very different ways. Whereas Marx believes the antagonism can be overcome only by the revolutionary expropriation of the means of production, Simondon would like to overcome what he sees as our cultural fear of and hostility towards the machine, by persuading us that '(t)he most powerful cause of alienation in the world of today is based on misunderstanding of the machine.' [31] This alienation is caused not by the machine but by the fact that it is absent from 'the world of meanings.' We are estranged from the human in the machine, which is 'locked in, unrecognized, materialized and enslaved, but human nonetheless.'

Simondon argues, on the same lines as Marx, that progress in the eighteenth-century left the human individual intact, because he remained a 'technical individual' among his tools, 'whose centre and whose bearer he was.' What distinguishes the factory from the craftsman's workshop is a change in the relationship between the technical object and the human being; 'the factory is a technical ensemble comprising automatic machines whose activity parallels human activity, whereas in the workshop it is man who lends his individuality to the performance of technical actions.' The human individual was unable to experience this as progress because he was no longer centralized 'as the core of command and perception in the adapted action.' The human individual became a mere spectator of mechanical operations or a manager of technical ensembles, in relation to the functioning of 'internally self-regulating technical individuals.'

[31] Gilbert Simondon, *Du mode d'existence des objets techniques*, (Paris: Aubier, 1989), p. 9.

Simondon's account here notably elides the stage in which, in the manufacturing workshop, the division of labour had already, for Marx, destroyed human individuality in the labour process. The essential antagonism is presented as that between the human individual and the machine, instead of that between the working class and capital, as materialized in the organization of the instruments of labour.

Simondon goes on to argue, *contra* Marx, that the alienation between worker and machine did not arise solely because the worker no longer owned his means of production. Beneath the legal and economic relation with ownership, there is, he believes, a more fundamental discontinuity between the human individual and the technical individual. The alienation of man from machine has more than a socio-economic meaning, it also has 'a psycho-physiological meaning,' by no means restricted to the working class. In what could be construed as a statement of the 'proletarianization' thesis, Simondon claims:

> The bankers whose social role was exalted by mathematicians such as the Saint-Simonians and August Comte are just as alienated from the machine as are the members of the new proletariat. By this we wish to say that there is no need to postulate a master and slave dialectic to account for alienation in the propertied classes. The relation of ownership with regard to the machine involves as much alienation as the non-ownership relation, even though it pertains to a very different social state.[32]

Because the focus of Simondon's attention is the understanding of technical reality, he is able to argue that the managers of a business,

[32] Simondon, p. 117.

who understand the machine in terms of costs and output, and the scientist who sees the machine only as the practical application of a theoretical law, are both as 'alienated' from the machine as the worker who has become its appendage or been replaced by it. One might object here that there is a difference between being alienated *from* the machine and being alienated *by* the machine. However, both owners and workers are said to lack a 'true' relationship with the machine. In Simondon's view, capital and labour are equally imperfect modes of *being* in relation to the technical object. Alienation will not disappear, he believes, with any resolution of the conflict between capital and labour, since, their different understandings of the technical object, as, on one side, 'man-of-elements' and, on the other, 'man-of-ensembles,' when brought together, are not complementary and cannot constitute the basis for a 'true' relationship with the technical object. Both are behind the times, not truly contemporary with the technical individual. Collective ownership of the means of production would not resolve or reduce our fundamental alienation from the machine. This can only be achieved by a cultural change in which we begin to grasp the technical object as an *individual*, not merely a means to an end. That is to say, if we recognize the automatism and self-regulation of the machine as a centre of command, but an autonomism which is not closed or complete. The ideal functioning of a machine demands a margin of indetermination, allowing for a sensitivity to outside information. Similarly, an 'open' technical ensemble assumes a human presence as 'permanent organizer and as a living interpreter of the inter-relationship of machines, in the same way that the musicians in an orchestra need a conductor. In this way, Simondon declares, with what might be an Heideggerian flourish, man is '*among* the machines that work with him.' [33]

---

[33] Simondon, p. 4.

Exteriorization and objective mind

There is at work in the line of thought that leads from Leroi-Gourhan to Simondon to Stiegler an interpretation of human development as a species, summed up in the following statement by the palaeontologist, Leroi-Gourhan:

> The whole of our evolution has been oriented toward placing outside ourselves what in the rest of the animal world is achieved *inside* by species adaptation. The most striking material fact is certainly the "freeing" of tools, but the fundamental fact is really the freeing of the word and our unique ability to transfer our memory to a social organism outside ourselves. [34]

In *Homo sapiens*, 'technicity is no longer geared to cell development but seems to exteriorize itself completely – to lead, as it were, a life of it own.' [35] If, as Leroi-Gourhan suggests, the origin of language in anthropoids preceding *Homo sapiens* was closely linked with the technical motor function, then, he continues, 'we are entitled to visualize language too, in the form of operating sequences limited to the expression of concrete situations, at first concurrently with them and later involving the deliberate preservation and and reproduction of verbal sequences going beyond immediate situations.' [36] This

[34] André Leroi-Gourhan, *Gesture and Speech*, trans. Anna Bostock Berger, (Cambridge, Mass and London: MIT Press, 1993), p. 235.
[35] *GS*, pp. 138-139.
[36] *GS*, 115-116.

would provide the basis for what Auroux describes as the process of *grammatization.*

It is difficult not to see behind these arguments the role of the Hegelian concept of externalization [*Entäusserung*] through which human development takes place as 'work' or objectification. In Marx, because of the emergence of the capitalist mode of production this externalization comes to take the form of alienation or estrangement [*Entfremdung*]. In Hegel also, the externalization of human creative powers leads to alienation, but this alienation is produced to the extent that the human subject has not yet achieved full self-consciousness of its own activity in the objectified world. This is close to what Simondon calls grasping the human reality in technical reality. We have, as he puts it, to find the proper place of technicity in our world of meanings, our symbolic order.

Stiegler begins from the same starting-point of what he calls, '*the pursuit of the evolution of the living by other means than life* – which is what the history of technics consists in,' under the concept of epiphylogenesis (the preservation in technical objects of epigenetic experience), through which he attempts to think the birth – or the 'invention' - of the human.[37] In this relation between the human and technics, there is a 'who' and a 'what,' but it is an open question which is the 'who' and which is the 'what.' It is a relation which, he insists, must be understood entirely independently of all 'anthropologism.' Exteriorization, as Stiegler understands it, is fundamentally the exteriorization of memory. The first tools are already a form of memory *support* in that they materialize and facilitate the exercise of human skills and capacities, although they are not as such intended to

---

[37] Bernard Stiegler, *Technics and Time 1: The Fault of Epimetheus*, tr. Richard Beardsworth and George Collins, (Stanford: Stanford University Press, 1998), p. 135.

store memory in the manner of later mnemotechnics, which emerge only with grammatization.

Stiegler is wary therefore of the term 'means of production,' insofar as it suggests a Marxist distinction between 'means of production' and 'relations of production' or between 'infrastructure' and 'superstructure,' in which the latter is determined by the former. Technical devices and equipment are, he believes, more correctly thought of as 'retentional supports, inscribed in a process of grammatization.'[38] Analysis of the 'relations of production' must also account for the dynamic that characterizes the evolution of the 'means of production,' of which the development of the 'relations of production' is the translation at the level of social organization. That is to say, the dynamic of their 'transductive' relation, in which neither can be reduced to the other, can only be comprehended within a general theory of technics. He continues:

> In short, therc is a *tension* between between the supports and relations of production, and the thought of this tension is called *political economy* – but in this political economy technics, which is the 'effective reality' of the relations of production, requires a specific analysis that would lead, precisely, to the impossibility of describing it simply as a 'means', while psychic individuation is the condition of the passage to the actuality (that is, the expression) of this tension.[39]

Proletarianization as disindividuation

[38] Bernard Stiegler, *The Lost Spirit of Capitalism*, trans. Daniel Ross, (Cambridge: Polity, 2014), p. 37.
[39] *Lost Spirit*, p. 39.

The concept of individuation, derived from Simondon, thereby comes to the fore. There is, Stiegler observes, a process of becoming 'older than that of *the division of social classes*,' that Marx was 'unable to think,' because he had failed to grasp the importance of mnemotechnics.[40] These mnemo-techniques 'constitute the characteristic pre-individual funds of the psychic and collective individuation process in which the West consisted,' and, at present form the basis of cultural capitalism. Individuation consists in a selection, based upon primary retention, of what I retain and which constitutes my present and thereby my past, as an arrangement of secondary retentions. Only on this basis do I *exist*, because my retentional process is unique, and is protentional, that is, constitutes an horizon of expectation. There are also *collective* secondary retentions forming a pre-individual fund, inherited by everyone in my group as the past of everyone in my group, by means of which the group individuates itself as a 'we,' with a shared horizon of expectation, but only to the extent that the *I*s psychically individuate themselves.[41] In cultural capitalism, however, the function of the cultural and programming industries has been to take control of the processes constituting secondary retentions and to replace pre-individual funds with cultural products adapted to the needs of marketing. 'Such funds cannot form the object of symbolic participation for those who are thereby distracted from *their own* individuation,' by a process which homogenizes individual pasts, short-circuiting traditional process of cultural transmission within the social group.

Secondary retentions which are objectivated and materialized, thus 'transmissible, inheritable and adoptable,' including bodily techniques, are constituted as *tertiary retentions*, providing a

[40] *Decadence*, p. 41.

[41] *Decadence*, p. 113

mnemotechnics. This tertiary retention exists in all societies, conditioning individuation and, as symbolic sharing 'makes possible the exteriorization of individual experience in epiphylogenetic traces.' When it becomes 'industrial,' however, Stiegler argues, 'tertiary retention constitutes technologies of control that fundamentally alter symbolic exchange,' and give rise to *dis*individuation.[42]

Fundamental to Stiegler's attachment to the concept of proletarianization is that the continuity which links its nineteenth-century origins to its contemporary forms rests upon an assault upon the (skilled) *work* which is essential to individuation. In the nineteenth century this assault was accomplished through mechanization and automation, whereby the worker was deprived of the work through which s/he individuated himself or herself. The contemporary capitalist economy is, on the other hand, based upon the incitement to *consume*. Both, however, involve the degradation of work. Stiegler declares, 'The capitalist economy, strictly speaking, *no longer works*.'[43] Not all employment can be considered as work in this sense, 'because not all jobs are conducive to the acquisition and development of knowledge and therewith, to individuation, that is, the process whereby you can make a place for yourself in society as a producer, *and not only as a consumer whose job furnishes the employee a salary which in turn confers buying power.* Individuation is on the contrary *what takes work beyond mere employment* if one understands that 'work' *consists in action in the world in order to transform it on the basis of the knowledge one has of it.*'[44]

Simondon's ontological theory which challenges the ontological privilege granted to the already constituted individual and then works

42 *Decadence*, p. 118.
43 *For a New Critique*, p. 63.
44 *La Télécratie*, pp. 243-244.

backwards to develop an ontogenesis 'in reverse', is thereby linked to a theory of ongoing self-individuation through work, resembling the Marxist theory of *praxis*. But, whereas in Marx, the self-realization of the individual is that of a revolutionary subject, a member of a class who transcends class-determination in the creation of a free society, Stiegler here understands the work of the worker in pre-capitalist terms as the activity through which the individual is individuated and 'makes a place' for him/herself in the social order.

In the palaeontological thought of Leroi-Gourhan, based upon an *evolutionary* perspective, it makes perfect sense to detect a fundamental continuity in the exteriorization of human 'memory,' understood, as he states, not as a property of the intelligence, but as 'a medium for action sequences,' including species-memory, ethnic memory, and artificial memory, without reference to instinct or thought.[45] But Stiegler's attempt to establish a continuity between the worker's loss of *savoir-faire* reduced to labour-power, and the consumer's loss of *savoir-vivre* reduced to purchasing power,[46] through the concept of proletarianization, necessarily fails, because it contains both too much and too little to be generalized in this way.

At the centre of Stiegler's psycho-social theory is the condition of those *'(p)roletarians of the nervous system* (who) are no less deprived of knowledge than are the *proletarians of the muscular system.'*[47] The engineer who developed, installed and managed a system has disappeared, as *hypomnemata* extend ever-deeper into the productive process. Cognitive labour-power has become devoid of knowledge, and the cognitive reduced to calculability. The middle classes, Stiegler argues, will soon disappear because they have suffered *symbolic*

[45] *GS*, p. 413.
[46] For example, in *Réenchanter le monde*, (Paris: Flammarion, 2006), p. 45.
[47] *For a New Critique*, p. 45.

immiseration, an '*aesthetic and noetic proletarianization*.'[48] Leaving aside the question of whether a social class can dissolve because of its changed noetic and aesthetic activity, this is proletarianization in the sense outlined at the beginning of this essay, in which Marx anticipated that the *petit-bourgeoisie* would 'sink' into the proletariat, although not for the reasons Marx predicted. The problem is that whereas the term 'proletarianization' here suggests that the *petit-bourgeoisie* would suffer a fate previously endured by the proletariat, Stiegler's concept of proletarianization seems rather to function in the opposite direction, that is, to transfer retrospectively an analysis of the psycho-social condition of the present-day middle-classes onto the nineteenth-century working class in order to propose a continuity which never existed. The considerable insights yielded by Stiegler's works are disrupted by an organizing concept which contributes nothing to his theory and serves only to produce logical incoherence.

---

[48] *For a New Critique*, pp. 63-64.

Politics and the Problem of Evil

The problem of evil, although it originated as an attempt to account for the existence of suffering in a world created by an omnipotent God, remains, I hope to show, a genuine *problem*. The problem, as I shall understand it here, is that of how we are to make sense of the world given the presence of what we call 'evil' within it. Historically, of course, the problem presented itself in a theological form, but my primary concern is to show how the problem of evil re-presented itself within the overwhelmingly secular thought of the twentieth century as thinkers attempted to make sense of the phenomenon which came to be known as 'totalitarianism' and, in particular, of the experience of the Nazi death camps.

The problem of evil can be traced back to the question, 'Why do terrible things happen?' As such it does not distinguish between what we would now regard as natural misfortunes and suffering brought about by the actions of other human beings. The individual whose family, home and life's work have been wiped out in an instant by an earthquake, and who asks, 'Why did this happen?' is not asking for an explanation of the cause of this event but for its meaning. Similarly, when, as we sometimes see, there is among the flowers at the site of a child's murder a sign asking 'Why?' the question is not directed at psychologists or the killer but towards the world in which such things happen. That such questions have no obvious answer does not in the least diminish their force or necessity. While originally the world put into question was God's creation, we can, as a first approximation, say that in a secular age our questions are directed to the void where God used to be and express the conviction that there may be a fundamental fault in the world.

The problem of evil was understood by the early Christian thinkers as the problem of *malum*, signifying the opposite of *bonum*, that is, as 'bad' in its widest sense. We should in the same way resist any attempt to draw too quickly a distinction between 'human' or 'moral' evil and 'physical' or 'natural' evil, since, as I have suggested, physical evil does not present itself to us as fully intelligible in physical terms. A rigid distinction between the two is often accompanied by a tendency to subjectivize evil, that is, to think of it primarily or exclusively in relation to the human will. As Marcel Gauchet has observed, with the withdrawal of God, 'Evil still existed, but it said nothing about the ultimate nature of things or of the being of humans. It no longer originated in ontology but in pathology.'[1] A widely recognized effect of this is to draw attention away from evil as something *suffered* to evil as something *practised.*

The Christian existentialist philosopher Gabriel Marcel argued that evil is to be understood as evil suffered: 'I can grasp it as evil only in the measure in which it *touches* me – that is to say in the measure in which I am *involved.*'[2] In the attempt to comprehend evil as suffering we may infer that first-person accounts are necessarily privileged and, in some sense, *inviolable*, for who are we, who have not suffered, to explain to those who have what their suffering means? We are entitled, I would argue, to put questions to those accounts and to interpret them,

---

[1] Marcel Gauchet, *The Disenchantment of the World: A Political History of Religion*, tr. Oscar Burge, (Princeton: Princeton University Press, 1997), p.168.

[2] Gabriel Marcel, 'The Philosophy of Existentialism', quoted in John Hick, *Evil and the Love of God*, (London: Macmillan, 1977), p. 10.

but never simply to eradicate them by overwriting them with our own. I shall return to this issue with regard to the significance of the testimony of concentration camp survivors, who survived a very real attempt to wipe all trace of them from the face of the earth. Nevertheless, the occurrence of evil touches not only its direct victims but many more, at least in some measure, and it is perhaps to the extent that we have been ourselves been touched in this way that we are ready to grant a kind of authority to those at the centre of this pain.

Marcel argues that the phenomenon of evil dissolves when we try to make it a theoretical object, most notably in the form of a theodicy. Levinas, in his phenomenology of evil, has written that theodicy functions:

> by invoking the proper sense of a metaphysical order, an ethics which is invisible in the immediate lessons of moral consciousness. This is a kingdom of transcendent ends, willed by a benevolent wisdom, by the absolute goodness of a God who is in some way defined by this super-natural goodness; or a widespread invisible goodness in Nature and History, where it would command the paths which are, to be sure, painful, but which lead to the Good. Pain is henceforth meaningful, subordinated in one way or another to the metaphysical finality envisaged by faith or by a belief in progress.[3]

Leibniz's *Theodicy* (1709) is remarkable for the fact that, as has been pointed out, in this display of ratiocination what is so clearly missing is the brute fact of human suffering. There are few who could be

---

[3] Emmanuel Levinas, 'Useless Suffering', trans. Richard Cohen in *The Provocation of Levinas*, ed. Robert Bernasconi and David Wood, (London: Routledge, 1998), p. 160.

convinced by Leibniz's assurance: 'It is true that one often suffers through the evil actions of others; but when one has no part in the offence one must look upon it as a certainty that these sufferings prepare us for a greater happiness'?[4]

As is well known, the Lisbon earthquake of November 1755 which brought about the destruction of a densely populated European city, including many Christian churches, and with great loss of life, prompted Voltaire to denounce such belief in a providential order, declaring:

> *Elements, animaux, humains, tout est en guerre*
> *Il le faut avouer, le* mal *est sur la terre.*

(Elements, animals, humans, everything is at war/ It has to be admitted, evil is upon the earth.)

The most notable consequence of the Lisbon earthquake was, according to Voltaire, to make human beings apprehensive about their mortality and their ultimate destiny, faced by a silent God:

> *On a besoin d'un Dieu qui parle au genre humain.*
> *Il n'appartient qu'à lui d'expliquer son ouvrage,*
> *De consoler le faible, et d'éclairer le sage.*[5]

(We need a God who speaks to humankind/It's up to him to explain his work/To comfort the weak and to enlighten the wise.)

Like all rational theodicies, that of Leibniz springs not from an attempt to grasp the nature of human suffering but from the enterprise

---

[4] G. W. Leibniz, *Theodicy*, Illinois: Open Court, La Salle, 1997, p. 276.

[5] *Poème sur le Désastre de Lisbonne*. See T. D. Kendrick, *The Lisbon Earthquake*, (Philadelphia: J. B. Lippincott Co.,1955).

of trying to justify God, in trying to conceive of, in Leibniz's absurd formulation, 'a God worthy of our love.' The most powerful counterpart to such arguments in the Judaeo-Christian tradition is undoubtedly *The Book of Job*. Job's sufferings originate with God's boast to Satan that Job is above all others, 'a perfect and an upright man, one that feareth God, and escheweth evil.' When Satan responds that Job has nothing to fear since God has always bestowed every blessing upon him, God allows Satan to test Job with every form of suffering, provided he keeps him alive.

Stripped of his wealth by thieves and natural disasters, his children dead, his body covered with boils, Job curses the day he was born. His 'comforters' all try in one way or another to justify God and to rationalize divine justice, each provoking an increasingly violent response from Job, who continues to affirm his own moral integrity and challenges God to answer him directly. For Elie Wiesel, Job, who in the telling of the tale has become Israel itself, makes 'this outcry which, from generation to generation, through pogroms and massacres, reverberates from one end of exile to the other: *Eretz al tekhast dami* – Earth, do not absorb my blood!'[6]

As Wiesel puts it:

> Job spoke his outrage, his grief; he told God what He should have known for a long time, perhaps since always, that something was amiss in His universe. The just were punished for no reason, the criminal rewarded for no reason. The just and the wicked were subjected to the same fate – God having turned

[6] Blood, if not covered with earth, cries out to heaven to be avenged.

> His back on them, on everyone. God had lost interest in His creation; He was absent.[7]

In *The Book of Job*, God, provoked by Job's outburst, answers him 'out of the whirlwind,' in a declaration of His almighty power as Creator of the world and everything in it, a power against which no human concept of self-righteousness can stand. Asked to choose whether he will place his own judgment before God's, Job capitulates and humbles himself before God, and, in reward, God restores his wealth and happiness twice over. For Wiesel, however, inverting the message of the story, which is the incommensurability of divine and human justice, Job is first of all the hero who finds in his sense of injustice the courage and the power to challenge God but then, having humbled himself, becomes 'a broken defeated man.'

Wiesel would 'prefer to think that the Book's true ending was lost. That Job died without having humiliated himself; that he succumbed to his grief an uncompromising and whole man.' In explanation of this reading, he adds, 'And then why not say it? I was preoccupied with Job, especially in the early days after the war. In those days he could be seen on every road of Europe. Wounded, robbed, mutilated. Certainly not happy. Nor resigned.' If Job had the right to forgive God for himself, Wiesel insists, he did not have the right to forgive God for his dead children. He prefers to think that Job did not believe his own confession, that he continued to interrogate God, and that 'thanks to him, we know that it is given to man to transform divine injustice into human justice and compassion.'

This Promethean re-interpretation of *The Book of Job* echoes the rebellion of Ivan Karamazov against divine (in)justice in

[7] Elie Wiesel, 'Job Our Contemporary' in *Messengers of God,* (New York: Simon and Schuster, 1994), pp. 229-230.

Dostoyevsky's *The Brothers Karamazov*, where, after presenting a long and harrowing catalogue of cruelty practised against children, Ivan declares the impossibility that such suffering can be expiated, and that without such atonement[8] the moral harmony of the universe cannot be restored.

In Ivan's words:

> They must be expiated for otherwise there can be no harmony. But how, how are you going to expiate them? Is it possible? Not surely, by their being avenged? But what do I want them avenged for? What do I want a hell for torturers for? What good can hell do if they (the children) have already been tortured to death? And what sort of harmony is it, if there is a hell? I want to forgive. I want to embrace. I don't want any more suffering. And if the sufferings of children go to make up the sum of sufferings which is necessary for the purchase of truth, then I say beforehand that the entire truth is not worth such a price. And finally, I do not want a mother to embrace the torturer who had her child torn to pieces by his dogs! She has no right to forgive him! If she likes, she can forgive him for herself, she can forgive the torturer for the immeasurable suffering he has inflicted upon her as a mother; but she has no right to forgive for the sufferings of her tortured child…Is there in the whole world a being who could or would have the right to forgive? I don't want harmony. I don't want it, out of the love I bear to mankind. I want my suffering to remain unavenged. I'd rather remain with my suffering unavenged and my indignation unappeased, *even if I were wrong*. Besides, too high a price has been placed on harmony. We cannot afford to pay so much for

[8] 'Atonement' is literally, 'bringing into harmony with.'

> admission. And, indeed, if I am an honest man, I'm bound to hand it back as soon as possible. This I am doing. It is not God that I do not accept, Alyosha. I merely most respectfully return him the ticket.[9]

Wiesel, like Ivan, feels it has become necessary to defend man against God, to insist that human suffering has exceeded the limit within which it could be given meaning within a divinely ordained universal order. Terrible suffering inflicted upon the entirely innocent cannot be accepted or given any sense, and if this is God's world then human beings may rightly refuse to live in it.

Evil, justice and the Law

Philippe Nemo in his reading of *The Book of Job* takes a diametrically opposite view to that of Wiesel, insisting that far from divine injustice forcing mankind back upon its own conception of justice, the presence of evil reveals the limits of the human attempt to impose order and meaning upon the world. He rejects what he describes as 'collectivist' interpretations of evil and insists upon the individual character of suffering in which those who have died in collective catastrophes are 'first of all private souls, each of whom saw death approaching for himself or herself alone.'[10] Collectivist interpretations therefore conceal the truth that lies at the heart of evil.

Approaching the phenomenology of evil through the experiences of Job, Nemo argues that everything begins with the question, 'Why do

[9] Fyodor Dostoyevsky, *The Brothers Karamazov*, Vol. I, trans. David Magarshack, (London: Penguin, 1993), p. 287.

[10] Philippe Nemo, *Job and the Excess of Evil*, trans. Michael Kigel, (Pittsburgh: Duquesne University Press, 1998).

you make me suffer?' addressed to a capricious intent that is responsible for my suffering; capricious in that it does not follow from the existence of Law. This is an existential question posed not by a *subject* but by a *soul*, and, since it presupposes intentionality it concerns an evil which is not natural in origin. Indeed, the soul is said to come into existence only in response to this intention. It is an intention that '*reveals itself* in its insistence on hurting us. If we did not suffer, or if we suffered according to the algebra of a Law of pleasures and pains, we would undoubtedly content ourselves with existing as world and as Earth. But would we exist?'[11]

For Nemo evil exists as an *excess*, 'a madness, an Other Scene that *exceeds* the Law of the world, exceeds the scene of the world as a technical world.'[12] Evil lies beyond the sphere that can be resolved by human know-how and precipitates the appearance of 'the abyss in which the whole world sinks.' This does not mean that there is a finite realm in which technique (or technology) retains its mastery. Rather, evil discloses a transcendent will which reaches back into the realm of technique to instigate an originary disorder there:

> In classical political theories, which impute the origin of disorder and the consequent institution of Law to a state of nature imbued with an intrinsic disorder, the question translates as: Where does an intrinsic natural disorder come from? In psychological theory: How is it that all psychic processes do not undergo normal development? The fact is, *there is always* disturbance, and always more disturbance than the amount needed to disturb the disturbance and thus return it to order. So that disorder reappears, and with it the Law that has to bring it

[11] Nemo, p. 115.
[12] Nemo. P. 81.

> to an end. Technique, the human effort to dominate the world, is a response to the human impotence that is always already there.[13]

The world human beings inhabit is fundamentally disordered and unjust, but, in Nemo's reading of *The Book of Job*, the existence of evil, rather than disproving the existence of God, is that which transcends the world dominated by human 'technique' and, in a Heideggerian manner, in the depth of anxiety, opens the 'clearing' in which the soul discovers itself in addressing the '*You*' which is the soul of God. 'We state, with Job, that … without all this evil, God would not exist. It is this evil that places us on the path of something like "God," and that opens up an Other Scene for us. Evil "demonstrates" God.'[14] Instead of a theodicy we are presented with a theophany leading to the discovery of the Good. The experience of God's 'capricious' intent does not *justify* His actions, which remain *unjustifiable*, but rather provides human thinking with a means of becoming aware of the presence of a will and a power which transcend earthly Law.

It can be seen that, ultimately, what is central to the problem of evil, and the arguments which take place in *The Book of Job*, is the question of justice. Leibniz may have been the first to coin the term 'theodicy' from the Greek *theos* (God) and *dike* (justice), but from the earliest times *dike* had been understood in terms of a pre-established order and harmony in the *kosmos*. The demand that divine justice be overthrown by human justice involves a rebellion not only against God but against justice as formerly understood. But what exactly is the nature of this human justice with regard to a suffering which allows neither

---

[13] Nemo, p. 90.
[14] Nemo, p. 142.

retribution, atonement nor forgiveness? It would seem to be a tragic posture, a demand that can never be realized, directed at a silent God. If justice cannot be found through God, is it likely to be found through man, so often the perpetrator as well as the victim?

Rousseau, perhaps more than any other thinker believed that, in relation to this dual role of perpetrator and victim, the problem of evil could be redefined and resolved in purely secular, political terms. Ernst Cassirer argues that the primacy of politics in Rousseau's thought results directly from his interpretation of the problem of evil. Cassirer maintains that what other Enlightenment thinkers merely identified as defects in social organization requiring correction, 'Rousseau saw rather as the guilt of society, and with flaming words, again and again, he reproached society with this guilt and called for atonement.'[15]

As Cassirer indicates, the problem of theodicy was of 'deep and central concern' to the thinkers of the seventeenth and eighteenth centuries, and it was this issue more than any other which divided Rousseau from the leading figures of the Enlightenment, as well as being the point on which he was most implacably condemned by the religious authorities because of his rejection of the doctrine of original sin.

The opening words of *Emile* state that, 'Everything is good as it leaves the hands of the Author of things; everything degenerates in the hands of man.' In the *Profession of Faith of the Savoyard Vicar*, insofar as this can be taken as an expression of Rousseau's own view, he states:

[15] Ernst Cassirer, *The Question of Jean-Jacques Rousseau*, (Bloomington: Indiana University Press, 1963), p. 71.

> Our sorrows, our cares, and our sufferings come to us from ourselves. Moral evil is incontestably our own work, and physical evil would be nothing without our vices, which have made us sense it .... Man, seek the author of evil no longer. It is yourself. No evil exists other than that which you do or suffer, and both come to you from yourself .... Take away our fatal progress, take away our errors and our vices, take away the work of man, and everything is good.[16]

Original sin is not the source of evil; it is, in a move that is entirely original to Rousseau, *society* which is to blame. As Cassirer puts it, 'Rousseau's solution of this dilemma lies in his placing responsibility at a point where no one before him had looked for it. He created, as it were, a new subject of responsibility, of "imputability." This subject is not individual man, but human society.'[17] In Rousseau's anthropology it is not 'Man' as such who bears the responsibility for evil but socialized man. The transition from natural man to social man is Rousseau's secularized version of the Fall. Society converts innocent *amour de soi* into selfish *amour propre*, creating needs and passions that far exceed those created by nature. But the society which has so damaged us can also be our saviour. When the coercive form of society is replaced by a free society in which individuals have learned to subordinate their private interests to the general will, man will have saved himself.

The problem of theodicy was in this way placed upon an entirely new foundation. As Cassirer puts it, 'He had carried it beyond the realm of metaphysics and placed it in the centre of ethics and politics.'

---

[16] Jean-Jacques Rousseau, *Emile* or *On Education*, trans. Allan Bloom, (London: Penguin, 1991), pp. 281-282.
[17] Cassirer, p. 75.

But it would be more accurate to say that Rousseau transposed this metaphysical problem *into* the centre of ethics and politics. The burden of responsibility for evil was removed from God and placed upon human society. As Cassirer puts it, for Rousseau:

> The theodicy problem can be solved only in and through the state. It is man's business and it is his loftiest task to accomplish the justification of God – not by means of metaphysical broodings over happiness and unhappiness and over good and evil but by freely creating and freely shaping the order in accordance with which he wants to live.[18]

The idea of providence was rescued by transforming it into the idea of progress, to be accomplished not by God but by human society. But at a price. Cassirer perceptively contrasts Voltaire's playful pessimism with Rousseau's *tragic* optimism. As Rousseau wrote to Voltaire in 1756, 'The optimism you consider so horrible consoles me in the very misery you set forth as unbearable.'[19] Rousseau's optimism gained its emotional force from the fact that he *felt* the misery of the world that much more deeply than Voltaire. But far from eliminating 'metaphysical broodings' over happiness and suffering and good and evil their transformation into the central concerns of modern 'rational' politics brought with it profoundly destabilizing effects.

As Lucio Colletti observes, this transposition of the problem of evil into society released 'a stimulus of unprecedented power.' Society is now responsible not only for perdition, but is also the site of human salvation. Morality is resolved into politics, which is to say that

[18] Cassirer, p. 82.
[19] Qu. Cassirer, *Rousseau, Kant and Goethe*, (New York: Harper and Row, 1963), p. 37.

'politics itself is the solution to the moral problem.'[20] In a fateful move, the problem of the elimination of evil comes to coincide with the idea of revolution. The nature of 'Man' himself, poised between good and evil, is put at stake in this reconception of state power.

The *Book of Job*, as we have seen, like Hobbes' *Leviathan* which invokes it, raises the question of the relation between power and justice. How, one might ask, does God's statement of His overwhelming power, manifested in the creation of the world, entail the justice of His actions? But every dispensation of justice, whether human or divine, presupposes the establishment of a power which cannot itself be justified. An appeal to justice is implicitly an appeal to the power which lies behind that justice, or else it implies the demand to establish a different power which will dispense a different kind of justice.

Theodicies, it was argued earlier, suppress rather than resolve the problem of evil, and we may include here also the logic of secular theodicies which, in practice at least, seek to convince us that past and present sufferings 'prepare us for a greater happiness.' Insofar as revolutionary movements seek to persuade us that suffering can be fully explained in terms of social causes and resolved by political action they also suppress the problem of evil. At the other extreme there is a view of suffering as surd and inexpiable which breaks the bounds of sense altogether and threatens the very idea of justice in which it claims to base itself. Ivan Karamazov is that distinctively modern hero, the man of such acute moral sense that he finds life unliveable.

Evil, excess and world-openness

[20] Lucio Colletti, *From Rousseau to Lenin*, (London: NLB, 1976), p. 145.

If theodicy begins with an already framed conception of an objective moral order into which the fact of suffering is integrated, achieving an inauthentic reconciliation by *negating* the reality of suffering, can we not begin with the experience of suffering itself and from that, work towards making it in some way intelligible? Hick has argued that the problem of evil arises only for the spectator while the sufferer is overwhelmed with more practical concerns.[21] As I have already indicated, I do not believe this is so. Every sufferer is inclined to ask, 'Why is this happening to me?', a question which transcends practical concerns, the asking of which readily opens into the more general question of why suffering exists at all, and the answer to which can only possibly be found in the way it is lived through, since it is a question that touches upon our very existence.

The problem of evil arises only for beings who inhabit a *world*, and puts into question our very being-in-the-world. But, to suggest, as Ivan does, that the price of entry is too high, to assert that it would have been better never to have existed, is radically to misrepresent the character of our being-in-the-world, since such a choice never was and never could be available to us. What Heidegger calls our thrownness [*Geworfenheit*] into the world means that to imagine a situation in which we could make a decision as to whether 'the price of entry' is too high is the product of a moral imagination that has become disconnected from our being-in-the-world. This is, of course, a quite different situation from that in which we try to decide whether or not we can bear to *continue* existing. More generally, to take a stand against God or against the divinely ordained order of the world on behalf of man is a form of moral reasoning which, as Dostoyevsky is

[21] John Hick, *Evil and the God of Love*, (London: Palgrave Macmillan, 2010), p. 10.

suggesting, leads into a crisis which cannot be resolved, the inverse of Leibnizian complacency.

Man's 'world-openness' [*Welthoffenheit*] is such that there are background conditions of intelligibility which forever elude our control and which, providing the basis for our judgments, can never themselves be made the objects of judgment. It signifies an openness not to the already known world but to what lies beyond it. This is nowhere more evident than in relation to the concept of justice. The project of overthrowing divine justice and replacing it with human justice involves a fundamental transgression against the meaning of justice itself, insofar as it implies a human law and an earthly city intelligible purely in their own terms.

The problem of evil must be understood against this background of our inability as human beings to frame a closed and self-sufficient account of our world. The worldliness [*Weltlichkeit*] of human beings is such that we experience the bad things that befall us against a background or horizon which normally bestows meaning upon those events. If, for example, I interpret my misfortunes as the result of, or retribution for, my own bad actions, the structure of my world is confirmed: similarly, if I understand my poverty as the result of capitalist or imperialist exploitation. As yet there may be evil [*malum*] but no *problem* of evil. The problem of evil arises not when the degree of suffering becomes too intense, but when evil appears as *senseless*, which is to say, it creates a rift within our understanding of the world. At this level, the problem of evil, arising out of an authentic experience of evil, threatens the integrity of 'world' itself. The experience of the surd, inexpiable character of suffering is an effect of this crisis of 'world'.

My argument here is not that the occurrence of evil *causes* this rift in our understanding of the world but that at certain times evil is experienced in such a way as to generate the problem of evil by breaking through the understanding of world and revealing its lack of self-sufficiency, its dependency on that which is beyond its grasp or control. The problem of evil then necessarily appears as a mystery or enigma. It may take the form of manifestations of nature which appear to be beyond the control of a Creator, or of an overwhelming malevolence incompatible with the idea of man as a created being or as the inhabitant of a moral world, but in all cases it refers us to something *inexplicable* that we urgently feel the need to have explained.

Levinas, in his dialogue with Nemo, has written that the 'excess' of evil is not an excessive evil; that is to say, its excessive character is not to be understood in terms of its quantitative intensity, as a 'degree surpassing measure,' beyond that which is endurable. Rather, 'The break with the normal and the normative, with order, with synthesis, with the world, already constitutes its qualitative essence.' Evil is 'the non-integratability of the non-integratable,' that which no categorical form can retain in its framework.[22]

Evil should be understood, then, neither as an objective force external to man, nor, in the Augustinian manner, as a self-originating act of will; neither as substance nor as privation. And since the problem of evil manifests itself at the level of world, the possibility of overcoming evil arises only at the same level, through an intervention that comes from outside the known world and transforms it. In the orthodox Christian view that intervention has already occurred, with the incarnation of God as Christ, who 'took upon himself the suffering of the world' and redeemed it through his death.

Where was God in Auschwitz?

---

[22] Emmanuel Levinas, *Collected Philosophical Papers*, trans. Alphonso Lingis, Phenomenologica 100, (Dordecht: Martinus Nijhoff, 1987), p.180.

As an alternative to theodicy, the presence of God in a suffering world can, some theologians have argued, be sustained through an *imitatio Christi*, through the practical resolution to be always on the side of the victim and never that of the oppressor. One highly *un*orthodox, theological development of this idea is that of the *theologia crucis*, or the 'crucified God.' On this view, premised upon the passibility of God, that is, the capacity of God to suffer, Christ's suffering and that of all human beings are to be understood as the suffering of God Himself.

To help understand this view we can consider Elie Wiesel's recollection of an event he witnessed in Auschwitz:

> One day when we came back from work, we saw three gallows rearing up in the assembly place, three black crows. Roll call. SS all around us, machine guns trained: the traditional ceremony. Three victims in chains – one of them, the little servant, the sad-eyed angel.
>
> The SS seemed more preoccupied, more disturbed than usual. To hang a young boy in front of thousands of spectators was no light matter. The head of the camp read the verdict. All eyes were on the child. He was lividly pale, almost calm, biting his lips. The gallows threw its shadow over him.
>
> This time the Lagerkapo refused to act as executioner. Three SS replaced him.
>
> The three victims mounted together on the chairs. The three necks were placed at the same moment within the nooses.
>
> 'Long live liberty!' cried the two adults.
>
> But the child was silent.
>
> 'Where is God? Where is He?' someone behind me asked.

> At a sign from the head of the camp, the three chairs tipped over.
>
> Total silence throughout the camp. On the horizon the sun was setting.
>
> 'Bare your heads!' yelled the head of the camp. His voice was raucous. We were weeping.
>
> 'Cover your heads!'
>
> Then the march past began. The two adults were no longer alive. Their tongues hung swollen, blue-tinged. But the third rope was still moving; being so light, the child was still alive…
>
> For more than half an hour he stayed there, struggling between life and death, dying in slow agony under our eyes. And we had to look him full in the face. He was still alive when I passed in front of him. His tongue was still red, his eyes were not yet glazed.
>
> Behind me I heard the same man asking:
>
> 'Where is God now?'
>
> And I heard a voice from within me answer him:
>
> 'Where is He? Here He is – He is hanging here on this gallows…' [23]

In answer to the question, 'Where was God in Auschwitz?' the Christian theologians Dorothee Soelle and Jürgen Moltmann have taken up Wiesel's account and argued that God was Himself a co-sufferer hanging on the gallows, since, assuredly, He was not to be

[23] Elie Wiesel, *Night*, trans. Stell Rodway, Penguin, London, 1981, pp. 76-77. See the discussion of this passage in Kenneth Surin, *Theology and the Problem of Evil*, (Oxford: Basil Blackwell, 1986), pp. 116-136.

found anywhere else in Auschwitz.[24] If God was neither executioner nor spectator then, in some sense, they argue, He must have suffered along with the helpless victim. But we immediately run into the difficulty referred to earlier. By what right does Christian theology appropriate the suffering of this Jewish child to explicate itself – a project made all the more dubious given that Auschwitz would not have been possible without centuries of Christian persecution of the Jews? Should this victim not be left with his own suffering without it being interpreted as an incarnation of the Christian God?[25] The only authentically victim-centred account of this suffering could come from his co-sufferers in Auschwitz itself.

Although Wiesel's description suggests a number of parallels with Christ's crucifixion, the meaning of the event for Wiesel is clarified by a passage in which he movingly describes the night of his initiation as a child into the terrors of Auschwitz, where the bodies of children were being tipped into burning pits:

> Never shall I forget that night, the first night in camp, which has turned my life into one long night, seven times cursed and seven times sealed. Never shall I forget that smoke. Never shall I forget the little faces of the children, whose bodies I saw turned into wreaths of smoke beneath a silent blue sky.
>
> Never shall I forget those flames which consumed my faith forever.

---

[24] Dorothee Soelle, *Suffering*, Darton, Longman & Todd, London, 1975. Jürgen Moltmann, *The Crucified God*, trans. R. A. Wilson and John Bowden, (London: SCM,1974).

[25] This has been argued by J-B. Metz, 'Facing the Jews: Christian Theoogy after Auschwitz', *The Holocause as Interruption*, (Edinburgh: T. & T. Clark, 1984). See Surin, p. 124.

> Never shall I forget that nocturnal silence which deprived me, for all eternity, of the desire to live. Never shall I forget those moments which murdered my God and my soul and turned my dreams to dust. Never shall I forget these things, even if I am condemned to live as long as God himself. Never.[26]

Wiesel's account, therefore, is by no means an affirmation of the indwelling, suffering God, of the *Shekinah*, the God who is with the Israelites even in their exile. Moltmann writes, 'God is not absent. He is present. God is not hidden. He is there, visible to everyone in the dying child.'[27] But, although Wiesel later expressed himself in different terms, here the 'voice' that spoke through him from within the experience is clear. It says that God is dead and that what is visible in the dying child is for him the death of belief.

Moltmann, in his argument for the indwelling God, even makes the disturbing claim that 'like the cross of Christ, even Auschwitz is in God himself,'[28] a doctrine which surely comes close to 'justifying' Auschwitz. Indeed, the whole theology of the 'crucified God' is of dubious relevance to Auschwitz. Whereas Christ's death on the cross is, in Christian doctrine, a self-chosen mission, full of religious significance, no-one chose the gas chambers and we struggle in their wake to revive any sense of meaning at all. Despite its name, the 'Holocaust' was not a sacrifice but an extermination.

This part of Moltmann's argument can be separated from that which insists that the crucial question for the sufferer is, as Surin puts it, not the intelligibility of theism but the question of whether there is a God

---

[26] *Night*, p. 45.
[27] Jürgen Moltmann, 'The Pit – Where was God?' in *God for a Secular Society: the Public Relevance of Theology*, (London: SCM Press, 1999), p. 179.
[28] p. 278.

who can save him. The question of evil is thus turned away from rational theodicy and re-directed towards an eschatology of hope. This is quite different from claiming that evil has a place in a divinely ordained teleology or that present suffering prepares us for future happiness. To assimilate Auschwitz into the being of God, however, is to suggest that evil can be assigned a place within a divine scheme of salvation. To avoid this it is necessary to maintain the externality of the saving power, to think of it as breaking into a disintegrating world.

The problem of evil arises when we seek reassurance from our existing beliefs that would provide suffering with a meaning and a value and we fail to find it. The attempt to incorporate the sufferings of Auschwitz into the divine being is a desperate and doomed theological manoeuvre, since the more we identify God with the suffering of helpless victims the less we are able to conceive of a saving power, and we run the risk of extinguishing hope itself. Only in the soteriological or redemptive possibility of a new world can we imagine the overcoming of evil, and this world cannot be thought of in purely human terms or produced by purely human agency. The image of happiness, as Walter Benjamin wrote, is 'inseparably bound up with the image of redemption,' the eschatological hope of every generation nourished by the memory of past suffering.[29] This idea of the redemption of past suffering is quite different from the idea of rationalist theodicy that suffering is a means to an end, since it posits an intervention which transforms the meaning of everything that has happened in the past.

Understandably, Moltmann rejects the idea of an omnipotent and impassive God, fashioned in the image of the victors and marching alongside their triumphal procession. But this is not the Judaeo-

[29] Walter Benjamin, 'Theses on the Philosophy of History' in *Illuminations*, trans. Harry Zohn, ed. Hannah Arendt, (London: Fontana,1967), p. 437.

Christian God of History. That God is, in Benjamin's words, the one who comes as the Messiah, the 'subduer of Antichrist,' who might enter human history at any second. Soelle, by contrast, rejects the idea that redemption comes to us 'from outside or from above,' while, for Moltmann, God is still 'the determining subject of redemption,' but only as a co-sufferer. Following Bonhoeffer, Moltmann argues that 'God does not help through his omnipotence but through his powerlessness.'[30] Since this subject of redemption does not appear to be in any sense the agent of redemption, it is difficult to see how Moltmann's position here differs significantly from Soelle's humanistic approach.

Total domination and absolute power

The claim that God was killed in Auschwitz reappears in political form in the concept of 'total domination' developed by Hannah Arendt in *The Origins of Totalitarianism*. After first maintaining that the essence of totalitarianism is to be found in the concentration camps, Arendt argues that the camps were 'the laboratories in which the fundamental belief of totalitarianism that everything is possible is being verified.'[31] Total domination as she explains it, involves, through the indoctrination of elites and the use of absolute terror, the systematic destruction of human individuality and spontaneity, so that human beings become mere things whose reactions can be completely manipulated and predicted.

Whereas Dostoyevsky argued that without God '*everything is permitted*,' total domination, she believes, transcends this 'nihilistic'

---

[30] *God for a Secular Society*, p. 184.

[31] Hannah Arendt, *The Origins of Totalitarianism*, (London: George Allen & Unwin, 1967), p. 437.

principle, which still implicitly recognizes the claims of self-interest and utility, towards the new and more drastic principle that '*everything is possible*,' that is, towards a realm 'that cannot be limited by either utilitarian motives or self-interest.' Although Arendt herself does not do so, it is necessary, as the parallel with Dostoyevsky suggests, to add the (hidden) condition, '*without God…everything is possible*.' Human self-assertion can become infinite only in the absence of or through the death of God.

The project of total domination, as Arendt understands it, surpasses all the established categories through which we have attempted to make sense of the world. What does the word 'murder' *mean* when corpses are produced by the thousand? All our concepts relating to crime and punishment are rendered 'inadequate and absurd.' Psychology is useless to understand those whose *psyches* have been destroyed. Morality and conscience became impossible for those who could only choose between forms of evil. As Arendt points out, almost every writer attempting to describe the 'madness and unreality' of the camps has had recourse to images drawn from life after death. It 'became evident that things which for thousands of years the human imagination had banished to a realm beyond human competence can be manufactured right here on earth.'

Arendt rejects the possibility of any political theodicy and seeks to 'dissolve the sophistical-dialectical interpretations of politics which are all based upon the superstition that something good might result from evil.' Instead, she argues:

> It is the appearance of some radical evil, previously unknown to us, that puts an end to the notion of developments and transformations of qualities. Here, there are neither political nor simply moral standards but, at the most, the realization that something seems to be involved in modern politics that actually

> should never be involved in politics as we used to understand it, namely all or nothing…'[32]

The radical evil which totalitarianism expresses cannot, Arendt claims, be understood in terms of human suffering. She writes, 'Suffering, of which there has always been too much on earth, is not the issue, nor the number of victims. Human nature as such is at stake…'[33] This radical evil cannot be grasped either by the philosophical tradition or by Christian theology. She continues, 'Therefore, we have nothing to fall back on in order to understand a phenomenon that nevertheless confronts us with its overpowering reality and breaks down all standards we know. There is only one thing that seems to be discernible: we may say that radical evil has emerged in connection with a system in which all men have become equally superfluous.'

She writes of the death camps, 'The insane mass manufacture of corpses is preceded by the historically and politically intelligible preparation of living corpses.' If, then, the mass murder perpetrated in the death camps lies beyond all possibility of historical or political explanation, we are able to grasp what made it possible. If the essence of totalitarianism for Arendt lies in its systematic assault upon human nature and human dignity, its condition of possibility is the emergence of 'rootless human masses' with little to lose and, consequently, little fear of death, either their own or that of others. In the Europe of that time millions had been made homeless and stateless. Political disintegration and mass unemployment had made millions 'economically superfluous and socially burdensome.' This state of 'worldlessness' [*Weltlosigkeit*] prepares the basis for totalitarianism.

---

[32] *OT*, p. 443.
[33] *OT*, pp. 458-459.

But Arendt does not pretend that this is the *cause* of radical evil. The evil she has in mind escapes all political, philosophical or theological categories, and cannot be rationalized.

Arendt's concept of total domination arises, then, out of the problem as outlined above. Faced with the irruption of an undeniable and unprecedented manifestation of evil which cannot be assimilated into and which therefore subverts the categories of the existing 'world', Arendt rejects the possibility of any rational solution of the problem by means of a theodicy, and refers us instead to a kind of demonic will released from any human limits or inhibitions, governed by an implacable *logos* the aim of which is the destruction of human being itself.

An essential feature of this argument is the claim that despite the cataclysmic defeat of Nazism the project of total domination *succeeded.* It succeeded because, although the concentration camps were overthrown and opened to the gaze of the world, the experiment 'proved', according to Arendt, what it set out to prove – a conclusion that must now somehow be assimilated into our knowledge – namely, that human dignity can be completely destroyed and man reduced to something lower than a beast. Man has surpassed what were previously held to be the limits of his world and demonstrated the power to destroy his own spirit. Seen in this light, the concentration camps mark the *beginning* of a new age.

Vasily Grossman in his essay 'The Hell of Treblinka', one of the first accounts in any language of the death camps, wrote:

> We must remember that Fascism and racism will emerge from this war not only with the bitterness of defeat but also with sweet memories of the ease with which it is possible to commit mass murder. It has turned out that it is really not so very difficult to kill entire nations. Ten small chambers – hardly

> enough space, if properly furnished, to stable a hundred horses – ten such chambers turned out to be enough to kill three million people.
>
> Killing turned out to be supremely easy – it does not entail any uncommon expenditure.
>
> It is possible to build five hundred such chambers in only a few days. This is no more difficult than constructing a five-storey building.
>
> It is possible to demonstrate with nothing more than a pencil that any large construction company with experience in the use of reinforced concrete can, in the course of six months and with a properly organized labour force, construct more than enough chambers to gas the entire population of the earth.[34]

Wolfgang Sofsky's justly renowned study of the organization and methods of the concentration camp is centred upon the concept of 'absolute power' [*Absolute Macht*], clearly a descendant of Arendt's 'total domination'.[35] But whereas Arendt's argument belongs to a realm that could be classified as political theology, the avowedly *sociological* character of Sofsky's study commits him to a 'scientific' approach, setting aside any search for historical meaning or philosophical interpretation as well, of course, of the concept of evil. He insists that since the camps were the product of human action they must be 'amenable to analysis and rational comprehension,' briefly dismissing the 'caveat of incomprehensibility' as 'a barrier erected to

---

[34] Vasily Grossman, *The Road: Short Fiction and Articles*, trans. Robert and Elizabeth Chandler, MacLehose Press, (London: Quercus, 2010), p. 179.
[35] Wolfgang Sofsky, *The Order of Terror: the Concentration Camp*, trans. William Templer, (Princeton: Princeton University Press, 1997). Arendt's influence is acknowledged by Sofsky, with certain reservations concerning the significance of work and ideology in the camps, p. 293, n. 5.

block perception.' In place of Arendt's 'fearful imagination', prepared to 'dwell on horrors,' Sofsky seeks to provide us with a clear and meticulous factual record.

Yet the limits of this scientific approach are immediately made clear as Sofsky tells us that the camps 'made obsolete the very concepts with which we attempt to make society intelligible: social action and reciprocity, work and power.'[36] What purchase one might ask can sociology have on a form of organization which is the very opposite of a society, a sociological account of the destruction of sociality? Sofsky also readily concedes the singularity of these events which cannot be compared with British concentration camps in the Boer War, nor even with previous instances of genocide, and opts instead for 'interpretive depth' or 'thick description' of these singular events. His use of the concept of 'absolute power' seems at once, however, to reassert the claims of sociological reason.

The paradoxical character of this concept is evident. It is, he states, a new kind of power, 'a power structure *sui generis*,' discontinuous with any other manifestation of power, involving a 'historical and anthropological rupture.'[37] The concentration camp, he claims, is not to be confused with any other form of the total institution where the aim of power is to create the totally disciplined individual. He explains:

> Absolute power as realized in the concentration camp differs from all this. Here, power does not shed its shackles until after all opponents have long since been vanquished. It does not forego violence, but liberates it from all inhibitions and impediments, intensifying it by organization. Where the terror

[36] Sofsky, p. 10.
[37] Sofsky, p. 16.

> of tyranny ends, it begins. Absolute power is not bent on achieving blind obedience or discipline, but desires to generate a universe of total uncertainty, one in which submissiveness is no shield against even worse outcomes...Terror dissolves the link between transgression and punitive sanction. It requires neither occasions nor reasons and has no interest in obligating itself by threat. Absolute power goes on a rampage whenever it so desires. It does not wish to limit freedom but to destroy it. It does not seek to guide action, but to demolish it. It drains human beings, depleting them by labor both useful and senseless. It sets economic goals from which it then breaks free. It liberates itself from ideological convictions after first having organized camp society in accordance with its ideological model of social classes. Even killing, that final reference point of all power, is not sufficient. Absolute power transforms the universal structures of human relatedness to the world: space and time, social relations, the connection with work, the relation to the self. It seizes on various elements and methods of traditional forms of power, combining and intensifying them, while casting off their instrumentality. In this way, it becomes a form of power of a distinctive, singular kind.[38]

Like Arendt, Sofsky claims to have discovered a kind of power which is non-instrumental; 'not a means to an end but an end in itself.' It seeks and requires no legitimation. 'Power would not be absolute if it had to justify itself.' He continues:

> Terror does not need to justify itself. Its basis is fear, an anxiety that it unceasingly generates. It is its own objective, self-

---

[38] Sofsky, pp. 17-18.

> contained. It proves itself by the act of its own exercise. And it remains effective by constant intensification, by self-exponentiation. Absolute power does not obey the pattern of of purposeful, result-oriented action. It is purposeless; not poesis, but negative praxis. Ideology here is not just superfluous, but obstructive. It ties power to certain aims, degrading it to a mere instrument. Terror that allowed itself to be guided by aims and purposes would by calculable. It would no longer be terror. To take recourse in ideology is a false interpretation *post festum*, nourished by the mistaken belief that there always has to be an intellectual reason, that everything has some historical meaning.

In dismissing the role of ideology Sofsky has clearly radicalized Arendt's argument even further. It was an essential element of Arendt's analysis of total domination that it involved the imposition of an 'ideological supersense' upon a recalcitrant reality, a ruthless and paranoid logic determined to make the world conform to its own 'key to history.' For Arendt it was part of the radical novelty of totalitarianism that it was driven by this logic, hence irreducible to any of the traditional political motivations, such as *libido dominandi*, self-interest or *ressentiment*. Sofsky, on the other hand, appears to regard this as a comforting, retrospective illusion, designed to restore sense where there is none. For him, in regard to those most Arendtian terms, *poesis* and *praxis*, absolute power becomes the very opposite of political action; that is, the exercise of a purely arbitrary and and destructive freedom in a rigidly demarcated and completely controlled space that is the opposite of political space.

Like Arendt he regards the concentration camp as a 'laboratory of violence,' and again, like Arendt, he argues that the aim of this violence was the complete dehumanization of the victim. The violence of the camps, he points out, cannot be explained as the violence of punishment or the calculated, purposeful technology of torture. It is rather to be explained through the concept of 'excess', but understood in a quite different way from Nemo and Levinas:

> Excess is not a punishment, not an instrument of punitive power. In any event, it seeks grounds and reasons after the fact. But excess provides the perpetrator with a distinctive sense of self-esteem. It vaults all internal and external barriers. By making the victim into a defenceless body and ultimately a nonreactive object, the culprits gain the certainty that they are capable of anything, any outrage. Excess is an act of uninhibited self-expansion, one that simultaneously extinguishes sociality. Cruelty wishes from its victims nothing further....Absolute power in action does not aim at subjugation. All it wishes is to achieve fear and terror for its own sake; all it seeks to demonstrate is how it can obliterate the human being as a personal and social being.[39]

As in the case of Arendt's concept of total domination, it appears to be true by definition that absolute power *succeeds*, a success made problematic by the fact that it is supposed to have no aims other than its own self-establishment. Sofsky writes, 'The strength of absolute power is manifested in the transformation and destruction of the human condition.' And, 'In sharp contrast with all earlier forms of power, absolute terror creates nothing. Its work is totally negative, a project of obliteration without trace. It realizes its freedom in the complete and total annihilation of the human being.'

The *Musselman* as the embodiment of evil

[39] Sofsky, pp. 23-24.

This work of annihilation is embodied in its extreme form in the figure of the *Musselman*, described by a number of camp survivors. Of the *Musselmänner*, the walking dead, Primo Levi write, 'They crowd my memory with their faceless presences, and if I could enclose all the evil of our time in one image, I would choose this image which is familiar to me: an emaciated man, with head dropped and shoulders curved, on whose face and in whose eyes not a trace of thought is to be seen.'[40]

Sofsky describes their corporeal state as follows:

> The mere external appearance of the *Musselmänner* bespoke profound dehumanisation. In a final stage of emaciation, their skeletons were enveloped by flaccid, parchmentlike sheaths of skin, edema had formed on their feet and thighs, their posterior muscles had collapsed. Their skulls seemed elongated; their noses dripped constantly, mucus running down their chins. Their eyeballs had sunk deep into their sockets; their gaze was glazed. Their limbs moved slowly, hesitantly, almost mechanically. They exuded a penetrating, acrid odor; sweat, urine, liquid feces trickled down their legs. The rags that covered their freezing frames were full of lice; their skin was covered with scabies. Most suffered from diarrhea. They ate anything they could lay their hands on – moldy bread, cheese wriggling with worms, raw bits of turnip, garbage fished from the bins.[41]

---

[40] Primo Levi, *If This is a Man and The Truce*, trans. Stuart Woolf, (London: Abacus, 2007), p. 96. The term was camp argot, of uncertain origin, but possibly a reference to the alleged fatalism of Muslims.
[41] Sofsky, p. 199.

These men, whom Levi also calls 'the drowned', were, he emphasizes, by no means exceptional. They were simply those who through incapacity or misfortune failed to acquire the skills of survival quickly enough; thereafter, 'they followed the slope down to the bottom, like streams that run down to the sea.' They were 'an anonymous mass, continually renewed and always identical, of non-men who march and labour in silence, the divine spark dead within them, already too empty to really suffer.'

In Sofsky's view, 'The *Musselman* embodies the anthropological meaning of absolute power in an especially radical form.' Despised by their captors, shunned by their fellow-prisoners who could not bear to look at them, and lost to themselves, they represent the extreme point of human misery. However, Sofsky immediately concedes that these, the most extreme victims of absolute power, were beyond the reach of power understood in its usual sense. As a result of their utterly degraded state, 'Orders accomplished nothing. Even violence fell flat; it was ineffective. The passivity of the *Musselman* was an insult to power.'[42] The most extreme manifestation of power thus at the same time revealed its limit in these, perhaps the *least* tractable inmates in the camps.

The following incident, recorded by a survivor, may serve to illustrate the point:

> The SS man went past slowly, and looked in the direction of the *Musselman* who was coming straight at him. All of us squinted to the left to see what would happen. And this creature bereft of will and thought, slouching along in his clattering wooden clogs, walked right into the SS man. The SS man shouted and

[42] Sofsky, p. 204.

> struck him over the head with his riding whip. The *Musselman* stopped, not quite sure what was happening. When he'd been given a second and third blow with the whip for not removing his cap, he shit his pants (he had diarrhea). When the SS man saw the black spot that was spreading round the wooden clogs of the *Musselman*, he was beside himself with rage. He pounced on him, kicking him in the abdomen, and after he lay there on the ground in his own excrement, he kicked the man's head and thorax. The *Musselman* did not resist. A few more kicks and he was dead.[43]

On the one hand, this may certainly be considered a manifestation of power, insofar as the SS man took a human life without a second thought or the possibility of retribution. But isn't it true that his rage was provoked by the fact that his nameless victim had been reduced to a state in which he was incapable of either fear or obedience? Although Sofsky states that it is not the aim of absolute power to instil discipline and obedience, is there not a limit to power here, such that we cannot speak of *absolute* power? The 'excess' which Sofsky describes as the certainty that one is capable of anything, of 'uninhibited self-expansion,' is clearly a version of Arendt's characterization of the radical evil for which 'everything is possible,' but, at the same time, this also threatens to exceed the limits which enable the political and sociological functions of power. It may be that the fundamental difficulty here is the impossibility of encompassing the ideas of absolute power or total domination, which are founded upon the notion of pure evil – evil for its own sake – within the categories of social theory. If, as Arendt frequently warned, the introduction of the absolute, either of good or of evil, 'spells doom to

---

[43] Testimony quoted by Sofsky, p. 330, n. 11.

everyone when it is introduced into the political realm,'[44] might not the same be said of its introduction into political theory?

Even more fundamentally, there is a problem with the idea that man is capable of attaining the absolute. It is true that camp survivors have often written in this way. Primo Levi wrote that the experience of the camps 'would prove that man, the human species – we, in short – were potentially able to construct an infinite enormity of pain, and that pain is the only force that is created from nothing, without cost and without effort. It is enough not to see, not to listen, not to act.' Levi seems to suggest that the age of man, when man finally frees himself from God, and manifests his own power to create a world *ex nihilo*, is the age in which man becomes capable of subjecting himself to an infinite torment. The essential object of man's newly won and infinitely destructive power proves to be himself.

Any suggestion that the camps manifested man's absolute power over his fellow man must also deal with the issue of resistance. Understandably, Wiesel and Levi do not want us to think of the death camps as a stage for heroic acts. Auschwitz and Treblinka were not battlegrounds but sites of industrial genocide. Nevertheless there were, as is well known, uprisings and acts of resistance, which again, set a limit upon power. If the language of heroism is inappropriate how can we describe, for example, the actions of one such as Mala Zimetbaum who, sentenced to death for her attempted escape, slashed her wrists on the gallows of Auschwitz and, shouting defiance, sprayed blood on the faces of her executioners, before being beaten to death?[45]

---

[44] Hannah Arendt, *On Revolution*, (London: Penguin, 1973), p. 84.
[45] The incident is described in Tzvetan Todorov, *Facing the Extreme: Moral Life in the Concentration Camps*, (New York: Metropolitan Books, 1996), pp. 63-64.

Bare life and the limits of testimony

'Absolute power' may also be said to encounter a limit in the testimony of survivors such as Wiesel and Levi, in whom this experience of evil is, with the utmost difficulty, lived through, communicated, and somehow assimilated into a changed understanding of the world. But although this may be true for us, it raised the greatest difficulties for the survivors themselves. Just as the victim asks, 'Why is this happening to me?', the same question is asked by the survivor. Dismissing the idea that he survived because he was somehow touched by grace, Levi writes:

> Such an opinion seemed monstrous to me. It pained me as when one touches an exposed nerve, and kindled the doubt I spoke of before. I might be alive in the place of another, at the expense of another; I might have usurped, that is, in fact, killed. The 'saved' of the Lager were not the best, those predestined to do good, the bearers of a message. What I had seen and lived through proved the exact contrary. Preferably, the worst survived, the selfish, the violent, the insensitive, the collaborators of the 'grey zones', the spies. It was not a certain rule (there were none, nor are there certain rules in human matters), but it was nevertheless a rule. I felt innocent, yes, but enrolled among the saved and therefore in permanent search of a justification in my own eyes and those of others. The worst survived – that is the fittest; the best all died.[46]

---

[46] Primo Levi, *The Drowned and the Saved*, trans. Raymond Rosenthal, (London: Abacus, 2013), pp. 62-63.

This is Levi's darkest thought, written shortly before his suicide. The survivors, he states, those who have testified, are not the true witnesses. They were in no sense 'chosen' as the bearers of truth and, Levi suggests, the full truth may never be known. The survivors are 'not only an exiguous but also an anomalous minority: we are those who by their prevarications or abilities or good luck did not touch bottom.' Those who 'saw the Gorgon' bore no witness. Only the *Musselmänner* would be able to convey to us the full depth of the evil they encountered, but 'they were struck dumb.'

Giorgio Agamben has drawn attention to the fact that the *Musselman* was hardly mentioned in historical studies on the destruction of European Jewry and suggests that only now is the figure of the *Musselman* starting to become visible. The paradigm of extermination in Holocaust studies is now coming to be accompanied by another paradigm, making it even more atrocious:

> Before being a death camp, Auschwitz is the site of an experiment that remains unthought today, an experiment beyond life and death in which the Jew is transformed into a *Muselmann* and the human being into a non-human. And we will not understand what Auschwitz is if we do not first understand who or what the *Muselmann* is – if we do not learn to gaze with him upon the Gorgon.[47]

The *Musselman*, according to Agamben, is 'not only or not so much a limit between life and death; rather, he marks the threshold between the human and the inhuman.' There is a point at which human beings cease to be human and this point is the *Musselman*. Hence the title of

---

[47] Giorgio Agamben, *Remnants of Auschwitz: The Witness and the Archive*, trans. Daniel Heller-Roazen, (New York: Zone Books, 2002), p. 52.

Levi's book, *If This is a Man* [*Se questo è un uomo*]. For Agamben this is not merely a question of the loss of human dignity, decency or a sense of shame, since these had to be abandoned by everyone who entered the camps. Rather, Agamben argues, 'the *Muselmann* 'is the site of an experiment in which morality and humanity themselves are called into question. The *Muselmann* is a limit figure of a special kind, in which not only categories such as dignity and respect but even the very idea of an ethical limit lose their meaning.'[48] Consequently, he goes on, 'if there is a zone of the human in which these concepts make no sense, then they are not genuine ethical concepts, for no ethics can claim to exclude a part of humanity, no matter how unpleasant or difficult that humanity is to see.'

In Auschwitz human beings were reduced to 'bare life', which 'itself is the only norm' and is 'absolutely immanent.'

> The good that the survivors were able to save from the camp – if there is any sense in speaking of a "good" here – is therefore not dignity. On the contrary, the atrocious news that the survivors carry from the camp to the land of human beings is precisely that it is possible to lose dignity and decency beyond imagination, that there is still life in the most extreme degradation. And this new knowledge now becomes that touchstone by which to judge and measure all morality and all dignity. The *Muselmann*, who is its most extreme expression, is the guard on the threshold of a new ethics, an ethics of a form of life that begins where dignity ends.[49]

[48] Agamben, p. 63.
[49] Agamben, p, 69.

Auschwitz teaches us that 'humans bear within themselves the mark of the inhuman, that their spirit contains at its very centre the wound of non-spirit, non-human chaos atrociously consigned to its own being capable of anything.' The *Musselman* appeared as both the being whose life is not truly life and whose death is not truly death, but only the production of a corpse. 'The *Muselmann* is the non-human who obstinately appears as human; he is the human that cannot be told apart from the inhuman.'[50]

Agamben seeks to bring together the insights of Arendt and Foucault, in that Foucault, while he grasped the nature of modern politics as biopolitics, failed to develop an analysis of totalitarian states, and Arendt's approach, for its part, was limited by its lack of a biopolitical perspective. She failed to see that 'Only because politics in our age had been entirely transformed into biopolitics was it possible for politics to be constituted as totalitarian politics to a degree hitherto unknown.'[51]

> Insofar as its inhabitants were stripped of every political status and wholly reduced to bare life, the camp was .... the most absolute biopolitical space ever to have been realized, in which power confronts nothing but pure life, without any mediation. This is why the camp is the very paradigm of political space at the point at which politics becomes biopolitics and *homo sacer* is virtually confused with the citizen. The correct question to pose concerning the horrors committed in the camps is, therefore, not the hypocritical one of how crimes of such atrocity could be committed against human beings. It would be

---

[50] Agamben, p. 82.

[51] Giorgio Agamben, *Homo Sacer: Sovereign Power and Bare Life*, trans. Daniel Heller-Roazen, (Stanford: Stanford University Press, 1998), p. 120.

> more honest and, above all, more useful to investigate carefully the juridical procedures and deployments of power by which human beings could be so completely deprived of their rights and prerogatives that no act committed against them could appear any longer as a crime. (At this point, in fact, everything had truly become possible.)[52]

While Arendt understands what happened in the camps as the intrusion of 'a radical evil, previously unknown to us,' which renders all previously established moral and political categories senseless, and inaugurates 'modern politics', Agamben approaches the concentration camp through the juridico-political concept of the 'state of exception' or 'state of emergency' [*Ausnahmezustand*], as theorized by the Nazi jurist, Carl Schmitt.[53] The first concentration camps in Germany were, as Agamben points out, established by Social-Democratic governments, interning thousands of communist militants during states of emergency that lasted for up to five months. When the Nazis took power, however, all the civil liberties guaranteed by the constitution were indefinitely suspended and remained so until the end of the Nazi regime. Agamben writes, 'Insofar as the state of exception is "willed," it inaugurates a new juridico-political paradigm in which the norm becomes indistinguishable from the exception. The camp is thus the structure in which the state of exception – the possibility of deciding on which founds sovereign power – is realized *normally*.'[54] The Nazi concept of race, framed within the concept of the political subject as a biopolitical body, operated as the site of sovereign

---

[52] *Homo Sacer*, p. 171.
[53] In particular in 'Staat, Bewegung, Volk', in Carl Schmitt, *Die Dreigliederung der politischen Einheit*, Hanseatische Verlagsanstalt, 1933.
[54] *Homo Sacer*, p. 170.

decision within 'the absolute indistinction of fact and law.'[55] For Agamben, the concentration camp is the realm where 'everything is possible' because of the biopolitical juridico-political foundation of the Nazi state upon which the camps were established. As Diels, the head of the Gestapo, stated, 'Neither an order nor an instruction exists for the origin of the camps: they were not instituted; one day they were there.'[56]

Arendt and the banality of evil

In Arendt's report on the Eichmann trial, *Eichmann in Jerusalem: the Banality of Evil,* she appears to develop a quite new and different concept of evil. This conception is perhaps best illustrated in the following passage:

> The trouble with Eichmann was precisely that so many were like him, and that the many were neither perverted nor sadistic, that they were, and still are, terribly and terrifyingly normal. From the point of view of our legal institutions and of our moral standards of judgment, this normality was much more terrifying than all the atrocities put together, for it implied – as had been said over and over again by the defendants and their counsels – that this new type of criminal, who is in actual fact *hostis generis humani*, commits his crimes under circumstances that make it well-nigh impossible for him to know or to feel that he is doing wrong.[57]

[55] As in Hitler's well-known statement, '*I* decide who is a Jew.'
[56] Quoted Agamben, *Homo Sacer*, p. 169.
[57] Hannah Arendt, *Eichmann in Jerusalem: the Banality of Evil*, (New York: Viking Press, 1965), p. 276.

In the *Postscript*, however, explaining the title of the book, she writes, 'when I speak of the banality of evil, I do so only on the strictly factual level, pointing to a phenomenon which stared one in the face at the trial.' If this were true, it would have been an extremely loose use of language for a philosopher of her stature. That she intended something more became clear in an exchange with Scholem, who had criticized the notion of the banality of evil as inferior to the concept of radical evil.

Arendt responded:

> You are quite right: I changed my mind and do no longer speak of "radical evil"...It is indeed my opinion now that evil is never "radical," that it is only extreme, and that it possesses neither depth nor any demonic dimension. It can overgrow and lay waste the world because it spreads like a fungus on the surface. It is "thought-defying," as I said, because thought tries to reach some depth, to go to the roots, and the moment it concerns itself with evil, it is frustrated because there is nothing. That is its "banality." Only the good has depth and can be radical.[58]

As Arendt subsequently made clear, what concerned her was the question of how to approach the problem of evil in an entirely secular setting. Villa suggests that in her attempted 'exorcism', there is a denial that, as Villa puts it, 'behind monstrous deeds there lies a monstrous or transhuman doer, a force or agency that transcends

---

[58] Quoted Dana R. Villa, *Politics, Philosophy, Terror: Essays on the Thought of Hannah Arendt*, (Princeton: Princeton University Press, 1999), pp. 55-56. The exchange with Scholem is to be found in *The Jew as Pariah*, ed. Ron H. Feldman, (New York: Grove Press, 1978), pp. 250-251.

human individuals or which expresses some deep, subterranean current of the West.'[59] In contrast to the radical, unfathomable evil that produces the infinite expansionism of total domination, banal evil 'spreads like a fungus.' It does not, it seems, possess the will, but rather stems from a contagion of bureaucratic 'thoughtlessness', providing nothing for authentic 'thinking' to grasp.

The same voice can be head in Sofsky when he writes, 'The face of modern systemic terror is not stamped by the all-powerful and inviolable master, but by the unbridled actions of the sedulous servants of power. It is an inconspicuous face, quite mean and shabby, without the grimace of wild frenzy, the ecstasies of brutality, the passions of sovereignty.'[60] It is, in short, the face of the Reich's faithful servant, Eichmann. There were, he assures us, 'no demonic monsters at work here, just simple supervisors and torturers (sic). For that reason the metaphor of hell is misplaced; it is misleading in the attempt to arrive at an appropriate notion of the radical transformation of power.'

Sofsky similarly invites us to analyse the work of the death factories in the terms of modern organization theory, of integrated work processes and sequences, exemplified in Auschwitz where a 'virtually trouble-free assembly line' was created, such that during the peak period in the summer of 1944, some 24,000 persons a day were killed and burned. 'While the last batch of the dead was burning down to ashes in the ovens or on the pyres, the next batch was already being slaughtered.'[61] While absolute power reigns supreme, its human agents quietly and efficiently perform their tasks.

But absolute power should not, Sofsky argues, be confused with the aims and objectives of the top organizational echelon of the SS. 'As in

---

[59] Villa, p. 50.
[60] Sofsky, p. 279.
[61] Sofsky, p. 262.

any social system, organization here was not a means to an end, but a dynamic field of action. The self-preservation of the system, the processes of power and terror, often had little if anything to do with the plans of the terror managers.'[62] Rather than understanding the death camp as a rational system, Sofsky's method of 'thick description' seeks to examine the dynamic process in which, out of varying interpretations of actions and situations, the processes and structures that crystallized as absolute power emerged.

While Sofsky seems to eliminate the concept of evil altogether, Arendt's later approach retains the concept of evil in order to secularize it as 'thoughtlessness', the absence from the modern world of *thinking* in the deep, Heideggerian sense. As in the Augustinian conception of evil, evil is understand as lack or privation, and the failure of the good to take action is what allows evil to triumph. Evil is retained as a concept but normalized, indeed *banalized*, from which it follows that the problem of evil as I have understood it here disappears. When evil has descended into ordinary, everyday life and become routinized it is no longer capable of provoking fundamental questioning about the meaning of existence.

Arendt's banalization of evil through the figure of Eichmann bears a curious resemblance to Ivan Karamazov's 'nightmare' in which he is visited by the devil and is profoundly disappointed by this 'stupid and vulgar' devil, who explains that when he assumes human form he 'suffers the consequences.'[63] Ivan's intellectual pride is wounded by this encounter which he at first takes to be a projection of the worst part of himself, but then insists that it must be a lesser devil and not Satan himself. Arendt draws the opposite conclusion, deciding that, Eichmann, this none too bright, former travelling salesman, a 'leaf in

---

[62] Sofsky, p. 13.

[63] Dostoyevsky, Vol. II, pp. 750-751.

the whirlwind of time,' his mind full of empty clichés, was indeed the unimpressive embodiment of evil. His embodiment is described in detail: 'medium-sized, slender, middle-aged, with receding hair, ill-fitting teeth, and nearsighted eyes, who throughout the trial keeps craning his scraggy neck toward the bench (not once does he face the audience), and who desperately and for the most part successfully maintains his self-control despite the nervous tic to which his mouth must have become subject long before this trial started.'[64]

The enigmatic nature of evil is such that even those who have studied or encountered it most closely find it strangely elusive and liable to disappear under their gaze. Was Eichmann merely a dim-witted transport official who happened to be in the service of a criminal state? The court psychiatrists all pronounced him sane. So where was the evil *in* him? But this is perhaps because we are looking in the wrong place. If we wish to form an *image* of evil then we find it not in the shape of demons and monsters but in the shape of the victim. As Levi observed, all the evil of his time was visible in the form of the *Musselman*. This was the true embodiment of evil. All of those who participated in reducing human beings to that condition acted in the service of evil, whether torturers or transport officials, whether sadists or those who chose to look the other way.

Questions of responsibility and guilt can, of course, under normal circumstances, be settled without reference to the concept of evil. The problem of evil arose in connection with the Eichmann trial because of the difficulty of making sense of events which threw into question the established moral and legal categories of the modern world. Arendt could hardly have made her 'report' without raising this issue. How can we then read *Eichmann in Jerusalem*, as Villa recommends, as

---

[64] *Eichmann in Jerusalem*, p. 5.

merely a judgment on the guilt of a particular individual, without grasping this dimension of the problem?[65]

Evil and obedience to authority

The Eichmann case, in particular, drew attention to that dimension of evil, first opened up by Rousseau, which originates in socialization, and here socialization as producing an unquestioning obedience to authority. While for Arendt the banalization of evil is understood in terms of the manner in which modern bureaucratic-technical rationality has eliminated the roots of authentic 'thinking', the banalization of evil can also be conceived as a sociological reduction of the problem of evil. Zygmunt Baumann, attaching considerable weight to the experiments conducted by Milgram and Zimbardo,[66] in which many of the participants showed themselves willing to inflict what they believed to be extreme pain upon helpless victims, considers that the most significant conclusion to be drawn from them is that 'cruelty correlates with certain patterns of social interaction much more closely than it does with personality features or other individual idiosyncrasies of the perpetrators.'[67] Bauman underlines the ease with which most people will demonstrate cruelty or moral blindness in the presence of a legitimizing authority. If cruelty is in this way socially determined, what is more difficult to explain, Baumann argues, is the capacity of some individuals to obey the call of conscience and to find

[65] Villa, pp. 58-60.

[66] Milgram's experiments, which are open to a number of criticisms, were conducted at Yale University between 1960 and 1963. See Stanley Milgram, *Obedience to Authority*, (London: Pinter & Martin, 1997).

[67] Zygmunt Bauman, *Modernity and the Holocaust*, (Cambridge: Polity Press, 1991), p. 166.

the courage to resist authority. Where immorality is socially produced the capacity to resist evil is undetermined, individual and unique.

Bauman, like many others, thinks of the Holocaust as a dramatic event on such a scale that it has caused a paradigm shift in our ethical thinking, and a challenge to sociological theory:

> *In the aftermath of the Holocaust, legal practice, and thus also moral theory, faced the possibility that morality may manifest itself in insubordination towards socially upheld principles, and in an action openly defying social solidarity consensus.*[68]

For sociology, he writes, the idea of pre-social grounds of moral behaviour is challenging. Nazism opened the question of the moral responsibility for resisting socialization in the most forceful way and showed that the human ability to tell right from wrong is not grounded in the (Durkheimian) *conscience collective* of society. The origin of the moral capacity must, Bauman argues, be sought in the realm of *being-with-others*, in a Levinasian pre-cognitive, 'inter-human', togetherness with the other, not in the *societal* sphere. The ethical is here understood as a primary structure of inter-subjectivity, not as a product of society.

It is a sense of (non-reciprocal) responsibility towards others that constitutes the individual as a moral subject, and that sense of responsibility towards other is reduced wherever separation replaces proximity. Bauman points to a growing consensus among historians that '*the preparation of the Holocaust required the neutralization of ordinary German attitudes toward the Jew, not their mobilization.*'[69] While there was widespread support for anti-Jewish legislation there

---

[68] Baumann, p. 177. Italics in original.
[69] Bauman, p. 185. Italics in original.

was little support for anti-Jewish violence of the kind practised by the SA. The *Kristallnacht*, the only officially planned large-scale pogrom against the Jews, was found by Nazi propagandists to be counter-productive and failed to incite the general public to anti-semitic violence. The 'Jew-next-door' was viewed with a measure of responsibility while Jews in the abstract were not. The wanton destruction of property was especially condemned by German public opinion.

Because of this the Holocaust could be accomplished only by 'isolating the machinery of murder from the sphere in which the moral drives remained active.' The 'Final Solution' had to become a rational bureaucratic-technical task, carried out by experts. But this required the 'depersonalization' of the Jew. Jews had to be systematically excluded from the 'universe of obligations.' This involved a progressive process of definition, exclusion, concentration, exploitation, starvation and, ultimately, annihilation, in which each step rendered rational the next step, even though the final end was not the guide. The essential conditions which made the Holocaust possible were the social production of distance, the substitution of technical for moral responsibility (problem-solving), and the technology of separation and segregation.

Christopher Browning, also drawing upon Milgram's experiments, similarly argues that obedience to authority made it possible for 'ordinary men' to commit atrocious crimes. His research, centred upon battalion 101 of the *Ordnungspolizei*, mostly family men whose average age was thirty-nine and 'had known political standards and moral norms other than those of the Nazis.[70] Drawn from the Hamburg area, not known for its sympathy to the National Socialists, they were

[70] Christopher R. Browning, *Ordinary Men: Reserve Police Battalion 101 and the Final Solution in Poland*, (London: Penguin, 1998), p. 48.

mainly working-class, poorly educated and had only minimal training or indoctrination.

Browning describes vividly, from historical records, how battalion 101 were driven to the Polish village of Józefów at dawn and informed of their task, which was to round up and escort all male Jews of working age to the work camps in Lublin and to shoot all the women, children and the elderly. As Major Trapp gave the men their orders, he wept and offered exemption to any man who felt unable to carry out the task. Some 10 or 12 took up the offer, and in the course of the executions a number of men asked to be reassigned or simply fled into the forest. Nevertheless, some 1500 Jews were shot that day, 80-90% of the men in the battalion taking part in the killing. Most of them had never fired a shot at a human being before and, despite instruction on how to kill efficiently by the battalion doctor, they frequently blew off the entire skullcap of their victims, covering themselves in blood, bone splinters and brains. The men returned to their barracks, 'depressed, angered, embittered, and shaken,' making considerable use of the free alcohol provided.[71]

The men who exempted themselves, with one exception, did not appeal to principles, but to 'weak nerves' or such, thereby not challenging their 'stronger' comrades, who 'had the stomach for it.' The largest group who carried out the killings described it as 'unpleasant work' but did not reflect upon it morally. Browning offers a multicausal sociological explanation of their motivation including conformity, peer pressure, and deference to authority. Coercion is ruled out since there is no recorded case of anyone suffering serious punishment for refusing to carry out such 'executions'. The *Hilfswillige*, on the other hand, recruited from Ukrainian, Latvian and Lithuanian POW camps and trained by the SS proved much more

[71] Browning, p. 69.

enthusiastic killers of Jews than these ordinary Germans, and where possible, mass killing was deputized to them. An exception was one Lieutenant Gnade who quickly degenerated into a drunken, brutal and sadistic killer who, by his second mission, forced elderly Jews to crawl around on the ground by their mass grave while being beaten with clubs.[72] The *cruelty* manifested by this individual was clearly the exception.

As mass killing became more organized the men were more often used to perform 'round-up' and deportation operations without any evidence of moral anxiety as they became separated from killing tasks. Organization was improved both to make the killing machine more efficient and to reduce the psychological burden upon the perpetrators, no longer *directly* confronted with questions of responsibility. Because the genocide was carried out in the main by 'ordinary', civilized, twentieth-century men and women there was a compelling imperative to make the killing as 'clean' and 'detached' as possible. Auschwitz was created to save such 'scruples'. But, paradoxically, Auschwitz is all the more shocking because of its technological character, a product of the same 'civilized' sensibility and the world we inhabit.

The banality of evil thesis and the attempt to explain the Holocaust in terms of bureaucratic rationality or uncritical obedience to authority have come under attack from Daniel Goldhagen's 'intentionalist' argument that they fail to grasp what is most essential, namely the malevolent intent of the perpetrators, which, in the case of the Holocaust, he attributes to the murderous anti-Semitism of German cultural history and its hold over the 'ordinary men' of German society. As he puts it, 'Comprehension and explanation of the perpetration of the Holocaust .... requires an explanation of the

[72] Browning, p. 83.

Germans' drive to kill the Jews.'[73] For Goldhagen the banality of evil thesis completely fails to explain the manner in which the virulent and deeply ingrained anti-Semitism of German society and of Nazi ideology in particular produced, among large sections of the German population, a freely chosen 'willingness to kill' Jews and the extraordinary degree of zeal and cruelty he claims they employed in doing so.[74] The *evil* of the Holocaust would seem to be firmly placed here, among the German people of the Third Reich who, we are told, were *not like us*. We must not assume, he warns, that they shared *our* values and sensibilities, but study them with 'anthropological' detachment.

Goldhagen's approach has led Browning to respond by accusing him of dehumanizing the perpetrators and thereby making it impossible for readers of his book to ask themselves, 'What would I have done in the situation in which the perpetrators found themselves?' Goldhagen's Manichean stance, by positivizing, particularizing, and situating evil in the will of the perpetrators obscures the true character of evil as a universal issue for human existence. It would be reassuring Browning writes, to think that only the Germans at a particular historical moment were capable of such atrocities, but he responds:

> I fear that we live in a world in which war and racism are ubiquitous, in which the powers of government mobilization and legitimization are powerful and increasing, in which a sense of of personal responsibility is increasingly attenuated by

[73] Daniel Jonah Goldhagen, *Hitler's Willing Executioners: Ordinary Germans and the Holocaust*, (London: Abacus, 1977), p. 6. Italics in the original.

[74] Daniel Jonah Goldhagen, 'The Evil of Banality', *The New Republic*, July 13-20, 1992.

> specialization and bureaucratization, and in which the peer group exerts tremendous pressures on behaviour and sets moral norms. In such a world, I fear modern governments that wish to commit mass murder will seldom fail in their efforts for being unable to induce "ordinary men" to become their "willing executioners."[75]

While the capacity of human beings to inflict suffering upon their fellow human beings is undeniable and daily confirmed, and political authorities are often responsible for such actions, social pressures and conformity to norms do not provide us with an adequate explanation when evil makes its appearance in the political realm. Nor can we explain the atrocities perpetrated by the Nazis by the fact that for historical and cultural reasons the Germans are 'not like us.'

Levinas, members of whose own family were killed in Auschwitz, has insisted that the 'failure of morality' in the twentieth century was not confined to Auschwitz or to the German people. It was also the century of Hiroshima, the Gulag, and Cambodia. But Levinas writes, 'the Holocaust of the Jewish people under the reign of Hitler seems to us the paradigm of gratuitous human suffering, where evil appears in its diabolical horror.' In Auschwitz the death of God took on the 'signification of a quasi-empirical fact.'[76]

Not only does Levinas state that all the dead of the Gulag and other places of torture 'are present when one speaks of Auschwitz',[77] but his book *Otherwise than Being* is dedicated '*To the memory of those who were closest among the six million assassinated by the National Socialists, and of the millions and millions of all confessions and all*

[75] Browning, 'Afterword', p. 223.
[76] 'Useless Suffering', p. 162.
[77] 'Useless Suffering', p. 167.

nations, victims of the same hatred of the other man, of the same anti-semitism.'[78] The exceptional character of the Holocaust appears to be simultaneously both affirmed and denied. 'Useless suffering' was not confined to the Jewish people, but the Holocaust is the 'paradigm' through which all other instances of useless suffering are to be understood. Similarly, the murderous ideologies which have claimed the lives of so many others are all named by Levinas as 'anti-semitism', as if it were the essence of all such ideologies, and the Jews were the essential victims.

In the twentieth century, he argues, suffering and evil were deliberately imposed by 'a reason become political and detached from ethics.' If God died in Auschwitz, ethics must not also fall victim to the experience of Nazism. Unlike Agamben, Levinas does not believe that genuine acknowledgement of the Holocaust involves the recognition that ethics has foundered and that we have entered a new form of (sub)human life in which dignity and respect have lost their meaning, since we have proved ourselves capable of inflicting and bearing limitless cruelty. He insists that ethics must continue unchanged, since 'when the perishability of so many values is revealed, all human dignity consists in believing in their return.'[79] This is surely true, but it must also be coupled with the belief that it is possible to recreate a politics which once again has an authentic ethical foundation.

---

[78] Emmanuel Levinas, *Otherwise than Being, or, Beyond Essence*, trans. Alphonso Lingis, (Pittsburgh: Duquesne University Press, 1999).
[79] Emmanuel Levinas, *Proper Names*, trans. Michael B. Smith, (London: Continuum, 1996), p. 121.

From Hegel's rabble to Marx's proletariat

In *Less Than Nothing* (2012)[1] Zizek argues that, although Hegel fails to see it, his unresolved difficulty with the problem of the 'rabble' [*Pöbel*] in the *Philosophy of Right* has consequences which bear upon the very foundations of Hegel's 'rational State'. The Hegelian rabble is also considered by Zizek as a precursor of Marx's subsequent concept of the proletariat. Like Marx, drawing upon the writings of the Scottish political economists, Hegel reveals in the *Philosophy of Right* a deep concern that the form of modern civil society, in which the division of labour and the system of needs both involve processes of universalization, brings about great increases in the accumulation of wealth, but, at the same time, intensifies 'the *dependence* and *want* of the class which is tied to such work; this in turn leads to an inability to feel and enjoy the wider freedoms, and particularly the spiritual advantages, of civil society.'[2]

The domination of the market economy, susceptible to rapid and unpredictable periods of both growth and recession, coupled with the specialization of labour, leaves the class that depends for its livelihood upon the sale of its labour in a position where 'a large mass' can suddenly fall into poverty. Significantly, however, Hegel maintains,

---

[1] Slavoj Zizek, *Less Than Nothing: Hegel and the Shadow of Dialecical Materialism*, (London and New York: Verso, 2012).
[2] G. W. F. Hegel, *Elements of the Philosophy of Right*, ed. Allen Wood, trans. H. B. Nisbet, (Cambridge: Cambridge University Press, 1991), §243.

'Poverty itself does not reduce people to a rabble; a rabble is created only by the disposition [*Gesinnung*] associated with poverty, by inward rebellion [*Empörung*] against the rich, against society, the government, etc.' Those who are, in this way, made dependent upon contingency, 'become frivolous and lazy,' this 'giving rise to the evil that the rabble do not have sufficient honour [*Ehre*] to gain their livelihood through their own work, yet claim that they have a right [*Recht*] to receive their own livelihood.' In civil society, hardship 'at once assumes the form of a wrong [*Unrecht*] inflicted on this or that class.'[3] The problem of how to remedy this situation, Hegel observes, 'is one which agitates and torments modern societies especially.'

Concerning Hegel's treatment of this intractable 'problem', Zizek writes:

> Hegel fails to take note of how the rabble, in its very status as the destructive excess of the social totality, its "part of no-part," is the "reflexive determination" of the totality as such, the immediate embodiment of its universality, the particular element in the guise of which the social totality encounters itself among its elements, and as such, the key constituent of its identity...If Hegel had seen the universal dimension of the rabble, he would have invented the symptom (as Marx – who saw in the proletariat the embodiment of the deadlocks of the existing society, the universal class – did. In other words, what makes the notion of the rabble symptomatic is that it describes a necessarily produced "irrational" excess of the modern rational state, a group of people for whom there is no place within the organized totality, although they formally belong to it – as such, they perfectly exemplify the category of singular

[3] *PR* §244.

universality (a singular which directly gives body to a universality, bypassing the mediation through the particular.)'[4]

The status of the 'rabble', then, is to be explained by means of Hegelian 'reflexive determination' and 'singular universality', Marx's concept of the proletariat, Rancière's 'part of no-part', and the Lacanian 'symptom'. The concept of reflexive determination [*Reflexionsbestimmungen*] is probably best recognized from Marx's reference in *Capital*[5] where he explains how, in exchange-value, a social relation established between two commodities, a commodity B comes to act as an equivalent for commodity A insofar as it functions as the form of appearance of the value of A, i.e. as a mirror in which the value of A is reflected back to it. Yet, mysteriously, this *relation*, in which B is a 'reflexive determination' of A, appears to exist *in* the commodity B, in an inverted (*alienated*) form, as the *property* of direct exchangeability, in a manner similar to its possession of physical properties.

To explain this relation further, Marx provides as an example: 'one man is king only because other men stand in the relation of subjects to him. They, on the other hand, imagine that they are subjects because he is king.' In this example of reflexive determination, then, an actual relation is presented as immediately embodied in its opposite – the predicate exchanging places with the subject. Zizek, however, has elsewhere criticized Marx's account of this phenomenon for not going far enough. If we take Hegel's controversial and much maligned philosophical legitimation of constitutional monarchy in the *Philosophy of Right*, Zizek has argued that the issue is not that of the reification or 'fetishistic illusion' of the monarch as incarnating the

---

[4] *LTN*, p. 431.

[5] Karl Marx, *Capital* Vol. 1, (London: Penguin), p. 149 fn.

state, requiring only a simple (Feuerbachian) inversion. Hegel's reflexive determination must instead be understood in *performative* terms: '*the very unity of our state, that which the king "embodies," actualizes itself only in the body of a king.*'[6] Only from the (limited) standpoint of the understanding is the king merely symbolic or representative. Nevertheless, his role is best accomplished the fewer his abilities, since it requires him not to *do* anything (except sign his name): it is simply to *be* king; the singular universal.

The essentials of Zizek's analysis can in fact be traced back to the opening chapter of *The Sublime Object of Ideology* (1989), entitled 'How Did Marx Invent the Symptom?', except that there Zizek appears to simply echo Marx's 'fetishistic misrecognition' analysis according to which the appearance of 'being-a-king' as a natural property of an individual is an ideological effect of (feudal) social relations.[7] With the transition from feudalism to capitalism, Zizek states, fetishism shifts from inter-subjective relations to relations between commodities:

> This is why one has to look for the discovery of the symptom in the way Marx conceived of the passage from feudalism to capitalism. With the establishment of bourgeois society, the relations of domination and servitude are *repressed*: formally, we are apparently concerned with free subjects whose interpersonal relations are discharged of all fetishism; the repressed truth – that of the persistence of domination and servitude – emerges in a symptom which subverts the

[6] Slavoj Zizek, *The Parallax View,* (Cambridge, Mass. and London: MIT Press, 2009), p. 108.
[7] Slavoj Zizek, *The Sublime Object of Ideology*, (London and New York: Verso, 1989), p. 25.

ideological appearance of equality, freedom and so on. This symptom, the point of emergence about the truth of social relations is precisely the 'social relation between things.

In the final pages of *The Sublime Object*, however, Zizek returns to consider 'reflection' in more detail, and, in particular, the passage from external to determinate reflection, rejecting the view that this simply requires a Feuerbachian-type inversion, whereby all man has to do is to recognize in God the alienated reflection of his own essence, thereby affirming himself as the absolute subject. Zizek proposes that determinate reflection be understood instead as reflection *redoubled*, in which essence reflects itself in itself, not as mere appearance but as 'an inverse-alienated image of the very essence, essence itself in the form its otherness.' It is only this movement that 'opens the space for the appearance in which the hidden essence can reflect itself.' That is to say, the 'substantial Entity must itself split and 'engender' the subject, 'God himself must become man.''[8] It follows, Zizek claims, that subjects alienated in the substantial State can come to 'recognize the State as ''their own work' only by reflecting free subjectivity into the very State at the point of the Monarch,' the point which confers its effectivity upon the State. Subjects can realize their freedom only insofar as they transpose their freedom into the heart of the substance opposed to them, as its own reflexive determination, 'into the person of the subject-Monarch.'

Zizek rounds off this argument by telling us that the conversion by which substance becomes subject is not through the dispersed multitude but can only be centred at 'some point of exception, in the One,' who takes up the burden of subjectivation in the form, 'This is my will.' Not surprisingly, the model of this conversion is the

---

[8] *SOI*, p. 228.

incarnation of God in Christ. At the core of Zizek's argument, however, is the claim that the passage from external to determinate reflection, the condition of our subjective freedom, must be reflected in advance into the substance itself, as its own 'reflexive determination.''[9] It is not sufficient that the subject, man, grasps the substantial entity, the State, as his own alienated essence; the political subject must grasp itself as engendered by the (necessary) failure of the State to actualize itself as universality, and itself as the bearer of that universality.

In *The Parallax View* (2009), Zizek has written:

> The Universal is not the encompassing container of the particular content, the peaceful medium-background of the conflict of particularities; the Universal "as such" is the site of an unbearable antagonism, self-contradiction and (the multitude of) its particular species are ultimately nothing but so many attempts to obfuscate/reconcile/master this antagonism. In other words, the Universal names the site of a Problem-Deadlock, of a burning question, and the Particulars are the attempted but failed Answers to this Problem. The concept of State, for instance, names a certain problem: how to contain the class antagonisms of a society? All particular forms of State are so many (failed) attempts to propose a solution to this problem.[10]

The symmetry of rabble and monarch

---

[9] *SOI*, p. 230.
[10] *PV*, pp. 34-35.

Returning now to the question of the rabble, Zizek is clearly seeking to establish a certain symmetry between, on the one hand, the reflexive determination of the monarch who, for Hegel, embodies and actualizes the unity of the state and, on the other, the rabble as the reflexive determination of the social totality, also embodying – in a different way - its universality. The 'excess' at the top – the apparently superfluous and irrational presence of the monarch – is 'supplemented' by the irrational 'destructive excess' at the bottom – that of the rabble, in which the 'identity' of the social totality is claimed to be revealed in the social group it has created as its opposite. The 'concrete universality' which comes into play here with regard to the rabble is not, Zizek underlines, that of the 'proto-fascist Hegel' in the advocacy of an organic, corporate state, but rather that of *dialectical negativity* in which 'the genus appears as one of its own species opposed to others, entering into a negative relationship with them.' It is a universality which includes itself among its species, 'in the guise of a singular moment lacking particular content.' Those without a proper place in the social edifice, 'the part of no-part', thereby 'stand for the universal dimension of the society which generates them.' This is why the problem of poverty cannot be eliminated without the transformation of the whole society.[11]

Zizek argues in *The Parallax View* that what the 'fetish' critique misses is the Lacanian notion of castration, which designates not only the empty gap which the element occupies (as in Claude Lefort's theory of democracy), but also reveals that this empty space of power, 'which lacks any "natural" element that would occupy it, is strictly correlative to an excessive element which wanders around, lacking its

[11] Slavoj Zizek, *The Politics of Negativity*, Introduction to Frank Ruda, *Hegel's Rabble: an Investigation into Hegel's Philosophy of Right*, (London and New York: Continuum, 2011), pp. xiv-xv.

"proper" place – the 'castrated' partial object.' Neither should we accept the view of the empty place of the impossible universal to be filled in, that is, hegemonized, by contingent particulars (as in Laclau) as the ultimate given; rather 'we should hazard a step further and ask how – through what cut in the texture of the living body – this empty place itself emerges.' Against the philosophy of finitude, Zizek asserts the 'materialist' view of the Lacanian '*objet petit a(utre)* as the "undead", "(noncastrated)" remainder which persists in its obscene immortality.'[12] The bond that attempts to hold together the social totality can never be wholly constituted from purely symbolic ties. There must be, in addition, 'a surplus of the Real' based in contingent materiality. The universal, for Hegel, must *appear as such* – it is not merely the abstract universal - and here it appears in the singular form of the rabble, the degraded, abject waste-product, the social excrement. 'As excluded, lacking recognition of its particular position, the rabble is the universal as such.'[13]

In his introduction to Ruda's *Hegel's Rabble*, entitled *The Politics of Negativity*, Zizek argues that there is a negative gesture of *subtraction* which opens the space for positive entities, the nothing that must be posited so that something can be present. For Lacan 'castration' is the primordial negation of this kind. In castration the lack of a signifier is turned into a signifier of lack. The *objet a* is the placeholder of this lack, a 'spectral positivization of this lack.'[14] Zizek continues, 'The deepest speculative insight is that a universality can only emerge when a flow of particularity gets stuck onto a singular moment.' In an object-symptom the subject reflexively registers a truth inaccessible to consciousness, an excess of negativity in which

---

[12] *PV*, p. 108.
[13] *LTN*, p. 433.
[14] *PN*, p. xi.

the core of the subject can be recognized. Freudian negativity, which Zizek here embraces, differs from Hegelian negativity in the manner in which it can become 'stuck' on a particular content and in pure repetition, while Hegelian negativity effects idealizing sublation. Freudian negativity thus, as Zizek puts it, provides the material base which underlies idealizing negativity, revealing its contingent pathological content. The 'rabble', then, is precisely such a singular negative universal, a material 'excess', stuck in pure repetition, permanently adrift, resisting the idealizing movement of sublation.

The symmetry between the monarch and the rabble, the 'excess' at the top and the 'excess' at the bottom, and their shared 'irrationality', is made particularly explicit in *For They Know Not What They Do* (2008) where Zizek provides yet another version of Hegel's account of monarchy. The monarch, Zizek states, functions as a pure Name (the Name s/he signs), embodying 'the function of the Master-Signifier at its purest,' a 'signifier without a signified', 'the One of Exception', the irrational surplus as condition of the rationality of the organic whole. In Hegel's words, '*Without* its monarch and that *articulation* of the whole which is necessarily and immediately associated with monarchy, *the* people is a formless mass.'[15] As hereditary monarch s/he occupies the point of coincidence between nature and culture; uniquely, the monarch's position is determined immediately by lineage.

However, Zizek states:

> At the very point where Hegel seems to praise monarchy, he carries out a kind of *separation* between S1 (the master-signifier) and (*objet*) *a* – on the illusion that the Master-Signifier covers, deep within itself, the precious object – Hegel separates

[15] *PR*, §279.

> them and shows us, on the one hand, S1 in its imbecilic tautology of an empty name; and, on the other, the object (the body of the monarch) as a pure excrement, a remainder appended to the Name.[16]

Zizek appears here to refer to the Lacanian *agalma*, the 'precious object' believed to be at the core of the beloved, quite separate from any particular properties possessed by the beloved, an excess reflexively posited by love itself; the subject's own desire inscribed in the object. The Greek *agalma* is originally the treasure hidden in a worthless box. Does this not indeed bear a marked similarity to that form of authority that Hegel calls 'majesty', one of the speculative names for the divine? If it seems that Zizek is claiming that Hegel is dispelling the illusion of monarchy in the act of philosophically 'comprehending' it, we should recall the Lacanian-Zizekian axiom that those who do not let themselves be caught in the symbolic deception are those who err most; that the domain of symbolic authority matters more than the reality of its spokesmen. As Zizek remarks in *The Sublime Object*, the Lacanian formula for the *agalma* is *objet petit a*, 'this point of the Real which cannot be symbolized, which is produced as a residue, a remnant, a leftover of every signifying operation'.[17]

Against the criticism which claims that Hegel's deduction of the monarchy is a failure of sublation, Zizek's point is that while the monarchy remains 'unaccounted for' by rational mediation, the monarch is precisely 'the element through which rational totality constitutes itself...on condition that this very power of absolute

---

[16] Slavoj Zizek, *For They Know Not What They Do: Enjoyment as a Political Factor*, (London and New York: Verso, 2008), p. 84.
[17] *SOI*, p. 180.

mediation is embodied anew in the form of its opposite; of an inert, non-rational residue of natural immediacy.' In fact, Hegel underlines the fact that monarchy is *not* deduced from anything else '*but entirely self-originating*.'[18] Hegel's account of monarchy begins with the power of the sovereign and 'the moment of ultimate *decision* as the *self-determination* to which everything else reverts and from which its actuality originates.'[19] Sovereignty can exist only as '*subjectivity* which is certain of itself', which 'attains its truth only as a *subject*, and personality only as a *person*,' thus 'in one individual, the *monarch*.' The monarch must occupy a position '*isolated for itself* and exalted *above everything particular and conditional*.' His 'I will' institutionalizes the contingent element in any decision while freeing it from arbitrary will (*Willkür*], and only by virtue of its inner and external immediacy is it saved from being dragged down into arbitrariness resulting from the strife of factions. The exercise of his will requires no justification since it is 'only the objective element in an action that can be justified.'

What might so far appear as an exposition of the legitimacy of absolute monarchy, however, turns into its opposite, since in the organic rational State, structured by the constitution and the separation of powers, 'the power of the sovereign presupposes the other moments, just as it is presupposed by each of them.'[20] The monarch is 'bound by the advice he receives.' All he has to do is to sign his name, but the name is 'the ultimate instance and *non plus ultra*.' As Hegel points out, 'Monarchs are not exactly distinguished by their physical powers or intellect.'[21] In fact, the less active, capable and intelligent

---

[18] *PR*, §279.
[19] *PR*, §275.
[20] *PR*, §285.
[21] *PR*, §281.

they are, the better, since then they are then so much less likely to exceed their minimal role. These negative determinations allow the monarch to be positively determined solely by the contingencies of birth and the ability to sign his name. The legitimacy of the constitutional monarch rests precisely in the complete absence of any other entitlement.

We are now in a position to assess the value of Zizek's account of the relation between Hegel's theory of monarchy and Hegel's concept of the 'rabble'. Both, as we have seen, occupy problematic and exceptional positions within the logical structure of the *Philosophy of Right*, neither being accommodated within what Zizek calls the 'proto-fascist' organic, corporate state, or within the logic of sublation. As 'irrational' 'excesses' Zizek is able to characterize both as the material 'excrement' concealed beneath the rational structures. As such they provide Zizek with essential resources for his 'Lacanian' reading of Hegel. Both monarch and rabble are claimed by Zizek to be 'singular universals', meaning that both give body to the universality of the State by virtue of their exclusion and absence of mediation through the particular. While it is clear that Hegel understands the monarch in this way, as thereby exempt from the particularity of factional interest, Zizek's parallel argument for the singular universality of the rabble is developed from within Lacanian theory. The existence of the rabble has a universal dimension because the position it occupies can be seen to be an expression of the fundamental antagonism that lies within the emerging capitalist order, an antagonism incapable of being resolved within the capitalist order. The argument is not the Lukàcsian one, concerning the proletariat, that it occupies a privileged site from which to grasp the social totality, but rather that the rabble constitutes a 'symptom' signifying the repressed truth of domination and servitude in a purportedly equal and just society. The symptom in *Sublime Object* is defined by Zizek in purely formal terms as 'a particular element which subverts its own universal foundation, a species subverting its own genus.'[22] Every ideological Universal - freedom, equality, etc. - is false 'in so far as it necessarily includes a specific case which breaks its unity, lays open its falsity.' The rabble is a symptom of this negativity in which a possible subject can be recognized along with the truth which emerges from this break. While the role of the monarch is that of the supernumerary element which would actualize the closure of the political order, the rabble remains a fixed, inassimilable moment of *dis*order.

Giorgio Agamben has similarly developed the concept of *homo sacer* or bare life which exists at the threshold of the political community, like the sovereign occupying 'the point of exception.' Both exist inside *and* outside the political order. Agamben distinguishes between exclusion and the exception, in that 'what is excluded in the exception maintains itself in relation to the rule in the form of the rule's suspension. *The rule applies to the exception in no longer applying, in withdrawing from it.*'[23] This involves the creation of a threshold and a zone of indistinction between nature and right which is 'the state of exception.' Just as in logic and mathematical set theory, 'non-belonging can be shown only at the centre of a class, by an exception,' so this issue comes into play 'every time the very sense of the belonging and commonality of individuals' in a social system is to be defined, involving the relation between inside and outside. This is clearly the case, it could be argued, with regard to the Hegelian rabble. The rabble are not a remnant of the pre-political Hobbesian multitude. They are subjected to the law but have learned to expect no

[22] *SOI* p. 21.

[23] Giorgio Agamben, *Homo Sacer: Sovereign Power and Bare Life*, trans. Daniel Heller-Roazen, (Stanford: Stanford University Press, 1998), pp. 17-18.

redress from the law; they are controlled by it without being protected by it. They know the rights they have but know that *de facto* these rights are not respected. The exception, as Agamben puts it, does not subtract itself from the rule, rather the rule withdraws from the exception and abandons it. What is captured is by the same stroke excluded and human life is politicized by subjection to an unconditional power. From this point of view, Agamben endorses the position of Badiou that, contra Hegel, '*the State is not founded as the expression of a social bond, which it would express, but rather upon un-binding* [déliaison] *which it prohibits*.'[24] This unbinding is Hegel's ultimate fear. In the rational state no moment in the state should appear as an unorganized crowd. 'The *many* as single individuals – and this is a favourite interpretation of [the term] 'the people' – do indeed live together but only as a crowd, i.e. a formless mass whose movement and activity can consequently only be elemental, irrational, barbarous, and terrifying.'[25]

Poverty and indignation

In the lectures appended to the *Philosophy of Right* attention is drawn to the 'division of emotion' [*Gemüt*] that has arisen between the rabble and civil society.

---

[24] *HS*, p. 90. Agamben's quotation from Alain Badiou, *Being and Event*, trans. Oliver Feltham, (London and New York: Continuum, 2007), p. 109 has been corrected.
[25] *PR* §303.

> The poor man feels excluded and mocked by everyone, and this necessarily gives rise to an inner indignation. He is conscious of himself as an infinite free being, and thus arises the demand that his external existence should correspond to this consciousness. In civil society it is not only natural distress against which the poor man has to struggle. The poor man is opposed not only by nature, a mere being, but also by my will. The poor man feels as if he were related to an arbitrary will, to human contingency, and in the last analysis what makes him indignant is that he is put into this state of division through an arbitrary will. Self-consciousness appears driven to the point where it no longer has any rights, where freedom has no existence. In this position, where the existence of freedom becomes something wholly contingent, inner indignation is necessary. Because the individual's freedom has no existence, the recognition of universal freedom disappears. From this condition arises the shamelessness that we find in the rabble. A rabble arises chiefly in a developed civil society…[26]

As indicated earlier, poverty within civil society does not itself create a rabble; it is rather the material precondition for the existence of a rabble. A rabble comes into existence only when there emerges the 'disposition' (*Gesinnung*) associated with poverty. While here above in the Nisbet translation of the lectures, we have 'inner indignation [*Empörung*]', in the main text of the *Philosophy of Right* that disposition is translated by Nisbet as 'inward rebellion [*Empörung*] against the rich, against society, the government, etc.' (§244) In this translation, therefore, the concept which lies at the centre of Ruda's interpretation, that of 'indignation' - most obviously in his article 'The

[26] *PR,* §244.

Indignant of the Earth' – is absent, replaced by 'rebellion'.[27] Ruda suggests that Hegel uses the word *Empörung* in 'a two-fold manner': as an affective determination of the rabble, but also 'in the (etymologically wrong) sense of rebellion, revolt, turmoil, insurrection,'[28] as when Hegel writes that rebellion in a province conquered by war is not the same as a rising [*Empörung*] in a well-organized state, the latter being, in Hegel's view, a crime against 'the state itself'.[29] For Ruda, 'This demonstrates that indignation is not simply characteristic of an inner attitude and has external effects,' thereby marking the transition from 'indignation-about (the condition of possibility of indignation)' to 'indignation-against (the reproduction and perpetuation of it).' But, clearly, indignation is not a crime. *Empörung* is, in the latter quotation, being used by Hegel in a different sense. 'Inward indignation', which is surely already directed *against* an object, would have given way to (active) insurrection.

Ruda's attempt to construct what he calls Hegel's 'theory of universal indignation,'[30] on the basis of Hegel's few uses of the term, leads to further complications. Indignation, Ruda claims, has a universal dimension since 'anyone is latently poor' and any poor person can become rabble when (s)he starts to be indignant. This is the basis for what Ruda calls 'the logic of double latency.' The rabble, Ruda states, demands a 'right without right', namely the right to subsist without working, demanded by the rabble as a *particular* right (i.e. for itself), but since, according to Ruda, every member of civil society 'is (or more precisely, will have been) latently rabble', this

---

[27] Frank Ruda,'The Indignant of the Earth', in *Crisis and Critique*, 1, 2013.
[28] *Crisis and Critique*, p. 84. See also *HR* p. 59.
[29] *PR* §281. Ruda refers to the Knox translation p. 275. In Nisbet's translation *Empörung* is translated here 'revolt'. *Crisis and Critique*, p. 84.
[30] *Crisis and Critique*, p. 73.

constitutes a 'latently' universal rights claim.[31] It must be objected that, first, it is not true, and certainly not part of Hegel's problem with poverty, that anyone is (or will have been shown to be) latently poor. Poverty does not strike indiscriminately and to state that anyone (or everyone) is 'latently' poor would mean that everyone lived in an existing state of poverty which was not yet actualized, which is absurd.

Secondly, Hegel does not say that the rabble unjustly claims a particular right for itself to be provided for without working. In the sections of the *Philosophy of Right* referred to by Ruda, Hegel writes, 'just as every human being has a right to demand a livelihood from society, so also must society protect him against himself...since civil society is obliged to feed its members, it also has the right to urge them to provide for their own livelihood.'[32] The problem – and this what makes it a problem for Hegel – is not the rabble's claim to a non-existent or unrecognized right but a conflict of already acknowledged rights. Hegel underlines the fact that civil society and property law, having *deprived* individuals of 'the natural means of acquisition,' dissolved the bonds of family, and denied the poor access to justice and health care, the 'universal authority' [*Macht*] must then assume the responsibilities which formerly attached to familial authority, both with regard to provision and, like the family, to dealing with the vices which, he believes, follow from such deprivation.[33] Contrary to Ruda's assertion, Hegel recognizes that the poor suffer from a socially created *lack*.[34] Hegel's difficulty, in common with present-day advocates of the market economy, is in conceding that this deprivation constitutes a 'wrong' [*Unrecht*], although he recognizes that the rabble

---

[31] *HR* p. 65.
[32] *PR* §240.
[33] *PR* §241.
[34] *HR*, p. 63.

must perceive it in this way. The indignation of the rabble is not therefore, as both Ruda and Zizek argue, expressed in the form of a claim to 'a right without right [*rechtlos*]'. It is a central element in Ruda's argument that 'the right which the rabble opposes to the existing right is one that is merely particular, particularized: it is valid for the rabble and for the rabble alone.'[35] Ruda insists upon this mistaken assertion, since his intention is to demonstrate that this particularized claim to a 'right without right,' 'impossible' in the existing order, is the bearer of a (latent) universality which can only be realized in a new, transformed political order.

Besides distinguishing between 'indignation-about' (the alleged condition of possibility of indignation) and 'indignation-against' (the reproduction and perpetuation of it), thereby attempting to link together the different senses of *Empörung* as forms of indignation, Ruda also tells us that 'it is important to note that indignation is directed against its own conditions of possibility. *Indignation is indignation against indignation*, against the condition of possibility of being indignant at all. It is hence not directed against an object of the world but against the world as it is. That is to say, indignation is directed against a world in which there is indignation. Indignation can therefore be read as a form of (latent) subjectivization of an injustice, which is not conceded to be one by the existing objective categories of right, since it concerns the very constitution of the world as such.'[36] It would seem, however, that 'indignation-about' is already 'indignation-against' the world as it is. Being-indignant about being-made-indignant, it must be said, seems an unlikely starting-point from which to adopt an insurrectionary posture. What Ruda seems to have in mind here is to establish a parallel (or a contrast) with Marx's

---

[35] *HR*, p. 61.
[36] *Crisis and Critique*, pp. 82-83.

argument that the proletariat, the class which is not a class, in overthrowing class society thereby abolishes itself. The logic of the rabble-attitude entails that, from its point of view, in perceiving the dissolution of ethical substance it sees reflected its own dissolution. But 'indignation', the attitude which is, according to Ruda, *not* an attitude, since it lacks ethical self-feeling, hardly provides us with the means to think this.[37]

The purpose of these distortions of the meaning of 'indignation' becomes clear when Ruda attempts to link Hegelian indignation with the Heideggerian-Lacanian affect of anxiety [*Angst, angoisse*], on the basis that both are said to effect a 'de-naturalization of the existing order, which opens up the dimension of true political action.' It is certainly true that Hegel, especially in his earlier, more radical, writings, gives full expression to the social and psychological stresses unleashed by the emergence of civil society. In the *Jenaer Realphilosophie* he writes:

> The contrast between great wealth and great poverty appears: the poverty for which it becomes impossible to do anything; the wealth which, like any mass, makes itself into a force... This inequality between wealth and poverty, this need and necessity, lead to the utmost dismemberment of the will, to inner indignation and hatred. This necessity, which is the complete contingency of individual existence, is at the same time its sustaining substance. State power enters and must see to it that each sphere is supported...[38]

---

[37] *HR*, pp. 117-118.

[38] *Hegel and the Human Spirit*, trans. Leo Rauch, (Detroit: Wayne State University Press, 1983), p. 140.

> [*Diese Ungleichheit des Reichtums und der Armuth, - diese Noth und Nothwendigkeit wird die höchste Zerrissenheit des Willens, - innre Empörung und Haß – Diese Nothwendigkeit, welche die vollkomme Züfalligkeit des einzelnen Daseyns ist, ist aber ebenso die erhaltende Substanz desselben*...]

Ruda, in his comments on part of this passage, argues that indignation is not the hatred of the poor towards the rich but 'rather what is generated when this splitting in poor and rich becomes a principle structuring the world. Indignation in its latent universal dimension names the affect that indicates the breaking of the social bond.' More precisely, it indicates that the social bond is already broken. As the passage in full makes clear, while not identifying inner indignation with hatred, as in Spinoza's well-known definition of indignation [*indignatio*] as 'hatred toward someone who has maltreated another,'[39] the two are for Hegel strongly associated. The 'dismemberment' or 'inner strife' [*Zerrissenheit*] of the will clearly refers to an *inner* subjective state, not, as Ruda claims, to a rupture within the social bond. While there can be no doubt that the problem of poverty constitutes, in Hegel's view, a fundamental antagonism within civil society and threatens an unbinding of the social bond, he does not appear to doubt, at any stage in his writings, the ability of the state to at least mitigate the most damaging effects of this contradiction. Indeed, it is one of the fundamental reasons why the state is considered essential.

Ruda sharply distinguishes his approach from the social pathology of Axel Honneth and the Frankfurt School's 'therapeutic critique' of social ills, but Honneth's *The Struggle for Recognition*, although not

---

[39] Spinoza, *Ethics*, trans, Andrew Boyle and revised by G. H. R. Parkinson (London: J. M. Dent & Sons), III, XX, p. 132.

explicitly concerned with 'the rabble', casts an interesting light on Hegel's treatment of the problems of social exclusion by means of the concept of inter-subjective recognition. In the early *Realphilosophie*, this is explained as follows:

> In recognition, the self ceases to be this individual. It exists by right in recognition, that is, no longer in its immediate existence. The one who is recognized is recognized as immediately counting as such, through his *being* – but this being is itself generated from the concept. It is recognized being [*annerkanntes Sein*].[40]

It could be argued that this is precisely what comes to be denied to the rabble. As Honneth points out, in Hegel's re-working of the Hobbesian state of nature he 'derives the reaction-formation of excluded subjects from a motivational situation whose core is formed by the disappointment of positive expectations vis-à-vis the partner to interaction. Unlike in Hobbes' depiction, the individual here reacts to the seizure of property not with the fear of having his survival subsequently threatened but rather with the feeling of being ignored by his social counterpart.'[41] The reason why the socially ignored and insulted person, in turn, seeks to damage the other's property 'is not because they want to satisfy their passions, but rather in order to make the others take notice of them.'

Hegel writes:

---

[40]G. W. F. Hegel, *Jenaer Realphilosophie*, (Hamburg: Meiner, 1969), p. 206, qu. Honneth, p. 42.

[41] Axel Honneth, *The Struggle for Recognition: The Moral Grammar of Social Conflicts*, trans. Joel Anderson, (Cambridge: Polity Press, 1995), p. 44,

> The excluded party spoils the other's possession, by introducing his excluded being-for-himself into it, his 'mine'. He ruins something in it – an annihilation like that of desire – in order to give himself his sense of self, yet not his empty sense of self but rather his self positing itself within another, in the knowing of another.[42]

However, as Honneth points out, in Hegel 'we did not find any indication as to how experiencing social disrespect [*Mißachtung*] can motivate a subject to enter a practical struggle or conflict. There was, as it were, a missing psychological link that would lead from mere suffering to action by cognitively informing the person in question of his or her social situation. I would like to defend the thesis that this function can be performed by negative emotional reactions, such as being ashamed or enraged, feeling hurt or indignant. These comprise the psychological symptoms on the basis of which one can come to realize that one is being illegitimately denied social recognition.'[43] These negative emotions caused by the disregard of one's claims to recognition create the possibility 'that the injustice done to one will cognitively disclose itself and become a motive for political resistance.' In the *Philosophy of Right*, however, Hegel appears preoccupied with the way in which shame is converted into 'shamelessness', impotence into idleness, and a sense of grievance into pure malevolence, rather than a desire for justice.

It is Honneth's missing link that Ruda attempts to fill with anxiety, despite the fact that there is nothing in Hegel to support this move, an association which appears to be made by Ruda solely to establish a connection with Badiou's political ontology. Ruda's 'formal

---

[42] *Realphilophie* p. 209.

[43] Honneth, pp. 135-136,

indignation', directed not against the rich, the system of rights and duties, or the state 'police', but against 'the world as it is', where 'world' is understood in Heideggerian-Lacanian terms, shifts us to a level at which it can be misleadingly identified with anxiety, the affect that 'never deceives' and reveals, as Ruda puts it, 'the non-necessity of the world,' a precondition for transforming it.

Ruda's position is based upon Badiou's adaptation of Lacan's concept of anxiety, in which anxiety plays a fundamental role in the way in which the Real is able to break through the formal impasse in the existing state of things, in the emergence of the (revolutionary) subject.[44] Anxiety, the reflexive affect which does not deceive (because it has no object), in its confrontation with the Real, involves 'the active failure of the whole apparatus of symbolic support provoked by what reveals itself therein, in a cut, as unnameable encounter.'[45] In anxiety, 'the real *kills* the symbolical rather than splitting it.'[46] But, anxiety is that side of subjectivization which, still 'caught in the web of the dead order,' makes an appeal to the law which no longer rules, to the superego. As Ruda observes, this 'point of impossibility' can then become the starting-point of a transition from, in Badiou's terms, anxiety to courage, and from courage to justice, which produces a new truth.

While it may well be the case that indignation and anxiety are both important concepts for understanding the rabble, they should not be confused with each other, not least because indignation is a conscious state while anxiety for Badiou is not a state of consciousness but a subject-effect. It should also be noted that, according to Lacan, anxiety

[44] See Bruno Bosteels, *Badiou and Politics*, (Durham and London: Duke University Press, 2012), p. 88.
[45] Alain Badiou, *Theory of the Subject*, trans. Bruno Bosteels, (London and New York: Continuum, 2009), p. 146.
[46] *TS*, p. 291.

is the *only* affect that never deceives, and indignation is not the same as anxiety. So far as Hegel's text is concerned, it provides no grounds for either a 'universal theory of indignation' or for a theory of anxiety.

Infinite unbinding and the absolute rabble

In a remark from the lectures included in the *Philosophy of Right*, it is observed that the 'rabble-disposition also appears where there is wealth. The rich man thinks that he can buy anything, because he knows himself as the power of the particularity of self-consciousness. Thus wealth can lead to the same mockery and shamelessness that we find in the poor rabble. The disposition of the master over the slave is the same as that of the slave...These two sides, poverty and wealth, thus constitute the corruption of civil society.'[47]

Despite the fact that he has identified the indignation produced by poverty as the defining characteristic of the rabble, Ruda makes every effort to extend the rabble-disposition to the rich, while conceding that the rich do not experience indignation. Although Ruda points out a number of similarities in Hegel's treatment of the rich and of the rabble – contingency, atomization, unbinding, shamelessness, lack of honour – it is grossly misleading to suggest that 'the rabble' has, as its sub-species, the 'pauper-rabble' and the 'luxury-rabble'. Both are said to 'claim a right without a right,' both disregard their duties within the ethical State. But it is difficult to see how Ruda's prolonged discussions of the practices of the unethical rich, gamblers, etc. contribute anything to our understanding of the rabble itself, except as part of his intention to 'universalize' the rabble-condition by any means possible.

---

[47] Note to *PR* §244, p. 454.

That this might appear feasible follows from Ruda's master-proposition that, 'anyone in the state is latently poor,' which appears to be a version of the proletarianization thesis, advanced in a limited form by Marx and in a more general form by Lacan.[48] Ruda explains, 'At the same time any poor (person) – because the rabble makes itself and is not subordinated to any other objective condition – can become rabble. For the rabble is rather the product of a genuinely subjective operation, a subjective act. The direct consequence of this is that anyone in the state is latently poor and therefore latently rabble.'[49] More precisely, he adds, in the future anterior, '*anyone* in the state will have been latently rabble.'

The claim that the rabble 'makes itself', repeatedly asserted by Ruda,[50] is based upon a single statement made by Hegel, which Ruda quotes only once accurately, as follows:

> The lowest subsistence level, that of a rabble of paupers, is fixed automatically [*machtsich von selbst*], but the minimum varies considerably in different countries. (*PR* 244 Addition, Knox translation)[51]
>
> The lowest level of subsistence [*Subsistenz*], that of the rabble, defines itself automatically, but this minimum varies greatly between different peoples. (Nisbet translation)

---

[48] 'There is but one social symptom: every individual is in effect a proletarian, that is to say, that no discourse is at the disposal of the individual by means of which a social bond could be established.'' (*La Troisième* in *La cause freudienne*, 2011, p. 79)
[49] *HR*, p. 47.
[50] See Ruda's, 'That Which Makes Itself: Hegel, Rabble and Consequences' in David James (ed.) *Hegel's Elements of the Philosophy of Right: A Critical Guide*, (Cambridge and New York: Cambridge University Press, 2017), pp. 160-176.
[51] Quoted in its full and correct form *HR*, p. 60.

In 'The Indignant of the Earth' Ruda explains that he has altered the 'misleading – false – translation 'fixed automatically,' and replaced it with 'makes itself.'[52] In *Hegel's Rabble*, however, the phrase is used extensively without explanation, as for example, when chapter nine opens with the question of how it is possible for the rabble 'to make itself' when 'everything is dissolved.' Later in the chapter, Ruda again quotes the above passage, this time in the form: 'The lowest subsistence level, that of a rabble of paupers, makes itself...Poverty in itself does not turn people into a rabble....' He adds, 'translation modified', without further explanation.[53] The remainder of the first sentence has been omitted because it would no longer make sense. The subject of the sentence is clearly not 'the rabble' but 'The lowest level of subsistence' (the minimum) which determines itself automatically (in line with the laws of political economy).

That the rabble 'makes itself' indicates first for Ruda that, in Hegel's view, the rabble opposes itself to the ethical state, an 'organ without body,' and that its purely oppositional attitude is *doxa* or mere opinion. Its indignation has a purely negative content, a position of untruth. Ruda continues, 'Therewith the rabble negates the ethical as such and also sociality as such: due to its attitude it is always a-social. At the same time the only thing that appears within the rabble-attitude is an infinite movement of negation from which nothing escapes.' Ruda quotes Hegel as follows:

> To take the merely negative as a starting-point and to make the willing of evil and the mistrust of such willing the primary

---

[52] *Crisis and Critique*, p. 77, fn. 38. The remainder of the sentence is eliminated.

[53] *HR*, p. 114.

> factor, and then on the basis of this presupposition slyly to construct dikes whose efficiency simply necessitates corresponding dislikes (*sic*) over against them, is characteristic of the negative understanding and in disposition of the outlook of the rabble.[54]

Ruda describes this passage as 'astonishing' because it 'draws a parallel between the rabble-attitude and the negative understanding.' More astonishing is the fact that this passage is actually concerned not with the rabble but with Montesquieu's doctrine of the separation of powers, hence the references to the construction of 'dikes', defences and counter-defences. Hegel is criticizing what the Nisbet translation refers to as the tendency of the separation of powers to produce a 'malevolent' attitude and mutual mistrust among the different divisions of the state; to relate to each other 'as if to an evil [*Übel*]'. Further, it is not the 'negative understanding' of these branches of the state which is being compared with the outlook of the rabble but the disposition they exhibit.

Ruda argues that the rabble-attitude which reflects its own dissolution is contagious. Because of the 'logic of double latency', anyone can become rabble, heralding a state of 'absolute putrefaction in which all determinations are dissolved.' It is laziness/foulness [*Faulheit*] which brings about this 'putrefaction' of the rabble, who become the 'absolutely inert,' living a present, insisting in-existence. It is for this reason that the rabble can be characterized as a singular universal. 'And this is precisely the point through which the rabble makes itself.'[55] The rabble, Ruda tells us, can now can 'make itself' in a different sense, as the 'first moment' in which the impossible starts

---

[54] *HR*, p. 115. *PR* §272, Knox trans. p. 285. Nisbet trans. pp. 306-307.
[55] *HR*, p. 120.

to become the possible. It is the bearer of a universality not, like the proletariat, through labour, not in fact through *doing* anything. The rabble 'as matter of the ethical space remains forever in this implicit dimension.' The rabble is not therefore merely a contingent irrationality, but because it is claimed to 'make itself' it can then be linked to the activity of the subject.

The rabble is also claimed to be equivalent to the empty set in post-Cantorian set theory, since it can only be explained through a series of negative determinations – it is 'morally deprived, shameless, evil, shy of work,' etc. - a subtraction from all determinations, which can, according to Ruda, be 'infinitely continued.' As a set without elements it is universally implied, as the empty set is implied as logically prior to any set which includes elements. Ruda claims, on this basis, that the 'in-existence' of the rabble, its appearance as disappearance, generates an insight into 'the matter of ethical space.'[56] It emerges as the 'irruption of the void' into the unity of Hegel's organic state, a state that prohibits the unbinding of this structured unity into the rabble's claim to what Ruda calls 'the equality of anyone.' In a similar way to that in which the name of the monarch is absolutely arbitrary and contingent but assures the symbolic unity of the state, as both individual and universal, the rabble appears as the 'name of nothing' in the ethical, as the 'matter' of the ethical which has no determinations and which is always already prior to the ethical. It is the irruption of an inconsistency into the ordered structure of the state, an insight into pure multiplicity of the *vulgus*, an indeterminacy which 'decomposes the state.'[57]

[56] *HR*, p. 156.
[57] *HR*, p. 164.

With the term '*vulgus*' we take a step back from the Hegelian rabble to the Kantian rabble. The *ignobile vulgus* [58] is for Kant, the *populus* (the multitude united into a whole) dissolved into a multitude or multiplicity. In Kant's anthropology the *vulgus* is the section of the population that exempts itself from the law and as an illegal association constitutes 'the mob' or *agere per turbas* – conduct excluding them from citizenship. The rabble, Ruda claims, is 'more vulgar' than Hegel thinks, since Hegel fails to grasp that, because of 'the logic of double latency', the infection borne by the 'fully putrefied rabble' threatens the very existence of the state, and raises the disturbing spectre of the 'absolute rabble.' In Hegelian terms, the 'in-and-for-itself' of the poor rabble is the absolute rabble, the beyond of the resentment-rabble with which Hegel ends.[59] The in and for itself of the rabble is also the universal identified by Marx as 'absolute poverty.' It constitutes an absolute unbinding, a privation free of all determinations. 'It will therefore be, will always already have been, as this Nothing, the universal which latently marks anyone.' The absolute rabble will always have been *present*. The name 'rabble' is then a synonym in Hegel for this unbinding and privation. It is able to 'make itself', Ruda claims, only from its position at what Badiou calls 'the edge of the void.' In the language of set theory, the rabble is a multiple beneath which there is 'nothing' because none of its terms are counted-as-one. Absolutely primary terms, they do not permit questioning as to their combinatory origin.[60] For Ruda the rabble is matter without form understood as a set, a multiplicity without unity; a Cantorian extensional set gathered together not on the basis of a property assignable to all its elements. It is a collection which happens

[58] *HR*, p. 118.
[59] *HR*, p. 73.
[60] Alain Badiou, *Being and Event*, p. 175.

externally, not by immanent determination, 'like fish caught in a fishing net.' As such it constitutes a permanent threat of dissolution, both to itself and to the wider collectivity.

The politics of the rabble

In 'The Indignant of the Earth' Ruda explains his attempt to construct Hegel's theory of universal indignation by the fact that, as currently exemplified by the Spanish *indignados*, indignation and indignant people 'can be seen and heard nearly everywhere.' 'Indignation' has become the political master-word. These remarks should be read against the background of the introductory observations to his article which, in Lacanian mode, dismiss the then recent London riots of 2012 as carried out under the imperative (of the superego), 'Enjoy and Consume!', a form of violent 'shopping' in which the rabble of today seek to emulate the rest of the population.[61] This contradictory desire to succumb to the social imperative from a position of impossibility is, for Ruda, the mark of the rabble. In designating indignation a 'pre-political affect', Ruda tells us, he wishes to emphasize his scepticism with regard to political affects as such.[62]

Despite, then, the complex and ultimately unsuccessful attempt to piece together a theory of indignation from the very limited textual sources provided by Hegel, it is clear that indignation, in the form given to it by Ruda, fails to reach the threshold of the political. At best,

[61] *Crisis and Critique*, pp. 67-68. Ruda refers here to Badiou's much more considered analysis of the 'immediate riot' in his *The Rebirth of History: Times of Riots and Uprisings*, trans. Gregory Elliot, (London and New York: Verso, 2012), pp. 16-26, although he describes the 'immediate riot' as 'not even pre-political.' (p. 26) Regarding the role of truth, see, for example pp. 60-61.
[62] *Crisis and Critique*, p. 74.

the rabble emerges as a 'possible' subject, 'latently' universal and 'latently' political, but currently occupied only in frenzied looting. Notable among the others named by Ruda who have raised the profile of indignation are Hardt and Negri who, in *Commonwealth*, have written in a quite different vein:

> Our task, then, is to investigate the organizational framework of antagonistic subjectivities that arise from below, based on the *indignation* expressed by subjects in the face of the unfreedoms and injustices of power, the severe forms of control and hierarchy, and the cruel forms of exploitation and expropriation in the disordered world of global governance. Indignation, as Spinoza notes, is the ground zero, the basic material from which movements of revolt and rebellion develop.[63]

Whereas Ruda's project is to demonstrate the *impasse* of political philosophy when confronted by politics, represented by Hegel's insoluble 'problem', a failure which both Zizek and Ruda attribute to the internal logic of the *Philosophy of Right*, Hardt and Negri describe their undertaking as a step back to a more '*philosophical*' standpoint, 'starting from the most basic, abstract point and building logically to arrive back with a fresh perspective at the formation of the multitude.' In indignation, they argue, citing Spinoza, we discover our power to act against the causes of oppression, and in 'the expression of indignation our very existence rebels.' Such indignation-based resistance, which necessarily includes a dimension of force, may, however, appear, in its immediate form, as spontaneous and naïve. *Jacqueries* of this kind are always prompted by a specific obstacle or

[63] Michael Hardt and Antonio Negri, *Commonwealth*, (Cambridge, Mass: Belknapp Press, Harvard University Press, 2009), p. 236.

violation but in them there is always a pressure to make them into the common action of the multitude. In the political anthropology of resistance *jacqueries* are not sufficient but they are necessary.

In the age of biopolitics, Hardt and Negri maintain, 'the proletariat is within society as a whole' and resistance must be 'directed against the society of capital in its entirety,' demanding 'a process of exodus, a kind of anthropological (and ontological) separation from the domination of capital.' They pose the question of how in these conditions indignation in revolt can be organized, adding that in their previous writings, 'we have often taken great pains to distinguish the multitude from the crowd, the mob, and the masses (but) here we see the possibility of recuperating these social formations when their indignation and revolts are directed and organized.'[64]

Negri, following Spinoza, has previously defined 'affect' as 'a *power to act* that is singular and at the same time universal, a power of appropriation, in which every obstacle that is overcome adds a greater force of action to the affect, a power beyond measure, a power of transformation, universal because it constructs a commonality among subjects.[65] Similarly in Spinoza, a *dispositio* signifies the means by which an individual confronts the dynamics of external forces, interiorizing them or resisting them in a process of adaptation. It is an affective dynamic which regulates the existence of a body. As indicated earlier, Spinoza defines indignation as 'hatred towards someone who has maltreated another,' which involves as Matheron puts it, a 'form of affective imitation,' insofar as it is 'the hate that we experience for the one who harms a being similar to ourselves, and we

[64] *Commonwealth*, p. 243.

[65] Antonio Negri, 'Value and Affect', *boundary* 2, 26:2, summer 1999, pp. 85-86. In Spinoza '*affectus*' involves an augmentation or diminution of the power to act.

experience it through imitation of the feelings of the victim.'[66] There are grounds then for understanding indignation not as a solitary, passive, affect but as an affect which binds the individual together with other victims of injustice into an affective commonality. Only when despotism assumes an extreme form is the indignant individual forced to withdraw into a solitary silence.

Whereas Hardt and Negri are concerned to make a sustained attempt to follow through the forms of resistance from indignation to insurrection, Ruda, having reduced the rabble to inert in-existence in the dimension of negative universality, offers only the thought that, in the rabble, indignation *about* the world 'rises itself up,' in the manner of Baron Münchhausen, to indignation *against* the world.

> Indignation is hence in Hegel an *anti-state*, literally an *a-social*, and therefore a pre-political affect. It is an affect of possible pre-political subjectivation; it is not an affect indicating political subjectivation in actu – hence the sole dimension that is present....in it is a latently universal one. But it indicates the place of politics...With regard to the rabble one may say: the true revolt of the rabble is the indignant unbinding of the alleged necessity of the world as it is. The rabble asserts, emphasizes and indignantly demonstrates the (impossible) possibility of politics.'[67]

Ruda claims that any political affect, 'if there are such, must be reflexive, but this is only a necessary and not a sufficient condition of its being political.' The reflexivity of an affect is no more than a

---

[66] Alexandre Matheron, '*Qu'est-ce que l'indignation?*', *Multitudes* 2011/3 (No. 46), pp, 24-25. My translation.

[67] *Crisis and Critique*, p. 85.

prerequisite of its political character, and indignation, although reflexive and directed against the world which makes indignation possible, is, in Ruda's view, not as such political. He adds that reflexive affects possess a degree of rationality which mere feelings lack. Since indignation is latently the indignation of anyone, the one who is indignant in the rabble sense aims to be latently the 'representative of the whole of humanity,' and therefore, 'indignation never deceives and it can become possibly a category of political action.'[68] It is not clear what it means to aim to be 'latently' the representative of the whole of humanity, nor why this 'reflexive' dimension of an affect would necessarily rule out such affects as those expressed in, for example, nativism and racism. Are those who experience such affects necessarily unreflective and do they not also sense that the world could be other than it is? In an age in which affects have increasingly become the substance of politics, what can justify Badiou and Ruda in restricting the terms 'political' to their own highly restrictive definitions? Indignation can take many forms and any of them may deceive. The investigation into the formation of the revolutionary rabble is at the same time the investigation into the formation of the reactionary rabble. The *truth* which Badiou claims to be a necessary attribute of genuine political action is here derived by Ruda solely from an illegitimate identification of indignation with anxiety, which itself cannot be directly linked with any particular form of political action.

From rabble to proletariat: Hegel to Marx

[68] *Crisis and Critique*, p. 84.

Ruda maintains that the difference between Hegel and Marx is the difference between the rabble and the proletariat.[69] Zizek declares, 'The rabble is the universal as such,' but it took Marx to grasp this in relation to the proletariat.[70] The aetiology of the social symptom thus retreats from the proletariat to the rabble. The part of no-part which was once that of the proletariat has now passed to the rabble. Hegel's philosophical representation of the poor as 'the rabble' is rediscovered as the precursor of Marx's philosophical transformation of the working-class into the 'proletariat'. Zizek reminds us that Hegel was closer to the mark than Marx in that the rage of the rabble was not converted into the triumph of the proletariat.[71] It is, of course, in Marx's *Contribution to the Critique of Hegel's Philosophy of Right* that the proletariat is *named* as the class which is not a class, which has a universal character because of its universal suffering, which claims no particular right because it suffers wrong in general, which is 'the total loss of humanity and which can therefore redeem itself only through *the total redemption of humanity*.'[72] In the *Contribution*, however, there is no indication that Marx has been influenced in any way by Hegel's concept of the 'rabble'; indeed, having discovered the proletariat Marx distinguished it in the strongest possible terms from the *lumpenproletariat*, the truly dehumanized 'social scum' which he considered the remnants of the previous age.

Why try to superimpose the figure of the Marxian proletariat upon Hegel's rabble? Because the actually existing working class is clearly no longer able to provide credible support for this role and a substitute must be found. Paradoxically, this involves going backwards to the

---

[69] *HR*, p. 170.
[70] *LTN*, p. 432.
[71] *LTN*, p. 437.
[72] Karl Marx, *Early Writings*, trans. Rodney Livingstone and Gregor Benton, (London: Penguin Books, 1975), p. 52.

pre-proletarian 'rabble', victims of the new forms of poverty and exclusion that capitalism brought to the world and are now engendered on a global scale. As Alain Badiou has put it:

> It's the question of finding something that is, paradoxically, a generic identity, the identity of no-identity, the identity which is beyond all identities. For Marx, "proletariat" was the name of something like that. In the Manuscripts of 1844, Marx writes that the very nature of the proletariat is to be generic. It's not an identity. It's something like an identity which is not an identity; it's humanity as such. That's why for Marx the liberation of the working class is the liberation of humanity as such, because the working class is something generic and not a pure identity. Probably that function of the working class is saturated. We cannot substitute a mere collection of identities for the saturated generic identity of the working class. I think we have to find the political determination that integrates the identities, the principles which are beyond identities. The great difficulty is to do that without something like the working class. Without something that was a connection between particularity and universality, because that's what the working class was. The particularity of the working class was its location in a singular place; the working class was generic. The solution of the problem for Marxism was the human group which is not really an identity, which is beyond identity…
>
> …Marx's solution is a sort of miracle: you find the group which is also a generic group. It was an extraordinary invention. The history of this Marxist invention, in its concrete political determination, was not so much the history of the generic group, of the working class as such, but rather history of the representation of this group in a political organization: it was

> the history of the party. The crisis now is the crisis of representation, and also the crisis of the idea of the generic group.[73]

The method of 'saturation', referred to here, is explained by Sylvain Lazarus in *Anthropology of the Name*. When, after an examination from within, one of the founding categories of a body of work is found to have 'lapsed' it must be re-identified in a new conjuncture, as an alternative to disavowal.[74] Lazarus identifies the Leninist concept of the Party and the 'worker-figure' as lapsed, along with the statist paradigm of the 'dictatorship of the proletariat'. Badiou makes it clear that, so far as he is concerned, the history of the actually existing working-class is quite secondary to that of its 'representation' (in the ontological sense) in the party. It should be pointed out immediately that this conception of the party has no foundation in Marx's thought. However, in the search for 'something like the working class,' the 'rabble' might be considered a possible substitute, save that whereas Negri finds something structural in the movement of emancipation itself, Badiou insists that the problem is the creation of a new form of organization and political discipline, for which 'the rabble' is clearly unsuitable.

The problem of the rabble has not yet been resolved. Although founded in a very real problem originally theorized in political economy, the Hegelian 'problem' was created by philosophy and remains unlikely to be resolved by philosophical means. Contrary to the assertions of Zizek and Ruda, the attempt to recast the problem of

---

[73] Alain Badiou, Interview February 2006, at a conference at the University of Washington entitled 'Is a History of the Cultural Revolution Possible?' https://chtodelat.org > Newspapers > 15: Reactionary Times

[74] Sylvain Lazarus, *Anthropology of the Name*, trans. Gila Walker, (London, New York, Calcutta: Seagull Books, 2015), pp. 25-26.

the rabble within Marxist theory – at least within their version of Marxist theory – does not involve a shifting of the problem into the logic of politics but remains entirely within the philosophical problematic which Marx constructed in transforming the working class into the 'proletariat'. The problem is not thereby solved but redoubled. In truth, it is the representation of the working class as the 'proletariat', to which Zizek, in particular, is so strongly attached, that is 'saturated', along with the 'proletarianization' thesis in its various manifestations which, instead of being dropped has been universalized, so that just as we are all proletarians now, we are all (virtual) rabble.